QUR'AN-BIBLE COMPARISON

A Topical Study of the Two Most
Influential and Respectful Books in
Western and Middle Eastern
Civilizations

Ami Ben-Chanan

 www.trafford.com

Acknowledgements

I am grateful for resources that were made available via the Internet through the following web sites:
The Humanities Text Initiative, a unit of the University of Michigan's Digital Library Production Service for texts of King James Bible and the Qur'an:

http://www.hti.umich.edu/

John Wesley's Christian Library for Non-Canonical Gospels resources:

http://wesley.nnu.edu/

Above all, the **Lord Jesus Christ**, without Whom this entire process would be unnecessary. All glory to God in the highest…. Maranatha, Lord Jesus!

"Be thou exalted, O God, above the heavens; let thy glory be above all the earth."

Psalm 57:5

CONTENTS

Part Three
COMPARISON OF THE NON-CANONICAL GOSPELS WITH THE BIBLE

Introduction

The attack and subsequent destruction of the World Trade Towers in New York City on September 11, 2001, motivated me to pose this question. Does the Qur'an mention a Holy War against those who do not believe in Allah as God and in Mohammed as God's Prophet? In studying the Qur'an, I discovered many biblical events and characters that seem to run parallel. Or do they? Intrigued, I decided to bring all references together into one file and compare them to each other. The result is this work, which I want to present to the reader for his/her scrutiny.

Preface

Over the course of a number of years, I have studied, debated, and discussed the Qur'an with Muslims. As one of the biggest and most rapidly growing religions, the Islamic faith attracts a lot of attention and debates. The last sixty years have been witness to innumerable conflicts between Muslims and Jews, and Muslims and the western world (Christians). Many famous people have accepted Islam, and increasing numbers of westerners are becoming Muslims every year.

Muslims scholars loudly proclaim that the Qur'an is the only Holy Book sent by God, and Islam is the "last religion", the purpose of which is to spread its tenets around the globe and to build a world-wide Caliphate.

I suggest for those who are considering becoming a Muslim to read very seriously the Qur'an and the Bible simultaneously.

Because the Qur'an mentions biblical stories a great number of times, the references should be read alongside the comparable passages in the Bible. I have attempted to accomplish this idea in this book and hope that it will be a useful tool for studying their differences and similarities. I hope that it will help the reader to understand the origin of these Books and find the Truth contained in its pages.

Part three is included to demonstrate the differences between the non-canonical texts and the Bible. I hope it will help the reader to understand why these texts were never included in the Canon of Scripture and where some traditions of certain Christian denominations mark their beginning.

Notes

The arguments of Muslim scholars:

1. The coming of the last Prophet Mohammed is predicted in the Old and New Testaments of the Bible.
2. The coming of Mohammed is predicted in sacred Christian and Jewish books.
3. Mohammed glorified Jesus and Mary, as predicted.
4. Muslim scholars point out that only Mohammed was sent for the entire human race, while Jesus and other prophets were sent only for Jews.
5. The corruption of the Bible leaves the Qur'an as the only book to be the true Word of God.
6. Many, if not all, of the Muslim witnesses of Mohammed's sayings and deeds are well known by their virtues and approved to be reliable sources of Truth. In contrast, the public, for example, does not know the people who wrote the New Testament, and nobody knows how well they were to be trusted.
7. The Qur'an records many facts about the nature of life and the nature of things which have since been proven by science today.
8. The Qur'an was given from Allah to Mohammed through a mediator angel known as Djibril (Gabriel).

The facts from the Bible:

1. The "last prophet" argument is based on speculation over two verses that Moses referred to about the next prophet who will come after him; Jesus was speaking about the Holy Spirit Who was yet to come upon believers in Him.
2. Christianity is based on the Canon of the Bible and not on the many non-canonical documents, for they are not considered inspired by God because they contradict each other and the Canon itself.
3. Mohammed actually glorified himself over every other messenger of God who came before him, speaking about himself as a "Seal of Prophets". But the Holy Spirit actually glorifies Jesus as the Son of God and the Only Saviour, Whose second coming all Christians await since His ascension into Heaven after His resurrection from the dead.
4. The history of Christian expansion shows that Christ was sent not only for Jews but for the entire world.
5. The Bible in its entirety has one consistent message about salvation, in spite of the fact that its 66 biblical books were written by 40 different authors over a period of 1500 years. There are no contradictions which might normally be present in books written by so many writers. It shows that One God is behind this Book. The character of God described identically by so many authors, as well as the plan of salvation through the blood sacrifice of an innocent and pure Being instead of us, a sinful and wicked people, to cover our sins. It starts at the very beginning of the Bible, in Genesis 3, when God Himself made a sacrifice of an innocent animal to cover the sin of Adam and Eve. God used the skin of this animal to cover their bodies, and the "covering of our sins" continues until the final book of the Bible, called Revelation, with the triumph of the Lamb of God who once was slain to be the sinless sacrifice for the entire human race.
6. The Bible teaches us not to trust human beings, for our hearts are corrupted and we need to rely only upon God Himself. Most of the prophets, kings, judges and apostles had a bad reputation even during time of their ministry. One had a mother who was

a prostitute, another committed immoral sins, some were afraid to witness, etc. In spite of their shortfalls and failures, God used them to glorify Himself, as He said to Paul in the second epistle to the Corinthians: *"My grace is sufficient for thee:* **for my strength is made perfect in (your) weakness.** *"*

We do not rely on the testimony of men simply because of their genealogy and credibility, but upon the Message itself, as to whether it really came from God.

7. The Bible itself speaks of many scientific facts. One of these facts concerns the shape of Earth as "hanging" in space without any support (not held up by a turtle, elephant or whale, etc. as we read in some of the earliest legends). We can find a description of dinosaurs and a "greenhouse effect" that influenced the growth of giant flora and fauna on antediluvian Earth. On the subject of science, the Qur'an cannot claim to be more "holy" than the Bible.

8. In many cases, God Himself spoke directly with His prophets like Abraham, Moses, and others. Jesus also communicated directly with the Father. In contrast, Mohammed never experienced the presence of Allah Himself.

Table of Equivalences

Qur'an	Bible
Tavrat	Torah
Injeel	Gospel
Shaitan	Lucifer/Satan
Djibril	Gabriel
Firon	Pharaoh
Nuh	Noah
Ayyub	Job
Ibrahim	Abraham/Abram
Lut	Lot
Ismail	Ishmael
Ishaq	Isaac
Yusuf	Joseph
Yaqoub	Jacob
Haroun	Aaron
Musa	Moses
Qaroun	Korah
Talut	Saul
Dawood	David
Jalut	Goliath
Sulaiman	Solomon
Yunus	Jonah
Uzair	Ezekiel
Marium	Miriam, Mary (mother of Jesus)
Zakariya	Zechariah/Zacharias
Yahya	John (the Baptist)
Muhammad	Mohammed
Isa	Jesus

Part One

THE GREAT PEOPLE OF THE BIBLE

Chapter One

ADAM

THE QUR'AN
"Adam Gives Names to the Animals"

Sura 2
The Cow

30. And when your Lord said to the angels, I am going to place in the earth a khalif, they said: **What! wilt Thou place in it such as shall make mischief in it and shed blood, and we celebrate Thy praise and extol Thy holiness?** [1]He said: Surely I know what you do not know.

31. And He taught Adam all the names, then presented them to the angels;[2] then He said: Tell me the names of those if you are right.

32. They said: Glory be to Thee! we have no knowledge but that which Thou hast taught us; surely Thou art the Knowing, the Wise.

33. He said: O Adam! inform them of their names. Then when he had informed them of their names, He said: Did I not say to you that I surely know what is ghaib in the heavens and the earth and (that) I know what you manifest and what you hide?

THE BIBLE
"Adam Gives Names to the Animals"

Genesis
Chapter 1

26. And God said, Let us make man in our image, after our likeness:[1] and let them have dominion over the fish of the sea, and over the fowl of the air, and over the cattle, and over all the earth, and over every creeping thing that creepeth upon the earth.

27. So God created man in his own image, in the image of God created he him; male and female created he them.

28. And God blessed them, and God said unto them, Be fruitful, and multiply, and replenish the earth, and subdue it: and have dominion over the fish of the sea, and over the fowl of the air, and over every living thing that moveth upon the earth.

Genesis

Chapter 2

19. And out of the ground the LORD God formed every beast of the field, and every fowl of the air; and brought them unto Adam to see what he would call them: and whatsoever Adam called every living creature, that was the name thereof.[2]

20. And Adam gave names to all cattle, and to the fowl of the air, and to every beast of the field; but for Adam there was not found an help meet for him.

COMMENTARY

In the Qur'an:

1. Adam was created by Allah as a creature lower than angels.
2. Allah taught Adam all the names of the animals in order to put the angels to shame.

In the Bible:

1. The creation of man was the **last and finest work** of Almighty God, because no other creatures, including angels, were made in the image of God
2. God brought to Adam, as ruler of the earth, all of the animals for him to give them names and Adam did his first job well. It had nothing to do with angels!

THE QUR'AN

"The Sin of Satan"

Sura 2

The Cow

34. And when We said to the angels: Make obeisance to Adam they did obeisance, but Iblis (did it not). He refused and he was proud, and he was one of the unbelievers.

Sura 7

The Elevated Places

11. And certainly We created you, then We fashioned you, then We said to the angels: Make obeisance to Adam. So they did obeisance except Iblis; he was not of those who did obeisance.

12. He said: What hindered you so that you did not make obeisance when I commanded you? He said: I am better than he: Thou hast created me of fire, while him Thou didst create of dust.

13. He said: Then get forth from this (state), for it does not befit you to behave proudly therein. Go forth, therefore, surely you are of the abject ones.

Sura 15

The Rock

28. And when your Lord said to the angels: Surely I am going to create a mortal of the essence of black mud fashioned in shape.

29. So when I have made him complete and breathed into him of My spirit, fall down making obeisance to him.

30. So the angels made obeisance, all of them together,

31. But Iblis (did it not); he refused to be with those who made obeisance.

32. He said: O Iblis! what excuse have you that you are not with those who make obeisance?

33. He said: I am not such that I should make obeisance to a mortal whom Thou hast created of the essence of black mud fashioned in shape.

34. He said: Then get out of it, for surely you are driven away:

35. And surely on you is curse until the day of judgment.

36. He said: My Lord! then respite me till the time when they are raised.

37. He said: So surely you are of the respited ones

38. Till the period of the time made known.

39. He said: My Lord! because Thou hast made life evil to me, I will certainly make (evil) fair-seeming to them on earth, and I will certainly cause them all to deviate

40. Except Thy servants from among them, the devoted ones.

Sura 17

The Children of Israel

61. And when We said to the angels: Make obeisance to Adam; they made obeisance, but Iblis (did it not). He said: Shall I make obeisance to him whom Thou hast created of dust?

62. He said: Tell me, is this he whom Thou hast honored above me? If Thou shouldst respite me to the day of resurrection, I will most certainly cause his progeny to perish except a few.

63. He said: Be gone! for whoever of them will follow you, then surely hell is your recompense, a full recompense:

64. And beguile whomsoever of them you can with your voice, and collect against them your forces riding and on foot, and share with them in wealth and children, and hold out promises to them; and the Shaitan makes not promises to them but to deceive:

65. Surely (as for) My servants, you have no authority over them; and your Lord is sufficient as a Protector.

Sura 18

The Cave

50. And when We said to the angels: Make obeisance to Adam; they made obeisance but Iblis (did it not). **He was of the jinn, so he transgressed the commandment of his Lord**. What! would you then take him and his offspring for friends rather than Me, and they are your enemies? Evil is (this) change for the unjust.

Sura 20

Ta Ha

116. And when We said to the angels: Make obeisance to Adam, they made obeisance, but Iblis (did it not); he refused.

117. So We said: O Adam! This is an enemy to you and to your wife; therefore let him not drive you both forth from the garden so that you should be unhappy;

Sura 38

Suad

71. When your Lord said to the angels; Surely **I am going to create a mortal from dust**:

72. So when I have made him complete and breathed into him of My spirit, then fall down making obeisance to him.

73. And the angels did obeisance, all of them,

74. But not Iblis: he was proud and he was one of the unbelievers.

75. He said: O Iblis! what prevented you that you should do obeisance to him whom I created with My two hands? Are you proud or are you of the exalted ones?

76. He said: **I am better than he**; Thou hast created me of fire, and him Thou didst create of dust.

77. He said: Then get out of it, for surely you are driven away:

78. And surely My curse is on you to the day of judgment.

THE BIBLE

"The Sin of Satan"

Ezekiel

Chapter 28

1. The word of the LORD came again unto me, saying,

2. Son of man, say unto the prince of Tyrus, Thus saith the Lord GOD; Because thine heart is lifted up, and thou hast said, I am a God, I sit in the seat of God, in the midst of the seas; yet thou art a man, and not God, though thou set thine heart as the heart of God:

3. Behold, thou art wiser than Daniel; there is no secret that they can hide from thee:

4. With thy wisdom and with thine understanding thou hast gotten thee riches, and hast gotten gold and silver into thy treasures:

5. By thy great wisdom and by thy traffick hast thou increased thy riches, and thine heart is lifted up because of thy riches:

6. Therefore thus saith the Lord GOD; Because thou hast set thine heart as the heart of God;

7. Behold, therefore I will bring strangers upon thee, the terrible of the nations: and they shall draw their swords against the beauty of thy wisdom, and they shall defile thy brightness.

8. They shall bring thee down to the pit, and thou shalt die the deaths of them that are slain in the midst of the seas.

9. Wilt thou yet say before him that slayeth thee, I am God? but thou shalt be a man, and no God, in the hand of him that slayeth thee.

10. Thou shalt die the deaths of the uncircumcised by the hand of strangers: for I have spoken it, saith the Lord GOD.

11. Moreover the word of the LORD came unto me, saying,

12. Son of man, take up a lamentation upon the king of Tyrus, and say unto him, Thus saith the Lord GOD; Thou sealest up the sum, full of wisdom, and perfect in beauty.

13. Thou hast been in Eden the garden of God; every precious stone was thy covering, the sardius, topaz, and the diamond, the beryl, the onyx, and the jasper, the sapphire, the emerald, and the carbuncle, and gold: the workmanship of thy tabrets and of thy pipes was prepared in thee in the day that thou wast created.

14. Thou art the anointed cherub that covereth; and I have set thee so: thou wast upon the holy mountain of God; thou hast walked up and down in the midst of the stones of fire.

15. Thou wast perfect in thy ways from the day that thou wast created, till iniquity was found in thee.

16. By the multitude of thy merchandise they have filled the midst of thee with violence, and thou hast sinned: therefore **I will cast thee as profane out of the mountain of God: and I will destroy thee, O covering cherub, from the midst of the stones of fire.**

17. Thine heart was lifted up because of thy beauty, thou hast corrupted thy wisdom by reason of thy brightness: I will cast thee to the ground, I will lay thee before kings, that they may behold thee.

18. Thou hast defiled thy sanctuaries by the multitude of thine iniquities, by the iniquity of thy traffick; therefore will I bring forth a fire from the midst of thee, it shall devour thee, and I will bring thee to ashes upon the earth in the sight of all them that behold thee.

19. All they that know thee among the people shall be astonished at thee: thou shalt be a terror, and never shalt thou be any more.

Isaiah

Chapter 14

12. How art thou fallen from heaven, O Lucifer, son of the morning! how art thou cut down to the ground, which didst weaken the nations!

13. For thou hast said in thine heart, I will ascend into heaven, I will exalt my throne above the stars of God: I will sit also upon the mount of the congregation, in the sides of the north:

14. I will ascend above the heights of the clouds; I will be like the most High.

15. Yet thou shalt be brought down to hell, to the sides of the pit.

16. They that see thee shall narrowly look upon thee, and consider thee, saying, Is this the man that made the earth to tremble, that did shake kingdoms;

17. That made the world as a wilderness, and destroyed the cities thereof; that opened not the house of his prisoners?

18. All the kings of the nations, even all of them, lie in glory, every one in his own house.

19. But thou art cast out of thy grave like an abominable branch, and as the raiment of those that are slain, thrust through with a sword, that go down to the stones of the pit; as a carcase trodden under feet.

20. Thou shalt not be joined with them in burial, because thou hast destroyed thy land, and slain thy people: the seed of evildoers shall never be renowned.

COMMENTARY

In the Qur'an:

1. A Jinn (who is not an angel according to **Sura 18:48**) named Iblis rejected Allah's order to bow down before Adam and was cast from Allah's presence until the Day of Judgment.

In the Bible:

1. Lucifer, a high-ranking angel called a cherub, sinned against God when he decided to be like God, and to usurp His place. Lucifer (later called Satan) deceived Eve by offering her the same idea- to be like God.

THE QUR'AN

"The Sin of Adam"

Sura 2

The Cow

35. And We said: O Adam! Dwell you and your wife in the garden and eat from it a plenteous (food) wherever you wish and do not approach this tree, for then you will be of the unjust.
36. But the Shaitan made them both fall from it, and caused them to depart from that (state) in which they were; and We said: Get forth, some of you being the enemies of others, and there is for you in the earth an abode and a provision for a time.
37. Then Adam received (some) words from his Lord, so He turned to him mercifully; surely He is Oft-returning (to mercy), the Merciful.
38. We said: Go forth from this (state) all; so surely there will come to you a guidance from Me, then whoever follows My guidance, no fear shall come upon them, nor shall they grieve.

Sura 7

The Elevated Places

19. And (We said): O Adam! Dwell you and your wife in the garden; so eat from where you desire, but do not go near this tree, for then you will be of the unjust.
20. But the Shaitan made an evil suggestion to them that he might make manifest to them what had been hidden from them of their evil inclinations, and he said: **Your Lord has not forbidden you this tree except that you may not both become two angels or that you may (not) become of the immortals.**
21. And he swore to them both: Most surely I am a sincere adviser to you.
22. Then he caused them to fall by deceit; so when they tasted of the tree, their evil inclinations became manifest to them, and they both began to cover themselves with the leaves of the garden; and their Lord called out to them: Did I not forbid you both from that tree and say to you that the Shaitan is your open enemy?

9

23. They said: Our Lord! We have been unjust to ourselves, and if Thou forgive us not, and have (not) mercy on us, we shall certainly be of the losers.

24. He said: Get forth, some of you, the enemies of others, and there is for you in the earth an abode and a provision for a time.

25. He (also) said: Therein shall you live, and therein shall you die, and from it shall you be raised.

26. O children of Adam! We have indeed sent down to you clothing to cover your shame, and (clothing) for beauty and clothing that guards (against evil), that is the best. This is of the communications of Allah that they may be mindful.

27. O children of Adam! let not the Shaitan cause you to fall into affliction as he expelled your parents from the garden, pulling off from them both their clothing that he might show them their evil inclinations, he surely sees you, he as well as his host, from whence you cannot see them; surely We have made the Shaitans to be the guardians of those who do not believe.

Sura 20

Ta Ha

117. So We said: O Adam! This is an enemy to you and to your wife; therefore let him not drive you both forth from the garden so that you should be unhappy;

118. Surely it is (ordained) for you that you shall not be hungry therein nor bare of clothing;

119. And that you shall not be thirsty therein nor shall you feel the heat of the sun.

120. But the **Shaitan made an evil suggestion to him**; he said: **O Adam! Shall I guide you to the tree of immortality and a kingdom which decays not?**

121. Then they both ate of it, so their evil inclinations became manifest to them, and they both began to cover themselves with leaves of the garden, and Adam disobeyed his Lord, so his life became evil (to him).

122. Then his Lord chose him, so He turned to him and guided (him).

123. He said: Get forth you two there from, all (of you), one of you (is) enemy to another. So there will surely come to you guidance from Me, then whoever follows My guidance, he shall not go astray nor be unhappy;

THE BIBLE

"The Sin of Adam"

Genesis

Chapter 2

16. And the LORD God commanded the man, saying, Of every tree of the garden thou mayest freely eat:

17. But of the tree of the knowledge of good and evil, thou shalt not eat of it: for in the day that thou eatest thereof thou shalt surely die.

Genesis

Chapter 3

1. Now the **serpent** was more subtil than any beast of the field which the LORD God had made. And he said unto the woman, **Yea, hath God said, Ye shall not eat of every tree of the garden?**

2. And the woman said unto the serpent, We may eat of the fruit of the trees of the garden:

3. But of the fruit of the tree which is in the midst of the garden, God hath said, Ye shall not eat of it, neither shall ye touch it, lest ye die.

4. And the serpent said unto the woman, Ye shall not surely die:

5. For God doth know that in the day ye eat thereof, then your eyes shall be opened, and ye shall be as gods, knowing good and evil.

12. And the man said, The woman whom thou gavest to be with me, she gave me of the tree, and I did eat.

13. And the LORD God said unto the woman, What is this that thou hast done? And the woman said, The serpent beguiled me, and I did eat.

14. And the LORD God said unto the serpent, Because thou hast done this, thou art cursed above all cattle, and above every beast of the field; upon thy belly shalt thou go, and dust shalt thou eat all the days of thy life:

15. And I will put enmity between thee and the woman, and between thy seed and her seed; it shall bruise thy head, and thou shalt bruise his heel.

16. Unto the woman he said, **I will greatly multiply thy sorrow and thy conception; in sorrow thou shalt bring forth children; and thy desire shall be to thy husband, and he shall rule over thee.**
17. And unto Adam he said, **Because thou hast hearkened unto the voice of thy wife, and hast eaten of the tree, of which I commanded thee, saying, Thou shalt not eat of it: cursed is the ground for thy sake; in sorrow shalt thou eat of it all the days of thy life;**
18. Thorns also and thistles shall it bring forth to thee; and thou shalt eat the herb of the field;
19. In the sweat of thy face shalt thou eat bread, till thou return unto the ground; for out of it wast thou taken: for dust thou art, and unto dust shalt thou return.
21. Unto Adam also and to his wife did the LORD God make coats of skins, and clothed them.
22. And the LORD God said, Behold, the man is become as one of us, to know good and evil: and now, lest he put forth his hand, and take also of the tree of life, and eat, and live for ever:
23. Therefore the LORD **God sent him forth from the garden of Eden, to till the ground from whence he was taken.**
24. So he drove out the man; and he placed at the east of the garden of Eden **Cherubim, and a flaming sword which turned every way, to keep the way of the tree of life.**

COMMENTARY

In the Qur'an:

1. There is no explanation of how sin first came into the world and resulted in the fall of mankind. Muslim scholars reject the fact that all humans are suffering because of Adam's sin.
2. The forbidden fruit belongs to the "Tree of Eternity".
3. Satan spoke directly to Adam.
4. Satan tempted Adam by saying: *"Your Lord has not forbidden you this tree except that you may not both become two angels or that you may (not) become of the immortals."*
5. Adam and Eve actually asked for forgiveness and admitted their sin.

In the Bible:

1. The Bible clearly speaks about the consequences of the first sin, namely death, and that all descendants of Adam and Eve are under this curse: *"... in sorrow thou shalt bring forth children; and thy desire shall be to thy husband, and he shall rule over thee... In the sweat of thy face shalt thou eat bread, till thou return unto the ground; for out of it wast thou taken: for dust thou art, and unto dust shalt thou return..."*

2. The forbidden fruit belongs to the "Tree of the Knowledge of Good and Evil", while the fruit of "Tree of Life" was never touched by Adam: *"... And the LORD God said, Behold, the man is become as one of us, to know good and evil: and now, lest he put forth his hand, and take also of the tree of life, and eat, and live for ever:..."*

3. Satan, in the guise of a serpent, spoke to Eve, and Eve transmitted the idea to Adam.

4. Satan, as the serpent, tempted Eve: *"...and ye shall be as gods, knowing good and evil."* Satan actually caused them to sin the same way he sinned in the first place; that is, by wishing to be god himself. Also, only after the fall God decided to expel Adam and Eve from Eden, to prevent them from becoming immortal, for no sin is allowed to be in the presence of the Lord in Paradise and Eternity.

5. Adam's response to God's inquiry was that he tried to blame Eve and eventually God Himself: *"...The woman whom thou gavest to be with me, she gave me of the tree, and I did eat..."*

THE QUR'AN

"The Story of Cain and Abel"

Sura 5

The Dinner Table

27. And relate to them the story of **the two sons of Adam** with truth when they both offered an offering, but it was accepted from one of them and was accepted from the other. **He said: I will most certainly slay you.** (The other) said: **Allah only accepts from those who guard** (against evil).

13

28. If you will stretch forth your hand towards me to slay me, I am not one to stretch forth my hand towards you to slay you surely I fear Allah, the Lord of the worlds:

29. Surely I wish that you should bear the sin committed against me and your own sin, and so you would be of the inmates of the fire, and this is the recompense of the unjust.

30. Then his mind facilitated to him the slaying of his brother **so he slew him**; then he became one of the losers

31. Then Allah sent a crow digging up the earth so that he might show him how he should cover the dead body of his brother. He said: Woe me! do I lack the strength that I should be like this crow and cover the dead body of my brother? *So he became of those who regret.*

THE BIBLE

"The Story of Cain and Abel"

Genesis

Chapter 4

1. And Adam knew Eve his wife; and she conceived, and bare Cain, and said, I have gotten a man from the LORD.

2. And she again bare his brother Abel. And Abel was a keeper of sheep, but Cain was a tiller of the ground.

3. And in process of time it came to pass, **that Cain brought of the fruit of the ground an offering unto the LORD.**

4. And Abel, he also brought of the firstlings of his flock and of the fat thereof. And the LORD had respect unto Abel and to his offering:

5. But unto Cain and to his offering he had not respect. **And Cain was very wroth, and his countenance fell.**

6. And the LORD said unto Cain, Why art thou wroth? and why is thy countenance fallen?

7. If thou doest well, shalt thou not be accepted? and if thou doest not well, sin lieth at the door. And unto thee shall be his desire, and thou shalt rule over him.

8. And Cain talked with Abel his brother: and it came to pass, when they were in the field, that Cain rose up against Abel his brother, and slew him.

9. And the LORD said unto Cain, Where is Abel thy brother? And he said, I know not: **Am I my brother's keeper?**

10. And he said, What hast thou done? **the voice of thy brother's blood crieth unto me from the ground.**

11. And now art thou cursed from the earth, which hath opened her mouth to receive thy brother's blood from thy hand;

12. When thou tillest the ground, it shall not henceforth yield unto thee her strength; a fugitive and a vagabond shalt thou be in the earth.

13. And Cain said unto the LORD, **My punishment is greater than I can bear.**

14. Behold, thou hast driven me out this day from the face of the earth; and from thy face shall I be hid; and I shall be a fugitive and a vagabond in the earth; and it shall come to pass, that every one that findeth me shall slay me.

15. And the LORD said unto him, Therefore whosoever slayeth Cain, vengeance shall be taken on him sevenfold. And the LORD set a mark upon Cain, lest any finding him should kill him.

16. And Cain went out from the presence of the LORD, and dwelt in the land of Nod, on the east of Eden.

First John

Chapter 3

11. For this is the message that ye heard from the beginning, that we should love one another.

12. Not as Cain, who was of that wicked one, and slew his brother. And wherefore slew he him? Because his own works were evil, and his brother's righteous.

Jude

Chapter 1

11. Woe unto them! for they have gone in the way of Cain, and ran greedily after the error of Balaam for reward, and perished in the gainsaying of Core.

COMMENTARY

In the Qur'an:

1. There is a conversation between two brothers, but we do not learn their names.
2. One brother repented for what he had done.

In the Bible:

1. We learn that two brothers called Cain and Abel offer God each their sacrifice. We have a record of a conversation between God and Cain before and after he murdered his brother Abel.
2. Cain only complained that his punishment from God was too severe to bear, and afterward he : "... *went out from the presence of the LORD...*", which means that he never regretted the murder and never reconciled with God. His generation (the next generation) became ungodly.

Chapter Two

NOAH

The Qur'an

"Noah and the Flood"

Sura 11

The Holy Prophet

36. And it was revealed to Nuh: That none of your people will believe except those who have already believed, therefore do not grieve at what they do:

37. And make the ark before Our eyes and (according to) Our revelation, and do not speak to Me in respect of those who are unjust; surely they shall be drowned.

38. And he began to make the ark; and whenever the chiefs from among his people passed by him they laughed at him. He said: If you laugh at us, surely we too laugh at you as you laugh (at us).

39. So shall you know who it is on whom will come a chastisement which will disgrace him, and on whom will lasting chastisement come down.

40. Until when Our command came and water came forth from the valley, We said: Carry in it two of all things, a pair, and your own family-- except those against whom the word has already gone forth, and those who believe. And there believed not with him but a few.

41. And he said: Embark in it, in the name of Allah be its sailing and its anchoring; most surely my Lord is Forgiving, Merciful.

42. And it moved on with them amid waves like mountains; and Nuh called out to his son, and he was aloof: O my son! embark with us and be not with the unbelievers.

43. He said: I will betake myself for refuge to a mountain that shall protect me from the water. Nuh said: There is no protector today from Allah's punishment but He Who has mercy; and a wave intervened between them, so he was of the drowned.

44. And it was said: O earth, swallow down your water, and O cloud, clear away; and the water was made to abate and the affair was decided, and the ark rested on the Judi, and it was said: Away with the unjust people.

45. And Nuh cried out to his Lord and said: My Lord! surely my son is of my family, and Thy promise is surely true, and Thou art the most just of the judges.

46. He said: **O Nuh! surely he is not of your family; surely he is (the doer of) other than good deeds, therefore ask not of Me that of which you have no knowledge; surely I admonish you lest you may be of the ignorant**

47. He said: My Lord! I seek refuge in Thee from asking Thee that of which I have no knowledge; and if Thou shouldst not forgive me and have mercy on me, I should be of the losers.

48. It was said: O Nuh! descend with peace from Us and blessings on you and on the people from among those who are with you, and there shall be nations whom We will afford provisions, then a painful punishment from Us shall afflict them.

49. These are announcements relating to the unseen which We reveal to you, you did not know them-- (neither) you nor your people-- before this; therefore be patient; surely the end is for those who guard (against evil).

Sura 26

The Poets

105. The people of Nuh rejected the apostles.

106. When their brother Nuh said to them: Will you not guard (against evil)?

107. Surely I am a faithful apostle to you;

108. Therefore guard against (the punishment of) Allah and obey me

109. And I do not ask you any reward for it; my reward is only with the Lord of the worlds:

110. So guard against (the punishment of) Allah and obey me.

111. They said: Shall we believe in you while the meanest follow you?

112. He said: And what knowledge have I of what they do?

113. Their account is only with my Lord, if you could perceive

114. And I am not going to drive away the believers;

115. I am naught but a plain warner.

116. They said: If you desist not, O Nuh, you shall most certainly be of those stoned to death.

117. He said: My Lord! Surely my people give me the lie!

118. Therefore **judge Thou between me and them with a (just) judgment, and deliver me and those who are with me of the believers.**

119. So We delivered him and those with him in the laden ark.

120. Then We drowned the rest afterwards.

Sura 29

The Spider

14. And certainly **We sent Nuh to his people, so he remained among them a thousand years save fifty years**. And the deluge overtook them, while they were unjust.

15. So We delivered him and the inmates of the ark, and made it a sign to the nations.

Sura 71

Nuh

21. Nuh said: My Lord! surely they have disobeyed me and followed him whose wealth and children have added to him nothing but loss.

22. And they have planned a very great plan.

23. And they say: By no means leave your gods, nor leave Wadd, nor Suwa; nor Yaghus, and Yauq and Nasr.

24. And indeed they have led astray many, and do not increase the unjust in aught but error.

25. Because of their wrongs they were drowned, then made to enter fire, so they did not find any helpers besides Allah.

26. And Nuh said: My Lord! leave not upon the land any dweller from among the unbelievers:

27. For surely if Thou leave them they will lead astray Thy servants, and will not beget any but immoral, ungrateful (children)

28. My Lord! forgive me and my parents and him who enters my house believing, and the believing men and the believing women; and do not increase the unjust in aught but destruction!

THE BIBLE

"Noah and the Flood"

Genesis

Chapter 6

1. And it came to pass, when men began to multiply on the face of the earth, and daughters were born unto them,

2. That the sons of God saw the daughters of men that they were fair; and they took them wives of all which they chose.

3. And the LORD said, My spirit shall not always strive with man, for that he also is flesh: yet his days shall be an hundred and twenty years.

4. There were giants in the earth in those days; and also after that, when the sons of God came in unto the daughters of men, and they bare children to them, the same became mighty men which were of old, men of renown.

5. And GOD saw that the wickedness of man was great in the earth, and that every imagination of the thoughts of his heart was only evil continually.

6. And it repented the LORD that he had made man on the earth, and it grieved him at his heart.

7. And the LORD said, I will destroy man whom I have created from the face of the earth; both man, and beast, and the creeping thing, and the fowls of the air; for it repenteth me that I have made them.

8. But Noah found grace in the eyes of the LORD.

9. These are the generations of Noah: Noah was a just man and perfect in his generations, and **Noah walked with God**.

10. And Noah begat three sons, Shem, Ham, and Japheth.

11. The earth also was corrupt before God, and the earth was filled with violence.

12. And God looked upon the earth, and, behold, it was corrupt; for all flesh had corrupted his way upon the earth.

13. And God said unto Noah, The end of all flesh is come before me; for the earth is filled with violence through them; and, behold, I will destroy them with the earth.

14. Make thee an ark of gopher wood; rooms shalt thou make in the ark, and shalt pitch it within and without with pitch.

15. And this is the fashion which thou shalt make it of: The length of the ark shall be three hundred cubits, the breadth of it fifty cubits, and the height of it thirty cubits.

16. A window shalt thou make to the ark, and in a cubit shalt thou finish it above; and the door of the ark shalt thou set in the side thereof; with lower, second, and third stories shalt thou make it.

17. And, behold, I, even I, do bring a flood of waters upon the earth, to destroy all flesh, wherein is the breath of life, from under heaven; and every thing that is in the earth shall die.

18. But with thee will I establish my covenant; and thou shalt come into the ark, thou, and thy sons, and thy wife, and thy' wives with thee.

Genesis

Chapter 7

1. And the LORD said unto Noah, Come thou and all thy house into the ark; for thee have I seen righteous before me in this generation.
6. And Noah was six hundred years old when the flood of waters was upon the earth.
13. In the selfsame day entered Noah, and Shem, and Ham, and Japheth, the sons of Noah, and Noah's wife, and the three wives of his sons with them, into the ark;

Genesis

Chapter 9

29. And all the days of Noah were nine hundred and fifty years: and he died.

COMMENTARY

In the Qur'an:

1. Noah asked Allah to destroy all those who did not listen to Noah, and asked for forgiveness for himself and his parents.
2. One of the sons of Noah was not in the Ark and died during the flood.
3. Noah was among the wicked generation for 950 years: " *so he remained among them a thousand years save fifty years…*".

In the Bible:

1. God Himself made the decision to destroy the human race, but saved Noah's immediate family – his wife, his three sons, and his three daughters-in-law (eight persons all together). There is no mention of Noah's parents.

2. One son became wayward. Ham sinned against Noah **after the flood**, having been saved earlier in the Ark; for God saved ALL Noah's family: *"Go into the ark, you and all your household..."*.

3. Noah was 600 years old before the coming of the flood and he lived 350 years after the flood while all other people of the world were destroyed; therefore Noah lived among the wicked generation for only 600 years.

Chapter Three

JOB

The Qur'an
"The Affliction of Job"

Sura 38
Suad

41. And remember Our servant Ayyub, when he called upon his Lord: The Shaitan has afflicted me with toil and torment.

42. Urge with your foot; here is a cool washing-place and a drink.

43. And We gave him his family and the like of them with them, as a mercy from Us, and as a reminder to those possessed of understanding.

44. And take in your hand a green branch and beat her with It and do not break your oath; surely We found him patient; most excellent the servant! Surely he was frequent m returning (to Allah).

The Bible
"The Affliction Of Job"

Job
Chapter 1

1. There was a man in the land of Uz, whose name was Job; and that man was perfect and upright, and one that feared God, and eschewed evil.

2. And there were born unto him seven sons and three daughters.

3. His substance also was seven thousand sheep, and three thousand camels, and five hundred yoke of oxen, and five hundred she asses, and a very great household; so that this man was the greatest of all the men of the east.

4. And his sons went and feasted in their houses, every one his day; and sent and called for their three sisters to eat and to drink with them.

5. And it was so, when the days of their feasting were gone about, that Job sent and sanctified them, and rose up early in the morning, and offered burnt offerings according to the number of them all: for

Job said, It may be that my sons have sinned, and cursed God in their hearts. Thus did Job continually.

6. Now there was a day when the sons of God came to present themselves before the LORD, and Satan came also among them.

7. And the LORD said unto Satan, Whence comest thou? Then Satan answered the LORD, and said, From going to and fro in the earth, and from walking up and down in it.

8. And the LORD said unto Satan, Hast thou considered my servant Job, that there is none like him in the earth, a perfect and an upright man, one that feareth God, and escheweth evil?

9. Then Satan answered the LORD, and said, Doth Job fear God for nought?

10. Hast not thou made an hedge about him, and about his house, and about all that he hath on every side? thou hast blessed the work of his hands, and his substance is increased in the land.

11. But put forth thine hand now, and touch all that he hath, and he will curse thee to thy face.

12. And the LORD said unto Satan, Behold, all that he hath is in thy power; only upon himself put not forth thine hand. So Satan went forth from the presence of the LORD.

13. And there was a day when his sons and his daughters were eating and drinking wine in their eldest brother's house:

14. And there came a messenger unto Job, and said, The oxen were plowing, and the asses feeding beside them:

15. And the Sabeans fell upon them, and took them away; yea, they have slain the servants with the edge of the sword; and I only am escaped alone to tell thee.

16. While he was yet speaking, there came also another, and said, The fire of God is fallen from heaven, and hath burned up the sheep, and the servants, and consumed them; and I only am escaped alone to tell thee.

17. While he was yet speaking, there came also another, and said, The Chaldeans made out three bands, and fell upon the camels, and have carried them away, yea, and slain the servants with the edge of the sword; and I only am escaped alone to tell thee.

18. While he was yet speaking, there came also another, and said, Thy sons and thy daughters were eating and drinking wine in their eldest brother's house:

19. And, behold, there came a great wind from the wilderness, and smote the four corners of the house, and it fell upon the young men, and they are dead; and I only am escaped alone to tell thee.

20. Then Job arose, and rent his mantle, and shaved his head, and fell down upon the ground, and worshipped,

21. And said, Naked came I out of my mother's womb, and naked shall I return thither: the LORD gave, and the LORD hath taken away; blessed be the name of the LORD.

22. In all this Job sinned not, nor charged God foolishly.

Job

Chapter 2

1. Again there was a day when the sons of God came to present themselves before the LORD, and Satan came also among them to present himself before the LORD.

2. And the LORD said unto Satan, From whence comest thou? And Satan answered the LORD, and said, From going to and fro in the earth, and from walking up and down in it.

3. And the LORD said unto Satan, Hast thou considered my servant Job, that there is none like him in the earth, a perfect and an upright man, one that feareth God, and escheweth evil? and still he holdeth fast his integrity, although thou movedst me against him, to destroy him without cause.

4. And Satan answered the LORD, and said, Skin for skin, yea, all that a man hath will he give for his life.

5. But put forth thine hand now, and touch his bone and his flesh, and he will curse thee to thy face.

6. And the LORD said unto Satan, Behold, he is in thine hand; but save his life.

7. So went Satan forth from the presence of the LORD, and smote Job with sore boils from the sole of his foot unto his crown.

8. And he took him a potsherd to scrape himself withal; and he sat down among the ashes.

9. Then said his wife unto him, Dost thou still retain thine integrity? curse God, and die.

10. But he said unto her, Thou speakest as one of the foolish women speaketh. What? shall we receive good at the hand of God, and shall we not receive evil? In all this did not Job sin with his lips.

11. Now when Job's three friends heard of all this evil that was come upon him, they came every one from his own place; Eliphaz the Temanite, and Bildad the Shuhite, and Zophar the Naamathite: for they had made an appointment together to come to mourn with him and to comfort him.

12. And when they lifted up their eyes afar off, and knew him not, they lifted up their voice, and wept; and they rent every one his mantle, and sprinkled dust upon their heads toward heaven.

13. So they sat down with him upon the ground seven days and seven nights, and none spake a word unto him: for they saw that his grief was very great.

Job

Chapter 3

1. After this opened Job his mouth, and cursed his day.

2. And Job spake, and said,

3. Let the day perish wherein I was born, and the night in which it was said, There is a man child conceived.

4. Let that day be darkness; let not God regard it from above, neither let the light shine upon it.

Job

Chapter 4

1. Then Eliphaz the Temanite answered and said,

17. Shall mortal man be more just than God? shall a man be more pure than his maker?

Job

Chapter 5

15. But he saveth the poor from the sword, from their mouth, and from the hand of the mighty.

16. So the poor hath hope, and iniquity stoppeth her mouth.

17. Behold, **happy is the man whom God correcteth**: therefore **despise not thou the chastening of the Almighty**:

Job

Chapter 6

1. But Job answered and said,

2. Oh that my grief were throughly weighed, and my calamity laid in the balances together!

3. For now it would be heavier than the sand of the sea: therefore my words are swallowed up.

4. For the arrows of the Almighty are within me, the poison whereof drinketh up my spirit: the terrors of God do set themselves in array against me.

Job

Chapter 7

17. What is man, that thou shouldest magnify him? and that thou shouldest set thine heart upon him?

18. And that thou shouldest visit him every morning, and try him every moment?

19. How long wilt thou not depart from me, nor let me alone till I swallow down my spittle?

20. I have sinned; what shall I do unto thee, O thou preserver of men? why hast thou set me as a mark against thee, so that I am a burden to myself?

Job

Chapter 8

1. Then answered Bildad the Shuhite, and said,

2. How long wilt thou speak these things? and how long shall the words of thy mouth be like a strong wind?

3. Doth God pervert judgment? or doth the Almighty pervert justice?

4. If thy children have sinned against him, and he have cast them away for their transgression;

5. If thou wouldest seek unto God betimes, and make thy supplication to the Almighty;

6. If thou wert pure and upright; surely now he would awake for thee, and make the habitation of thy righteousness prosperous.

20. Behold, God will not cast away a perfect man, neither will he help the evil doers:

21. Till he fill thy mouth with laughing, and thy lips with rejoicing.

Job

Chapter 9

1. Then Job answered and said,

2. I know it is so of a truth: but how should man be just with God?

3. If he will contend with him, he cannot answer him one of a thousand.

4. He is wise in heart, and mighty in strength: who hath hardened himself against him, and hath prospered?

16. If I had called, and he had answered me; yet would I not believe that he had hearkened unto my voice.

17. For he breaketh me with a tempest, and multiplieth my wounds without cause.

18. He will not suffer me to take my breath, but filleth me with bitterness.

19. If I speak of strength, lo, he is strong: and if of judgment, who shall set me a time to plead?

20. If I justify myself, mine own mouth shall condemn me: if I say, I am perfect, it shall also prove me perverse.

21. Though I were perfect, yet would I not know my soul: I would despise my life.

22. This is one thing, therefore I said it, He destroyeth the perfect and the wicked.

Job

Chapter 10

7. Thou knowest that I am not wicked; and there is none that can deliver out of thine hand.

Job

Chapter 11

1. Then answered Zophar the Naamathite, and said,

2. Should not the multitude of words be answered? and should a man full of talk be justified?

3. Should thy lies make men hold their peace? and when thou mockest, shall no man make thee ashamed?

4. For thou hast said, My doctrine is pure, and I am clean in thine eyes.

5. But oh that God would speak, and open his lips against thee;

Job

Chapter 27

1. Moreover Job continued his parable, and said,

2. As God liveth, who hath taken away my judgment; and the Almighty, who hath vexed my soul;

3. All the while my breath is in me, and the spirit of God is in my nostrils;

4. My lips shall not speak wickedness, nor my tongue utter deceit.

5. God forbid that I should justify you: till I die I will not remove mine integrity from me.

6. My righteousness I hold fast, and will not let it go: my heart shall not reproach me so long as I live.

Job

Chapter 32

1. So these three men ceased to answer Job, because he was righteous in his own eyes.

2. Then was kindled the wrath of Elihu the son of Barachel the Buzite, of the kindred of Ram: against Job was his wrath kindled, because he justified himself rather than God.

3. And Elihu the son of Barachel the Buzite answered and said, I am young, and ye are very old; wherefore I was afraid, and durst not shew you mine opinion.

Job

Chapter 34

5. For Job hath said, I am righteous: and God hath taken away my judgment.

6. Should I lie against my right? my wound is incurable without transgression.

7. What man is like Job, who drinketh up scorning like water?

8. Which goeth in company with the workers of iniquity, and walketh with wicked men.

9. For he hath said, It profiteth a man nothing that he should delight himself with God.

10. Therefore hearken unto me, ye men of understanding: far be it from God, that he should do wickedness; and from the Almighty, that he should commit iniquity.

11. For the work of a man shall he render unto him, and cause every man to find according to his ways.

12. Yea, surely God will not do wickedly, neither will the Almighty pervert judgment.

Job
Chapter 38

1. Then the LORD answered Job out of the whirlwind, and said,

2. Who is this that darkeneth counsel by words without knowledge?

3. Gird up now thy loins like a man; for I will demand of thee, and answer thou me.

4. Where wast thou when I laid the foundations of the earth? declare, if thou hast understanding.

5. Who hath laid the measures thereof, if thou knowest? or who hath stretched the line upon it?

6. Whereupon are the foundations thereof fastened? or who laid the corner stone thereof;

7. When the morning stars sang together, and all the sons of God shouted for joy?

Job
Chapter 40

7. Gird up thy loins now like a man: I will demand of thee, and declare thou unto me.

8. Wilt thou also disannul my judgment? wilt thou condemn me, that thou mayest be righteous?

9. Hast thou an arm like God? or canst thou thunder with a voice like him?

Job
Chapter 42

1. Then Job answered the LORD, and said,

2. I know that thou canst do every thing, and that no thought can be withholden from thee.

3. Who is he that hideth counsel without knowledge? therefore have I uttered that I understood not; things too wonderful for me, which I knew not.

4. Hear, I beseech thee, and I will speak: I will demand of thee, and declare thou unto me.

5. I have heard of thee by the hearing of the ear: but now mine eye seeth thee.

6. Wherefore I abhor myself, and repent in dust and ashes.

7. And it was so, that after the LORD had spoken these words unto Job, the LORD said to Eliphaz the Temanite, **My wrath is kindled against thee, and against thy two friends: for ye have not spoken of me the thing that is right, as my servant Job hath.**

8. Therefore take unto you now seven bullocks and seven rams, and go to my servant Job, and offer up for yourselves a burnt offering; and my servant Job shall pray for you: for him will I accept: lest I deal with you after your folly, in that ye have not spoken of me the thing which is right, like my servant Job.

9. So Eliphaz the Temanite and Bildad the Shuhite and Zophar the Naamathite went, and did according as the LORD commanded them: the LORD also accepted Job.

10. And the LORD turned the captivity of Job, when he prayed for his friends: also the LORD gave Job twice as much as he had before.

11. Then came there unto him all his brethren, and all his sisters, and all they that had been of his acquaintance before, and did eat bread with him in his house: and they bemoaned him, and comforted him over all the evil that the LORD had brought upon him: every man also gave him a piece of money, and every one an earring of gold.

12. So the LORD blessed the latter end of Job more than his beginning: for he had fourteen thousand sheep, and six thousand camels, and a thousand yoke of oxen, and a thousand she asses.

13. He had also seven sons and three daughters.

14. And he called the name of the first, Jemima; and the name of the second, Kezia; and the name of the third, Keren-happuch.

15. And in all the land were no women found so fair as the daughters of Job: and their father gave them inheritance among their brethren.

16. After this lived Job an hundred and forty years, and saw his sons, and his sons' sons, even four generations.
17. So Job died, being old and full of days.

COMMENTARY

In the Qur'an:

1. Job asked God to help him in his affliction. God responded to him: *"...Strike with thy foot: here is (water) wherein to wash, cool and refreshing, and (water) to drink...".* It is unclear why Job should strike something (his wife?) *"And take in thy hand a little grass, and strike therewith: and break not (thy oath)...".*
2. After Job's ordeal, God *"...gave him (back) his people, and doubled their number...".*

In the Bible:

1. The beginning of the book of Job states that Satan argued with God about the faithfulness of Job. God gave Satan permission to "touch" Job. However, even after losing all his wealth and family, excluding his wife, and became a leper, Job praised God and *"...did not sin with his lips...".* Along with four of his friends, Job tried to figure out why such evil had happened to him. He had insisted that he did not commit any sin worthy of such punishment, while his friends were sure that God would not have sent His wrath upon a righteous person, therefore Job must have inadvertently committed sin against God. After a lengthy discussion, God explained to them that no man can comprehend a full knowledge of God. All of them judged God's involvement wrongly, consequently *"...My wrath is kindled against thee, and against thy two friends: for ye have not spoken of me the thing that is right, as my servant Job hath...".* Then Job repented of what he had spoken about God. This book of the Bible is about God, who is in full control, and without His permission even Satan can do nothing. The attitude of Job was to praise and trust God no matter the circumstances in life.
2. In the end, God restored to Job his possessions, giving him *"... twice as much as he had before...",* and replaced his family with the exact same number as he had before: seven sons and three daughters.

CONCLUSION

It is difficult to compare the story as recorded in the Qur'an and in the Bible, for there are only a few common issues, such as:

a) the name of the person (Job),
b) the fact that he was afflicted,
c) God increased Job's possessions two-fold.

There is no explanation why the Qur'an says that God told Job to use the grass that was in his hand and to strike the ground with his foot in order to release a water fountain. In the Bible, we see a beautiful story of the man who trusted God even if it meant his own death.

Chapter Four

ABRAHAM

THE QUR'AN

"Ibrahim and his Father"

Sura 6

The Cattle

74. And when Ibrahim said to his sire, Azar: Do you take idols for gods? Surely I see you and your people in manifest error.

Sura 9

The Immunity

114. And Ibrahim asking forgiveness for his sire was only owing to a promise which he had made to him; but when it became clear to him that he was an enemy of Allah, he declared himself to be clear of him; most surely Ibrahim was very tender-hearted forbearing.

Sura 19

Marium

42. When he said to his father; **O my father! why do you worship what neither hears nor sees, nor does it avail you in the least:**
43. O my father! truly the knowledge has come to me which has not come to you, therefore follow me, I will guide you on a right path:
44. O my father! serve not the Shaitan, surely the Shaitan is disobedient to the Beneficent God:
45. O my father! surely I fear that a punishment from the Beneficent God should afflict you so that you should be a friend of the Shaitan.
46. He said: Do you dislike my gods, O Ibrahim? **If you do not desist I will certainly revile you, and leave me for a time.**
47. He said: Peace be on you, I will pray to my Lord to forgive you; surely He is ever Affectionate to me:
48. And I will withdraw from you and what you call on besides Allah, and I will call upon my Lord; may be I shall not remain unblessed in calling upon my Lord.

49. So when he withdrew from them and what they worshipped besides Allah, We gave to him Ishaq and Yaqoub, and each one of them We made a prophet.

50. And We granted to them of Our mercy, and We left (behind them) a truthful mention of eminence for them.

Sura 21

The Prophets

52. When he said to his father and his people: What are these images to whose worship you cleave?

53. They said: We found our fathers worshipping them.

54. He said: Certainly you have been, (both) you and your fathers, in manifest error.

55. They said: Have you brought to us the truth, or are you one of the triflers?

56. He said: Nay! your Lord is the Lord of the heavens and the earth, Who brought them into existence, and I am of those who bear witness to this:

57. And, by Allah! I will certainly do something against your idols after you go away, turning back.

58. So he broke them into pieces, except the chief of them, that haply they may return to it.

59. They said: Who has done this to our gods? Most surely he is one of the unjust.

60. They said: We heard a youth called Ibrahim speak of them.

61. Said they: Then bring him before the eyes of the people, perhaps they may bear witness.

62. They said: Have you done this to our gods, O Ibrahim ?

63. He said: Surely (some doer) has done it; the chief of them is this, therefore ask them, if they can speak.

64. Then they turned to themselves and said: Surely you yourselves are the unjust;

65. Then they were made to hang down their heads: Certainly you know that they do not speak.

66. He said:.What! do you then serve besides Allah what brings you not any benefit at all, nor does it harm you?

67. Fie on you and on what you serve besides Allah; what! do you not then understand?

68. They said: **Burn him and help your gods, if you are going to do (anything).**
69. We **said: O fire! be a comfort and peace to Ibrahim;**
70. And they desired a war on him, but We made them the greatest losers.

Sura 29

The Spider

16. And (We sent) Ibrahim, when he said to his people: Serve Allah and be careful of (your duty to) Him; this is best for you, if you did but know:
17. You only worship idols besides Allah and you create a lie surely they whom you serve besides Allah do not control for you any sustenance, therefore seek the sustenance from Allah and serve Him and be grateful to Him; to Him you shall be brought back.
24. So naught was the answer of his people except that they said: Slay him or burn him; then Allah delivered him from the fire; most surely there are signs in this for a people who believe.

Sura 29

The Rangers

95. Said he: What! do you worship what you hew out?
96. And Allah has created you and what you make.
97. They said: Build for him a furnace, then cast him into the burning fire.
98. And they desired a war against him, but We brought them low.

THE BIBLE

"Abram and his Father"

Genesis

Chapter 11

26. And Terah lived seventy years, and begat Abram, Nahor, and Haran.
31. And Terah took Abram his son, and Lot the son of Haran his son's son, and Sarai his daughter in law, his son Abram's wife; and

they went forth with them from Ur of the Chaldees, to go into the land of Canaan; and they came unto Haran, and dwelt there.
32. And the days of Terah were two hundred and five years: and **Terah died in Haran**.

Genesis

Chapter 12

1. Now the LORD had said unto Abram, Get thee out of thy country, and from thy kindred, and from thy father's house, unto a land that I will shew thee:
2. And I will make of thee a great nation, and I will bless thee, and make thy name great; and thou shalt be a blessing:
3. And I will bless them that bless thee, and curse him that curseth thee: and in thee shall all families of the earth be blessed.
4. So Abram departed, as the LORD had spoken unto him; and Lot went with him: **and Abram was seventy and five years old when he departed out of Haran**.

COMMENTARY

In the Qur'an:

1. Ibrahim (Abraham) is portrayed as the first person to defend monotheism in Ur.

In the Bible:

1. God first called Abram (Abraham) to follow Him; Abram was not looking for God. Abram followed God not from the city of Ur, but from the city of Haran after the death of his father.

The Bible does not mention anything about Abram's relationship to his father, but it seems to be more appropriate for Mohammed to put such emphasis on that to make a parallel with his own struggle for Allah against his relatives in Mecca. By doing so, Mohammed actually made himself equal to Abraham.

The Qur'an

"God's Covenant with Abraham"

Sura 2

The Cow

260. And when Ibrahim said: My Lord! show me how Thou givest life to the dead, He said: What! and do you not believe? He said: Yes, but that my heart may be at ease. He said: **Then take four of the birds, then train them to follow you, then place on every mountain a part of them, then call them, they will come to you flying; and know that Allah is Mighty, Wise.**

The Bible

"God's Covenant with Abram (Abraham)"

Genesis

Chapter 15

7. And he said unto him, I am the LORD that brought thee out of Ur of the Chaldees, to give thee this land to inherit it.

8. And he said, Lord GOD, whereby shall I know that I shall inherit it?

9. And he said unto him, Take me an heifer of three years old, and a she goat of three years old, and a ram of three years old, and a turtledove, and a young pigeon.

10. And he took unto him all these, **and divided them in the midst, and laid each piece one against another:** *but the birds divided he not.*

12. And when the sun was going down, a deep sleep fell upon Abram; and, lo, an horror of great darkness fell upon him.

13. And he said unto Abram, Know of a surety that thy seed shall be a stranger in a land that is not theirs, and shall serve them; and they shall afflict them four hundred years;

14. And also that nation, whom they shall serve, will I judge: and afterward shall they come out with great substance.

17. And it came to pass, that, when the sun went down, and it was dark, behold a smoking furnace, and a burning lamp that passed between those pieces.

18. In the same day the LORD made a covenant with Abram, saying, Unto thy seed have I given this land, from the river of Egypt unto the great river, the river Euphrates.

COMMENTARY

In the Qur'an:

1. Ibrahim asked Allah to show him a sign that He could bring life to the dead , and as a result, **parts of birds** reattached themselves together and flew to Ibrahim.

In the Bible:

1. Abraham (Abram) inquired of God how he could know that his seed will inherit the land that God had promised to him. God asked him to prepare a sacrifice. Every animal was cut into pieces, **except the birds**.

Here in the Bible we see that Abraham's question to God was different than the one asked in the Qur'an, and it resulted in a special covenant (agreement) that God made with Abraham and his descendants.

THE QUR'AN

"Abraham Meets the Lord in Mamre"

Sura 11

The Holy Prophet

69. And certainly Our messengers came to Ibrahim with good news. They said: Peace. Peace, said he, and he made no delay in bringing a roasted calf.

70. But when he saw that their hands were not extended towards it, he deemed them strange and conceived fear of them. They said: Fear not, surely we are sent to Lut's people.

71. And his wife was standing (by), so she laughed, then We gave her the good news of Ishaq and after Ishaq of (a son's son) **Yaqoub.**

72. She said: O wonder! shall I bear a son when I am an extremely old woman and this my husband an extremely old man? Most surely this is a wonderful thing.

73. They said: Do you wonder at Allah's bidding? The mercy of Allah and His blessings are on you, O people of the house, surely He is Praised, Glorious.

74. So when fear had gone away from Ibrahim and good news came to him, he began to plead with Us for Lut's people.

75. Most surely Ibrahim was forbearing, tender-hearted, oft-returning (to Allah):

Sura 51

The Scatterers

24. Has there come to you information about the honored guests of Ibrahim?

25. When they entered upon him, they said: Peace. Peace, said he, a strange people.

26. Then he turned aside to his family secretly and brought a fat (roasted) calf,

27. So he brought it near them. He said: **What! will you not eat?**

28. So he conceived in his mind a fear on account of them. They said: Fear not. And they gave him the good news of a boy possessing knowledge.

29. Then his wife came up in great grief, and she struck her face and said: An old barren woman!

30. They said: Thus says your Lord: Surely He is the Wise, the Knowing.

31. He said: What is your affair then, O messengers!

32. They said: Surely we are sent to a guilty people,

33. That we may send down upon them stone of clay,

34. Sent forth from your Lord for the extravagant.

35.Then We brought forth such as were therein of the believers.

36. But We did not find therein save a (single) house of those who submitted (the Muslims).

THE BIBLE
"Abraham Meets the Lord in Mamre"

Genesis
Chapter 18

1. And the LORD appeared unto him in the plains of Mamre: and he sat in the tent door in the heat of the day;

2. And he lift up his eyes and looked, and, lo, three men stood by him: and when he saw them, he ran to meet them from the tent door, and bowed himself toward the ground,

3. And said, My Lord, if now I have found favour in thy sight, pass not away, I pray thee, from thy servant:

4. Let a little water, I pray you, be fetched, and wash your feet, and rest yourselves under the tree:

5. And I will fetch a morsel of bread, and comfort ye your hearts; after that ye shall pass on: for therefore are ye come to your servant. And they said, So do, as thou hast said.

6. And Abraham hastened into the tent unto Sarah, and said, Make ready quickly three measures of fine meal, knead it, and make cakes upon the hearth.

7. And Abraham ran unto the herd, and fetcht a calf tender and good, and gave it unto a young man; and he hasted to dress it.

8. And he took butter, and milk, and the calf which he had dressed, and set it before them; and he stood by them under the tree, **and they did eat**.

9. And they said unto him, Where is Sarah thy wife? And he said, Behold, in the tent.

10. And he said, I will certainly return unto thee according to the time of life; and, lo, Sarah thy wife shall have a son. And Sarah heard it in the tent door, which was behind him.

11. Now Abraham and Sarah were old and well stricken in age; and it ceased to be with Sarah after the manner of women.

12. Therefore Sarah laughed within herself, saying, After I am waxed old shall I have pleasure, my lord being old also?

13. And the LORD said unto Abraham, Wherefore did Sarah laugh, saying, Shall I of a surety bear a child, which am old?

14. Is any thing too hard for the LORD? At the time appointed I will return unto thee, according to the time of life, and Sarah shall have a son.
15. Then Sarah denied, saying, I laughed not; for she was afraid. And he said, Nay; but thou didst laugh.

COMMENTARY

In the Qur'an:

1. A few of Allah's messengers came to Ibrahim.
2. Ibrahim offered them a meal, but they did not eat.
3. Ibrahim's wife loudly expressed her disbelief regarding her future pregnancy.

In the Bible:

1. God Himself, accompanied by two angels, met with Abraham.
2. Abraham offered them a meal, and they ate it.
3. Sara *"laughed to herself"* when she heard about a boy she would bring forth, and was afraid to acknowledge her quiet disbelief in God's promise.

THE QUR'AN

"Lot's Mission"

Sura 7

The Elevated Places

80. And (We sent) Lut when he said to his people: What! do you commit an indecency which any one in the world has not done before you?
81. Most surely you come to males in lust besides females; nay you are an extravagant people.
82. And the answer of his people was no other than that they said: Turn them out of your town, surely they are a people who seek to purify (themselves).
83 So We delivered him and his followers, except his wife; she was of those who remained behind.

84. And We rained upon them a rain; consider then what was the end of the guilty.

Sura 11

The Holy Prophet

77. And when Our messengers came to Lut, he was grieved for them, **and he lacked strength to protect them,** and said: This is a hard day.

78. And his people came to him, (as if) rushed on towards him, and already they did evil deeds. He said: O my people! these are my daughters-- they are purer for you, so guard against (the punishment of) Allah and do not disgrace me with regard to my guests; is there not among you one right-minded man?

79. They said: Certainly you know that we have no claim on your daughters, and most surely you know what we desire.

80. He said: Ah! that I had power to suppress you, rather I shall have recourse to a strong support.

81. They said: O Lut! we are the messengers of your Lord; they shall by no means reach you; **so remove your followers in a part of the night-- and let none of you turn back-- except your wife,** for surely whatsoever befalls them shall befall her; surely their appointed time is the morning; is not the morning nigh?

82. So when Our decree came to pass, We turned them upside down and rained down upon them stones, of what had been decreed, one after another.

83. Marked (for punishment) with your Lord and it is not far off from the unjust.

Sura 15

The Rock

61. So when the messengers came to Lut's followers,

62. He said: Surely you are an unknown people.

63. They said: Nay, we have come to you with that about which they disputed.

64. And we have come to you with the truth, and we are most surely truthful.

65. Therefore go forth with your followers in a part of the night and yourself follow their rear, and let not any one of you turn round, and go forth whither you are commanded.

66. And We revealed to him this decree, that the roots of these shall be cut off in the morning.

67. And the people of the town came rejoicing.

68. He said: Surely these are my guests, therefore do not disgrace me,

69. And guard against (the punishment of) Allah and do not put me to shame.

70. They said: Have we not forbidden you from (other) people?

71. He said: These are my daughters, if you will do (aught).

72. By your life! they were blindly wandering on in their intoxication.

73. So the rumbling overtook them (while) entering upon the time of sunrise;

74. Thus did We turn it upside down, and rained down upon them stones of what had been decreed.

75. Surely in this are signs for those who examine.

Sura 26

The Poets

160. The people of Lut gave the lie to the apostles.

161. When their brother Lut said to them: Will you not guard (against evil)?

162. Surely I am a faithful apostle to you;

163. Therefore guard against (the punishment of) Allah and obey me:

164. And I do not ask you any reward for it; my reward is only with the Lord of the worlds;

165. What! do you come to the males from among the creatures

166. And leave what your Lord has created for you of your wives? Nay, you are a people exceeding limits.

167. They said: If you desist not, O Lut! you shall surely be of those who are expelled.

168. He said: Surely I am of those who utterly abhor your conduct.

169. My Lord ! deliver me and my followers from what they do.

170. So We delivered him and his followers all,

171. Except an old woman, among those who remained behind.

172. Then We utterly destroyed the others.

173. And We rained down upon them a rain, and evil was the rain on those warned.

Sura 27

The Ant

54. And (We sent) Lut, when he said to his people: What! do you commit indecency while you see?

55. What! do you indeed approach men lustfully rather than women? Nay, you are a people who act ignorantly.

56. But the answer of his people was no other except that they said: **Turn out Lut's followers from your town; surely they are a people who would keep pure!**

57. But We delivered him and his followers except his wife; We ordained her to be of those who remained behind.

58. And We rained on them a rain, and evil was the rain of those who had been warned.

Sura 29

The Spider

26. And Lut believed in Him, and he said: I am fleeing to my Lord, surely He is the Mighty, the Wise.

28. And (We sent) Lut when he said to his people: Most surely you are guilty of an indecency which none of the nations has ever done before you;

29. What! do you come to the males and commit robbery on the highway, and you commit evil deeds in your assemblies? But nothing was the answer of his people except that they said: Bring on us Allah's punishment, if you are one of the truthful.

30. He said: My Lord! help me against the mischievous people.

31. And when Our messengers came to Ibrahim with the good news, they said: Surely we are going to destroy the people of this town, for its people are unjust.

32. He said: Surely in it is Lut. They said: **We know well who is in it; we shall certainly deliver him and his followers, except his wife; she shall be of those who remain behind.**

33. And when Our messengers came to Lut he was grieved on account of them, and he felt powerless (to protect) them; and they said: Fear not, nor grieve; **surely we will deliver you and your followers, except your wife; she shall be of those who remain behind.**

34. Surely We will cause to come down upon the people of this town a punishment from heaven, because they transgressed.

35. And certainly We have left a clear sign of it for a people who understand.

Sura 50

Qaf

12. (Others) before them rejected (prophets): the people of Nuh and the dwellers of Ar-Rass and Samood,

13. And Ad and Firon and Lut's brethren…

THE BIBLE

"Lot's Mission"

Genesis

Chapter 13

7. And there was a strife between the herdmen of Abram's cattle and the herdmen of Lot's cattle: and the Canaanite and the Perizzite dwelled then in the land.

8. And Abram said unto Lot, Let there be no strife, I pray thee, between me and thee, and between my herdmen and thy herdmen; for we be brethren.

9. Is not the whole land before thee? **separate thyself, I pray thee, from me: if thou wilt take the left hand, then I will go to the right; or if thou depart to the right hand, then I will go to the left.**

10. And Lot lifted up his eyes, and beheld all the plain of Jordan, that it was well watered every where, before the LORD destroyed Sodom and Gomorrah, even as the garden of the LORD, like the land of Egypt, as thou comest unto Zoar.

11. Then Lot chose him all the plain of Jordan; and Lot journeyed east: and they separated themselves the one from the other.

12. Abram dwelled in the land of Canaan, **and Lot dwelled in the cities of the plain, and pitched his tent toward Sodom.**

13. But the men of Sodom were wicked and sinners before the LORD exceedingly.

14. And the LORD said unto Abram, after that Lot was separated from him, Lift up now thine eyes, and look from the place where thou art northward, and southward, and eastward, and westward:

15. For all the land which thou seest, to thee will I give it, and to thy seed for ever.

16. And I will make thy seed as the dust of the earth: so that if a man can number the dust of the earth, then shall thy seed also be numbered.

17. Arise, walk through the land in the length of it and in the breadth of it; for I will give it unto thee.

18. Then Abram removed his tent, and came and dwelt in the plain of Mamre, which is in Hebron, and built there an altar unto the LORD.

Genesis

Chapter 14

11. And they took all the goods of Sodom and Gomorrah, and all their victuals, and went their way.

12. And they took Lot, Abram's brother's son, who dwelt in Sodom, and his goods, and departed.

Second Peter

Chapter 2

6. And turning the cities of Sodom and Gomorrha into ashes condemned them with an overthrow, making them an ensample unto those that after should live ungodly;

7. And delivered **just Lot**, vexed with the filthy conversation of the wicked:

8. (For that **righteous man dwelling among them**, in seeing and hearing, **vexed his righteous soul** from day to day with their unlawful deeds;)

9. The Lord knoweth how to deliver the godly out of temptations, and to reserve the unjust unto the day of judgment to be punished:

Genesis

Chapter 19

1. And there came two angels to Sodom at even; **and Lot sat in the gate of Sodom**: and Lot seeing them rose up to meet them; and he bowed himself with his face toward the ground;

2. And he said, Behold now, my lords, turn in, I pray you, into your servant's house, and tarry all night, and wash your feet, and ye shall rise up early, and go on your ways. And they said, Nay; but we will abide in the street all night.

3. And he pressed upon them greatly; and they turned in unto him, and entered into his house; and he made them a feast, and did bake unleavened bread, and they did eat.

4. But before they lay down, the men of the city, even the men of Sodom, compassed the house round, both old and young, all the people from every quarter:

5. And they called unto Lot, and said unto him, Where are the men which came in to thee this night? bring them out unto us, that we may know them.

6. And Lot went out at the door unto them, and shut the door after him,

7. And said, I pray you, brethren, do not so wickedly.

8. Behold now, I have two daughters which have not known man; let me, I pray you, bring them out unto you, and do ye to them as is good in your eyes: only unto these men do nothing; for therefore came they under the shadow of my roof.

9. And they said, Stand back. And they said again, This one fellow came in to sojourn, and he will needs be a judge: now will we deal worse with thee, than with them. And they pressed sore upon the man, even Lot, and came near to break the door.

10. But the men put forth their hand, and pulled Lot into the house to them, and shut to the door.

11. And they smote the men that were at the door of the house with blindness, both small and great: so that they wearied themselves to find the door.

12. And the men said unto Lot, Hast thou here any besides? son in law, and thy sons, and thy daughters, and whatsoever thou hast in the city, bring them out of this place:

13. For we will destroy this place, because the cry of them is waxen great before the face of the LORD; and the LORD hath sent us to destroy it.
14. And Lot went out, and spake unto his sons in law, which married his daughters, and said, Up, get you out of this place; for the LORD will destroy this city. But he seemed as one that mocked unto his sons in law.
15. And when the morning arose, then the angels hastened Lot, saying, **Arise, take thy wife, and thy two daughters, which are here; lest thou be consumed in the iniquity of the city.**
16. And while he lingered, the men laid hold upon his hand, and upon the hand of his wife, and upon the hand of his two daughters; the LORD being merciful unto him: and they brought him forth, and set him without the city.
17. And it came to pass, when they had brought them forth abroad, that he said, Escape for thy life; look not behind thee, neither stay thou in all the plain; escape to the mountain, lest thou be consumed.
18. And Lot said unto them, Oh, not so, my Lord:
19. Behold now, thy servant hath found grace in thy sight, and thou hast magnified thy mercy, which thou hast shewed unto me in saving my life; and I cannot escape to the mountain, lest some evil take me, and I die:
20. Behold now, this city is near to flee unto, and it is a little one: Oh, let me escape thither, (is it not a little one?) and my soul shall live.
21. And he said unto him, See, I have accepted thee concerning this thing also, that I will not overthrow this city, for the which thou hast spoken.
22. Haste thee, escape thither; for I cannot do any thing till thou be come thither. Therefore the name of the city was called Zoar.
23. The sun was risen upon the earth when Lot entered into Zoar.
24. Then the LORD rained upon Sodom and upon Gomorrah brimstone and fire from the LORD out of heaven;
25. And he overthrew those cities, and all the plain, and all the inhabitants of the cities, and that which grew upon the ground.
26. But his wife looked back from behind him, and she became a pillar of salt.
27. And Abraham gat up early in the morning to the place where he stood before the LORD:
28. And he looked toward Sodom and Gomorrah, and toward all the land of the plain, and beheld, and, lo, the smoke of the country went up as the smoke of a furnace.

29. And it came to pass, when God destroyed the cities of the plain, that God remembered Abraham, and sent Lot out of the midst of the overthrow, when he overthrew the cities in the which Lot dwelt.

30. And Lot went up out of Zoar, and dwelt in the mountain, and his two daughters with him; for he feared to dwell in Zoar: and he dwelt in a cave, he and his two daughters.

31. And the firstborn said unto the younger, Our father is old, and there is not a man in the earth to come in unto us after the manner of all the earth:

32. Come, let us make our father drink wine, and we will lie with him, that we may preserve seed of our father.

33. And they made their father drink wine that night: and the firstborn went in, and lay with her father; and he perceived not when she lay down, nor when she arose.

34. And it came to pass on the morrow, that the firstborn said unto the younger, Behold, I lay yesternight with my father: let us make him drink wine this night also; and go thou in, and lie with him, that we may preserve seed of our Father.

35. And they made their father drink wine that night also: and the younger arose, and lay with him; and he perceived not when she lay down, nor when she arose.

36. Thus were both the daughters of Lot with child by their father.

37. And the firstborn bare a son, and called his name Moab: the same is the **father of the Moabites unto this day**.

38. And the younger, she also bare a son, and called his name Benammi: the same is the father of the children of Ammon unto this day.

COMMENTARY

In the Qur'an:

1. God had sent Lut (Lot) to be a witness for Him before a sinful generation, but the people of Sodom rejected the message. Lot asked God to destroy them and save his family, to which God complies.

2. Lot's wife was predestined for destruction: "*...To her will happen what happens to the people.*"

3. Angels came to Ibrahim (Abraham) and announced the "good news" that Sodom will be destroyed.
4. The brothers (or neighbours) of Lot rejected the message.

In the Bible:

1. Lot chose Sodom not because he followed God's command, but because of the riches of that land. He became very prosperous there. The angels who came to Lot's house did not want to stay in his house. Contrary to Abraham, a picture of the mature spiritual believer, Lot is a picture of the **carnal believer.** Lot did not even leave with the angels after they told him about the plan to destroy Sodom; **they had to force him out of the city!** *"...And while he lingered, the men laid hold upon his hand, and upon the hand of his wife, and upon the hand of his two daughters; the LORD being merciful unto him: and they brought him forth, and set him without the city..."* Lot did not ask God to deliver him from Sodom, but actually liked this city and even lingered before leaving on the eve of its destruction.

2. The angels wanted to save all of Lot's immediate family: *"...the men laid hold upon his hand, and upon the hand of **his wife**, and upon the hand of his two daughters;".* They physically seized him, his wife and his daughters and forced them leave Sodom. Lot's wife perished (she turned into a pillar of salt) by the time they reached the city called Zoar. She had disobeyed God's command by looking back at the destruction behind them.

3. God Himself had told Abraham about the coming destruction of Sodom, and never referred to this as a "good" message. Abraham even pleaded with God not to destroy entire city for the sake of at least ten righteous persons. Although God agreed to Abraham's request, there could not be found at least ten righteous persons and therefore the city had to be destroyed.

4. The sons-in-law (not his brothers or neighbours) of Lot rejected the warning. Lot is not recorded as having any brothers. No other inhabitants of the city were warned by Lot about the coming destruction.

The Qur'an
"Abraham Sacrifices his Son"

Sura 37
The Rangers

99. And he said: Surely I fly to my lord; He will guide me.

100. My Lord! grant me of the doers of good deeds.

101. So We gave him the good news of a boy, possessing forbearance.

102. And when he attained to working with him, **he said: O my son! surely I have seen in a dream that I should sacrifice you; consider then what you see. He said: O my father! do what you are commanded; if Allah please, you will find me of the patient ones.**

103. So when they both submitted and he threw him down upon his forehead,

104. And We called out to him saying: O Ibrahim!

105. You have indeed shown the truth of the vision; surely thus do We reward the doers of good:

106. Most surely this is a manifest trial.

107. And We ransomed him with a Feat sacrifice.

108. And We perpetuated (praise) to him among the later generations.

110. Thus do We reward the doers of good.

111. Surely he was one of Our believing servants.

112. And We gave him the good news of Ishaq, a prophet among the good ones.

113. And We showered Our blessings on him and on Ishaq; and of their offspring are the doers of good, and (also) those who are clearly unjust to their own souls.

THE BIBLE

"Abraham Sacrifices his Son"

Genesis

Chapter 21

1. And the LORD visited Sarah as he had said, and the LORD did unto Sarah as he had spoken.

2. For Sarah conceived, and bare Abraham a son in his old age, at the set time of which God had spoken to him.

3. And Abraham called the name of his son that was born unto him, whom Sarah bare to him, Isaac.

4. And Abraham circumcised his son Isaac being eight days old, as God had commanded him.

5. And Abraham was an hundred years old, when his son Isaac was born unto him.

6. And Sarah said, God hath made me to laugh, so that all that hear will laugh with me.

7. And she said, Who would have said unto Abraham, that Sarah should have given children suck? for I have born him a son in his old age.

8. And the child grew, and was weaned: and Abraham made a great feast the same day that Isaac was weaned.

9. And Sarah saw the son of Hagar the Egyptian, which she had born unto Abraham, mocking.

10. Wherefore she said unto Abraham, Cast out this bondwoman and her son: for the son of this bondwoman shall not be heir with my son, even with Isaac.

11. And the thing was very grievous in Abraham's sight because of his son.

12. And God said unto Abraham, Let it not be grievous in thy sight because of the lad, and because of thy bondwoman; in all that Sarah hath said unto thee, hearken unto her voice; for in Isaac shall thy seed be called.

13. And also of the son of the bondwoman will I make a nation, because he is thy seed.

14. And Abraham rose up early in the morning, and took bread, and a bottle of water, and gave it unto Hagar, putting it on her shoulder, and the child, and sent her away: and she departed, and wandered in the wilderness of Beer-sheba.

15. And the water was spent in the bottle, and she cast the child under one of the shrubs.

16. And she went, and sat her down over against him a good way off, as it were a bowshot: for she said, Let me not see the death of the child. And she sat over against him, and lift up her voice, and wept.

17. And God heard the voice of the lad; and the angel of God called Hagar out of heaven, and said unto her, What aileth thee, Hagar? fear not; for God hath heard the voice of the lad where he is.

18. Arise, lift up the lad, and hold him in thine hand; for I will make him a great nation.

19. And God opened her eyes, and she saw a well of water; and she went, and filled the bottle with water, and gave the lad drink.

20. And God was with the lad; and he grew, and dwelt in the wilderness, and became an archer.

21. And he dwelt in the wilderness of Paran: and his mother took him a wife out of the land of Egypt.

22. And it came to pass at that time, that Abimelech and Phichol the chief captain of his host spake unto Abraham, saying, God is with thee in all that thou doest:

23. Now therefore swear unto me here by God that thou wilt not deal falsely with me, nor with my son, nor with my son's son: but according to the kindness that I have done unto thee, thou shalt do unto me, and to the land wherein thou hast sojourned.

24. And Abraham said, I will swear.

25. And Abraham reproved Abimelech because of a well of water, which Abimelech's servants had violently taken away.

26. And Abimelech said, I wot not who hath done this thing: neither didst thou tell me, neither yet heard I of it, but to day.

27. And Abraham took sheep and oxen, and gave them unto Abimelech; and both of them made a covenant.

28. And Abraham set seven ewe lambs of the flock by themselves.

29. And Abimelech said unto Abraham, What mean these seven ewe lambs which thou hast set by themselves?

30. And he said, For these seven ewe lambs shalt thou take of my hand, that they may be a witness unto me, that I have digged this well.

31. Wherefore he called that place Beer-sheba; because there they sware both of them.

32. Thus they made a covenant at Beer-sheba: then Abimelech rose up, and Phichol the chief captain of his host, and they returned into the land of the Philistines.

33. And Abraham planted a grove in Beer-sheba, and called there on the name of the LORD, the everlasting God.

34. And Abraham sojourned in the Philistines' land many days.

Genesis

Chapter 22

1. And it came to pass after these things, that God did tempt Abraham, and said unto him, Abraham: and he said, Behold, here I am.

2. And he said, Take now thy son, thine only son Isaac, whom thou lovest, and get thee into the land of Moriah; and offer him there for a burnt offering upon one of the mountains which I will tell thee of.

3. And Abraham rose up early in the morning, and saddled his ass, and took two of his young men with him, **and Isaac his son,** and clave the wood for the burnt offering, and rose up, and went unto the place of which God had told him.

4. Then on the third day Abraham lifted up his eyes, and saw the place afar off.

5. And Abraham said unto his young men, Abide ye here with the ass; and I and the lad will go yonder and worship, and come again to you,

6. And Abraham took the wood of the burnt offering, and laid it upon Isaac his son; and he took the fire in his hand, and a knife; and they went both of them together.

7. And Isaac spake unto Abraham his father, and said, My father: and he said, Here am I, my son. And he said, Behold the fire and the wood: but where is the lamb for a burnt offering?

8. And Abraham said, My son, God will provide himself a lamb for a burnt offering: so they went both of them together.

9. And they came to the place which God had told him of; and Abraham built an altar there, and laid the wood in order, **and bound Isaac his son, and laid him on the altar upon the wood.**

10. And Abraham stretched forth his hand, and took the knife to slay his son.

11. And the angel of the LORD called unto him out of heaven, and said, Abraham, Abraham: and he said, Here am I.

12. And he said, Lay not thine hand upon the lad, neither do thou any thing unto him: for now I know that thou fearest God, seeing thou hast not withheld thy son, thine only son from me.

13. And Abraham lifted up his eyes, and looked, and behold behind him a ram caught in a thicket by his horns: and Abraham went and took the ram, and offered him up for a burnt offering in the stead of his son.

14. And Abraham called the name of that place Jehovah-jireh: as it is said to this day, In the mount of the LORD it shall be seen.

15. And the angel of the LORD called unto Abraham out of heaven the second time,

16. And said, **By myself have I sworn, saith the LORD, for because thou hast done this thing, and hast not withheld thy son, thine only son**:

17. That in blessing I will bless thee, and in multiplying I will multiply thy seed as the stars of the heaven, and as the sand which is upon the sea shore; and thy seed shall possess the gate of his enemies;

18. And in thy seed shall all the nations of the earth be blessed; because thou hast obeyed my voice.

19. So Abraham returned unto his young men, and they rose up and went together to Beer-sheba; and Abraham dwelt at Beer-sheba.

20. And it came to pass after these things, that it was told Abraham, saying, Behold, Milcah, she hath also born children unto thy brother Nahor;

21. Huz his firstborn, and Buz his brother, and Kemuel the father of Aram,

22. And Chesed, and Hazo, and Pildash, and Jidlaph, and Bethuel.

23. And Bethuel begat Rebekah: these eight Milcah did bear to Nahor, Abraham's brother.

24. And his concubine, whose name was Reumah, she bare also Tebah, and Gaham, and Thahash, and Maachah.

COMMENTARY

In the Qur'an:

1. Ibrahim (Abraham) asked God for a son. And God *"...gave him the good news of a boy, possessing forbearance."*

2. Abraham saw a vision of his son being sacrificed and told his son about it. His son agreed with the will of God and encouraged his father to offer himself as a sacrifice.

3. God rewarded Abraham because of his obedience.

4. After that event, God gave Abraham *"...the good news of Ishaq, a prophet among the good ones."*

In the Bible:

1. God Himself gave Abraham this promise:

    *"....**I will make of thee a great nation**, and I will bless thee, and make thy name great; and thou shalt be a blessing"-* **(Genesis 12:2)**. *"...And God said unto Abraham, As for Sarai thy wife, thou shalt not call her name Sarai, but Sarah shall her name be. And I will bless her, **and give thee a son also of her**: yea, I will bless her, **and she shall be a mother of nations; kings of people shall be of her**. Then Abraham fell upon his face, and laughed, and said in his heart, Shall a child be born unto him that is an hundred years old? and shall Sarah, that is ninety years old, bear?"* **(Genesis 17:15-17)**

    Abraham did not expect to have a child from Sarah.

2. God said unto Abraham:

    *"...Take now thy son, **thine only son Isaac**, whom thou lovest, and get thee into the land of Moriah; **and offer him there for a burnt offering** upon one of the mountains which I will tell thee of...".* *"And Isaac spake unto Abraham his father, and said, My father: and he said, Here am I, my son. And he said, **Behold the fire and the wood: but where is the lamb for a burnt offering?**"*

    Isaac did not know until the last moment that it was he who was to be sacrificed.

3. God actually tested Abraham's faith and it became a great blessing not only for the nation of the Israel, but for all believers, regardless of nationality and race:

    "...That in blessing I will bless thee, and in multiplying I will multiply thy seed as the stars of the heaven, and as the sand which is upon the sea shore; and thy seed shall possess the gate of his enemies; And in thy

*seed shall **all the nations of the earth be blessed**; because thou hast obeyed my voice."* **(Genesis 22:18)**

4. In the Bible we read that Ishmael was sent away before Isaac was about to be sacrificed. Most, if not all Muslim scholars believe that it was Ishmael who was about to be sacrificed, not Isaac. The Qur'an does not mention any name, but in ayat 112 it looks as if Isaac was born after that event would have taken place. Meanwhile, the Bible gives us the exact sequence of events:

    a) Isaac was born.

    b) Later, Ishmael was caught mocking Isaac and Sarah demanded that Abraham send Hagar and Ishmael away. God approved it and it was done.

    c) After that event Abraham *"...sojourned in the Philistines' land many days..."*

    d) God specifically asked Abraham to sacrifice his son Isaac.

Chapter Five

JOSEPH

THE QUR'AN

"The Jealousy of Joseph's Brothers"

Sura 12

Yusuf

4. When Yusuf said to his father: **O my father! surely I saw eleven stars and the sun and the moon-- I saw them making obeisance to me.**

5. He said: O my son! do not relate your vision to your brothers, lest they devise a plan against you; surely the Shaitan is an open enemy to man.

6. And thus will your Lord choose you and teach you the interpretation of sayings and make His favor complete to you and to the children of Yaqoub, as He made it complete before to your fathers, Ibrahim and Ishaq; surely your Lord is Knowing, Wise.

7. Certainly in Yusuf and his brothers there are signs for the inquirers.

8. When they said: **Certainly Yusuf and his brother are dearer to our father than we, though we are a (stronger) company; most surely our father is in manifest error:**

9. Slay Yusuf or cast him (forth) into some land, so that your father's regard may be exclusively for you, and after that you may be a righteous people.

10. A speaker from among them said: **Do not slay Yusuf, and cast him down into the bottom of the pit if you must do (it), (so that) some of the travellers may pick him up.**

11. They said: O our father! what reason have you that you do not trust in us with respect to Yusuf? And most surely we are his sincere well-wishers:

12. Send him with us tomorrow that he may enjoy himself and sport, and surely we will guard him well.

13. He said: **Surely it grieves me that you should take him off, and I fear lest the wolf devour him while you are heedless of him.**

14. They said: Surely if the wolf should devour him notwithstanding that we are a (strong) company, we should then certainly be losers.

15. So when they had gone off with him and agreed that they should put him down at the bottom of the pit, **and We revealed to him: You will most certainly inform them of this their affair while they do not perceive.**

16. And they came to their father at nightfall, weeping.

17. They said: O our father! surely we went off racing and left Yusuf by our goods, so the wolf devoured him, and you will not believe us though we are truthful.

18. And they brought his shirt with false blood upon it. He said: Nay, your souls have made the matter light for you, but patience is good and Allah is He Whose help is sought for against what you describe.

19. And there came travellers and they sent their water-drawer and he let down his bucket. He said: O good news! this is a youth; and they concealed him as an article of merchandise, and Allah knew what they did.

20. And they sold him for a small price, a few pieces of silver, and they showed no desire for him.

THE BIBLE

"The Jealousy of Joseph's Brothers"

Genesis

Chapter 37

2. These are the generations of Jacob. Joseph, being seventeen years old, was feeding the flock with his brethren; and the lad was with the sons of Bilhah, and with the sons of Zilpah, his father's wives: **and Joseph brought unto his father their evil report.**

3. Now Israel loved Joseph more than all his children, because he was the son of his old age: and he made him a coat of many colours.

4. And when his brethren saw that their father loved him more than all his brethren, they hated him, and could not speak peaceably unto him.

5. And Joseph dreamed a dream, and he told it his brethren: and they hated him yet the more.

6. And he said unto them, Hear, I pray you, this dream which I have dreamed:

7. For, behold, we were binding sheaves in the field, and, lo, my sheaf arose, and also stood upright; and, behold, your sheaves stood round about, and made obeisance to my sheaf.

8. And his brethren said to him, Shalt thou indeed reign over us? or shalt thou indeed have dominion over us? And they hated him yet the more for his dreams, and for his words.

9. And he dreamed yet another dream, and told it his brethren, and said, Behold, I have dreamed a dream more; and, behold, the sun and the moon and the eleven stars made obeisance to me.

10. And he told it to his father, and to his brethren: and his father rebuked him, and said unto him, What is this dream that thou hast dreamed? Shall I and thy mother and thy brethren indeed come to bow down ourselves to thee to the earth?

11. And his brethren envied him; but his father observed the saying.

12. And his brethren went to feed their father's flock in Shechem.

13. And Israel said unto Joseph, Do not thy brethren feed the flock in Shechem? come, and I will send thee unto them. And he said to him, Here am I.

14. And he said to him, Go, I pray thee, see whether it be well with thy brethren, and well with the flocks; and bring me word again. So he sent him out of the vale of Hebron, and he came to Shechem.

15. And a certain man found him, and, behold, he was wandering in the field: and the man asked him, saying, What seekest thou?

16. And he said, I seek my brethren: tell me, I pray thee, where they feed their flocks.

17. And the man said, They are departed hence; for I heard them say, Let us go to Dothan. And Joseph went after his brethren, and found them in Dothan.

18. And when they saw him afar off, even before he came near unto them, they conspired against him to slay him.

19. And they said one to another, Behold, this dreamer cometh.

20. Come now therefore, and let us slay him, and cast him into some pit, and we will say, Some evil beast hath devoured him: and we shall see what will become of his dreams.

21. And Reuben heard it, and he delivered him out of their hands; and said, Let us not kill him.

22. And Reuben said unto them, Shed no blood, but cast him into this pit that is in the wilderness, and lay no hand upon him; that

he might rid him out of their hands, to deliver him to his father again.

23. And it came to pass, when Joseph was come unto his brethren, that they stript Joseph out of his coat, his coat of many colours that was on him;

24. And they took him, and cast him into a pit: and the pit was empty, there was no water in it.

25. And they sat down to eat bread: and they lifted up their eyes and looked, and, behold, a company of Ishmeelites came from Gilead with their camels bearing spicery and balm and myrrh, going to carry it down to Egypt.

26. And Judah said unto his brethren, What profit is it if we slay our brother, and conceal his blood?

27. Come, and let us sell him to the Ishmeelites, and let not our hand be upon him; for he is our brother and our flesh. And his brethren were content.

28. Then there passed by Midianites merchantmen; and they drew and lifted up Joseph out of the pit, and sold Joseph to the Ishmeelites for twenty pieces of silver: and they brought Joseph into Egypt.

29. And Reuben returned unto the pit; and, behold, Joseph was not in the pit; and he rent his clothes.

30. And he returned unto his brethren, and said, The child is not; and I, whither shall I go?

31. And they took Joseph's coat, and killed a kid of the goats, and dipped the coat in the blood;

32. And they sent the coat of many colours, and they brought it to their father; and said, **This have we found: know now whether it be thy son's coat or no.**

33. And he knew it, and said, It is my son's coat; an evil beast hath devoured him; Joseph is without doubt rent in pieces.

34. And Jacob rent his clothes, and put sackcloth upon his loins, and mourned for his son many days.

COMMENTARY

In the Qur'an:

1. Jacob encouraged Joseph not to tell his dream to his brothers and prophesied that Joseph would be an interpreter of dreams.

2. One of the brothers purposed not to kill Joseph but to throw him into a pit instead so that travelers would find him. They agreed to this plan even before Joseph came to them.

3. The brothers actually asked their father's permission to let Joseph go with them so that they might execute their plot against him.

4. Jacob did not believe their story that a wolf had devoured Joseph.

5. Travelers found Joseph by accident in the well.

6. His brothers somehow were able to sell Joseph to the travelers, in spite of fact that those travelers found Joseph on their own. Or perhaps travellers found him while brothers were far away from the well and sold Joseph to the Egyptians for a small amount of silver.

In the Bible:

1. Joseph had two dreams and recounted them to his father and his brothers. Jacob interpreted Joseph's dream and rebuked him.

2. His brothers had gone into the fields with their flocks and Jacob asked Joseph to find them and bring back news to him. As they saw Joseph approaching, the brothers plotted to get rid of him. Reuben, his oldest brother, tried to stop the other brothers from killing Joseph and proposed throwing him into the well, planning to rescue Joseph later and return him to his father. Reuben mourned over Joseph's fate after his brothers sold Joseph into slavery.

4. Jacob believed the story about the death of Joseph and "...*mourned for his son many days.*"

5, 6. His brothers saw travelers who happened to be descendants of Ishmael, and sold Joseph to them for twenty pieces of silver .

THE QUR'AN

"Potiphar's Wife"

Sura 12

Yusuf

21. And the Egyptian who bought him said to his wife: Give him an honorable abode, maybe he will be useful to us, or we may adopt

him as a son. And thus did We establish Yusuf in the land and that We might teach him the interpretation of sayings; and Allah is the master of His affair, but most people do not know.

22. And when he had attained his maturity, We gave him wisdom and knowledge: and thus do We reward those who do good.

23. And she in whose house he was sought to make himself yield (to her), and she made fast the doors and said: Come forward. He said: I seek Allah's refuge, surely my Lord made good my abode: Surely the unjust do not prosper.

24. And certainly she made for him, and he would have made for her, were it not that he had seen the manifest evidence of his Lord; thus (it was) that We might turn away from him evil and indecency, surely he was one of Our sincere servants.

25. And they both hastened to the door, and she rent his shirt from behind and they met her husband at the door. She said: What is the punishment of him who intends evil to your wife except imprisonment or a painful chastisement?

26. He said: She sought to make me yield (to her); and a witness of her own family bore witness: **If his shirt is rent from front, she speaks the truth and he is one of the liars**:

27. And if his shirt is rent from behind, she tells a lie and he is one of the truthful.

28. So when he saw his shirt rent from behind, he said: Surely it is a guile of you women; surely your guile is great:

29. O Yusuf! turn aside from this; and (O my wife)! ask forgiveness for your fault, surely you are one of the wrong-doers.

30. And women in the city said: The chiefs wife seeks her slave to yield himself (to her), surely he has affected her deeply with (his) love; most surely we see her in manifest error.

31. So when she heard of their sly talk she sent for them and prepared for them a repast, and gave each of them a knife, and said (to Yusuf): Come forth to them. So when they saw him, they deemed him great, and cut their hands (in amazement), and said: Remote is Allah (from imperfection); this is not a mortal; this is but a noble angel.

32. She said: This is he with respect to whom you blamed me, and certainly I sought his yielding himself (to me), but he abstained, and if he does not do what I bid him, he shall certainly be imprisoned, and he shall certainly be of those who are in a state of ignominy.

33. He said: My Lord! the prison house is dearer to me than that to which they invite me; and if Thou turn not away their device from me, I will yearn towards them and become (one) of the ignorant.
34. Thereupon his Lord accepted his prayer and turned away their guile from him; surely He is the Hearing, the Knowing.
35. Then it occurred to them after they had seen the signs that they should imprison him till a time.

THE BIBLE

"Potiphar's Wife"

Genesis

Chapter 39

1. And Joseph was brought down to Egypt; and Potiphar, an officer of Pharaoh, captain of the guard, an Egyptian, bought him of the hands of the Ishmeelites, which had brought him down thither.
2. And the LORD was with Joseph, and he was a prosperous man; and he was in the house of his master the Egyptian.
3. And his master saw that the LORD was with him, and that the LORD made all that he did to prosper in his hand.
4. And Joseph found grace in his sight, and he served him: and he made him overseer over his house, and all that he had he put into his hand.
5. And it came to pass from the time that he had made him overseer in his house, and over all that he had, that the LORD blessed the Egyptian's house for Joseph's sake; and the blessing of the LORD was upon all that he had in the house, and in the field.
7. And it came to pass after these things, that his master's wife cast her eyes upon Joseph; and she said, Lie with me.
8. But he refused, and said unto his master's wife, Behold, my master wotteth not what is with me in the house, and he hath committed all that he hath to my hand;
9. There is none greater in this house than I; neither hath he kept back any thing from me but thee, because thou art his wife: how then can I do this great wickedness, and sin against God?
10. And it came to pass, as she spake to Joseph day by day, that he hearkened not unto her, to lie by her, or to be with her.

11. And it came to pass about this time, that Joseph went into the house to do his business; and there was none of the men of the house there within.

12. And she caught him by his garment, saying, Lie with me: and he left his garment in her hand, and fled, and got him out.

13. And it came to pass, when she saw that he had left his garment in her hand, and was fled forth,

14. That she called unto the men of her house, and spake unto them, saying, See, he hath brought in an Hebrew unto us to mock us; he came in unto me to lie with me, and I cried with a loud voice:

15. And it came to pass, when he heard that I lifted up my voice and cried, that he left his garment with me, and fled, and got him out.

16. And she laid up his garment by her, until his lord came home.

17. And she spake unto him according to these words, saying, The Hebrew servant, which thou hast brought unto us, came in unto me to mock me:

18. And it came to pass, as I lifted up my voice and cried, that he left his garment with me, and fled out.

19. And it came to pass, when **his master** heard the words of his wife, which she spake unto him, saying, After this manner did thy servant to me; that **his wrath was kindled**.

20. And Joseph's master took him, and put him into the prison, a place where the king's prisoners were bound: and he was there in the prison.

COMMENTARY

In the Qur'an:

1. The man who bought Joseph hoped that a new slave would bring prosperity into his house.
2. Allah brought Joseph to Egypt in order to make him an interpreter of dreams.
3. One day when the Egyptian's wife asked Joseph to be with her, he refused and they both ran to the door where they met. the master of the house.
4. Joseph called for a witness of one of his household who offered to examine the manner in which his shirt had been ripped off. The master of the house examined the evidence and saw that Joseph was telling the truth and his wife was lying.

5. The man's wife asked other ladies in town to see for themselves that Joseph's handsomeness was a good reason for her desire to him and that she was innocent in her lust. The women testified in agreement.

6. The man's wife asked Joseph again to lie down with her and threatened him with imprisonment. Joseph chose prison. Somehow she managed to get him imprisoned, in spite of her husband's conviction of Joseph's innocence.

In the Bible:

1. God blessed Joseph and Potiphar saw that Joseph brought prosperity into his house.

2. As we will read in later chapters, God brought Joseph to the Egypt not to be an interpreter of dreams, but ultimately to save his family from famine in Canaan.

3. Potiphar's wife desired Joseph and asked him day after day to lie with her, without success. She used one chance when no other servants were in the house and asked him again, grabbing him by his garment. He tried to escape from her and left his garment in her hands. She called the other servants and concocted a story about Joseph's attempt to rape her. Then she waited for her husband to come home and she repeated her story to him. He believed his wife's words and angrily sent Joseph to prison.

4,5,6. There is no room in the Bible for stories like one in the Qur'an about the second attempt of Potiphar's wife to seduce Joseph and to threaten him with imprisonment.

THE QUR'AN

"Joseph in Prison"

Sura 12

Yusuf

36. And two youths entered the prison with him. One of them said: I saw myself pressing wine. And the other said: I saw myself carrying bread on my head, of which birds ate. Inform us of its interpretation; surely we see you to be of the doers of good.

37. He said: There shall not come to you the food with which you are fed, but I will inform you both of its interpretation before it comes to you; this is of what my Lord has taught me; surely I have forsaken the religion of a people who do not believe in Allah, and they are deniers of the hereafter:

38. And I follow the religion of my fathers, Ibrahim and Ishaq and Yaqoub; it beseems us not that we should associate aught with Allah; this is by Allah's grace upon us and on mankind, but most people do not give thanks:

41. O my two mates of the prison! as for one of you, he shall give his lord to drink wine; and as for the other, he shall be crucified, so that the birds shall eat from his head, the matter is decreed concerning which you inquired.

42. And he said to him whom he knew would be delivered of the two: Remember me with your lord; but the Shaitan caused him to forget mentioning (it) to his lord, so he remained in the prison a few years.

THE BIBLE

"Joseph in Prison"

Genesis

Chapter 39

21. But the LORD was with Joseph, and shewed him mercy, and gave him favour in the sight of the keeper of the prison.

22. And the keeper of the prison committed to Joseph's hand all the prisoners that were in the prison; and whatsoever they did there, he was the doer of it.

23. The keeper of the prison looked not to any thing that was under his hand; because the LORD was with him, and that which he did, the LORD made it to prosper.

Genesis

Chapter 40

1. And it came to pass after these things, that the butler of the king of Egypt and his baker had offended their lord the king of Egypt.

2. And Pharaoh was wroth against two of his officers, against the chief of the butlers, and against the chief of the bakers.

3. And he put them in ward in the house of the captain of the guard, into the prison, the place where Joseph was bound.

4. And the captain of the guard charged Joseph with them, and he served them: and they continued a season in ward.

5. And they dreamed a dream both of them, each man his dream in one night, each man according to the interpretation of his dream, the butler and the baker of the king of Egypt, which were bound in the prison.

6. And Joseph came in unto them in the morning, and looked upon them, and, behold, they were sad.

7. And he asked Pharaoh's officers that were with him in the ward of his lord's house, saying, Wherefore look ye so sadly to day?

8. And they said unto him, We have dreamed a dream, and there is no interpreter of it. And Joseph said unto them, Do not interpretations belong to God? tell me them, I pray you.

9. And the chief butler told his dream to Joseph, and said to him, In my dream, behold, a vine was before me;

10. And in the vine were three branches: and it was as though it budded, and her blossoms shot forth; and the clusters thereof brought forth ripe grapes:

11. And Pharaoh's cup was in my hand: and I took the grapes, and pressed them into Pharaoh's cup, and I gave the cup into Pharaoh's hand.

12. And Joseph said unto him, This is the interpretation of it: **The three branches are three days:**

13. Yet within three days shall Pharaoh lift up thine head, and restore thee unto thy place: and thou shalt deliver Pharaoh's cup into his hand, after the former manner when thou wast his butler.

14. But think on me when it shall be well with thee, and shew kindness, I pray thee, unto me, and make mention of me unto Pharaoh, and bring me out of this house:

15. For indeed I was stolen away out of the land of the Hebrews: and here also have I done nothing that they should put me into the dungeon.

16. When the chief baker saw that the interpretation was good, he said unto Joseph, I also was in my dream, and, behold, I had three white baskets on my head:

17. And in the uppermost basket there was of all manner of bakemeats for Pharaoh; and the birds did eat them out of the basket upon my head.

18. And Joseph answered and said, This is the interpretation thereof: The three baskets are three days:

19. Yet within three days shall Pharaoh lift up thy head from off thee, and shall hang thee on a tree; and the birds shall eat thy flesh from off thee.

20. And it came to pass the third day, which was Pharaoh's birthday, that he made a feast unto all his servants: and he lifted up the head of the chief butler and of the chief baker among his servants.

21. And he restored the chief butler unto his butlership again; and he gave the cup into Pharaoh's hand:

22. But he hanged the chief baker: as Joseph had interpreted to them.

23. Yet did not the chief butler remember Joseph, but forgat him.

COMMENTARY

In the Qur'an:

1. Two of Pharaoh's servants were put into prison and had dreams. Joseph interpreted both their dreams at once.

In the Bible:

1. God prospered Joseph even while he was in prison and he had won the favour of the prison keeper. Pharaoh's butler and baker were sent to prison and each had unusual dreams. Joseph first interpreted the butler's dream. The baker, having heard of the favourable interpretation, asked Joseph also to interpret his dream, receiving a bad report

THE QUR'AN

"Joseph and Pharaoh"

Sura 12

Yusuf

43. And the king said: Surely I see seven fat kine which seven lean ones devoured; and seven green ears and (seven) others dry: O chiefs! Explain to me my dream, if you can interpret the dream.

44. They said: **Confused dreams and we do not know the interpretation of dreams.**

45. And of the two (prisoners) he who had found deliverance and remembered after a long time said: I will inform you of its interpretation, so let me go:

46. Yusuf! O truthful one! explain to us seven fat kine which seven lean ones devoured, and seven green ears and (seven) others dry, that I may go back to the people so that they may know.

47. He said: **You shall sow for seven years continuously, then what you reap leave it in its ear except a little of which you eat.**

48. Then there shall come after that seven years of hardship which shall eat away all that you have beforehand laid up in store for them, except a little of what you shall have preserved:

49. Then there will come after that a year in which people shall have rain and in which they shall press (grapes).

50. And the king said: Bring him to me. So when the messenger came to him, he said: Go back to your lord and ask him, what is the case of the women who cut their hands; surely my Lord knows their guile.

51. He said: How was your affair when you sought Yusuf to yield himself (to you)? They said: Remote is Allah (from imperfection), we knew of no evil on his part. The chief's wife said: **Now has the truth become established: I sought him to yield himself (to me), and he is most surely of the truthful ones.**

52. This is that he might know that I have not been unfaithful to him in secret and that Allah does not guide the device of the unfaithful.

53. And I do not declare myself free, most surely (man's) self is wont to command (him to do) evil, except such as my Lord has had mercy on, surely my Lord is Forgiving, Merciful.

54. And the king said: Bring him to me, I will choose him for myself. So when he had spoken with him, he said: Surely you are in our presence today an honorable, a faithful one.

55. He said: **Place me (in authority) over the treasures of the land, surely I am a good keeper, knowing well.**

56. And thus did **We give to Yusuf power in the land-- he had mastery in it wherever he liked;** We send down Our mercy on whom We please, and We do not waste the reward of those who do good.

THE BIBLE

"Joseph and Pharaoh"

Genesis

Chapter 41

1. And it came to pass at the end of two full years, that Pharaoh dreamed: and, behold, he stood by the river.

2. And, behold, there came up out of the river seven well favoured kine and fatfleshed; and they fed in a meadow.

3. And, behold, seven other kine came up after them out of the river, ill favoured and leanfleshed; and stood by the other kine upon the brink of the river.

4. And the ill favoured and leanfleshed kine did eat up the seven well favoured and fat kine. So Pharaoh awoke.

5. And he slept and dreamed the second time: and, behold, seven ears of corn came up upon one stalk, rank and good.

6. And, behold, seven thin ears and blasted with the east wind sprung up after them.

7. And the seven thin ears devoured the seven rank and full ears. And Pharaoh awoke, and, behold, it was a dream.

8. And it came to pass in the morning that his spirit was troubled; and he sent and called for all the magicians of Egypt, and all the wise men thereof: and Pharaoh told them his dream; but there was none that could interpret them unto Pharaoh.

9. Then spake the chief butler unto Pharaoh, saying, I do remember my faults this day:

10. Pharaoh was wroth with his servants, and put me in ward in the captain of the guard's house, both me and the chief baker:

11. And we dreamed a dream in one night, I and he; we dreamed each man according to the interpretation of his dream.

12. And there was there with us a young man, an Hebrew, servant to the captain of the guard; and we told him, and he interpreted to us our dreams; to each man according to his dream he did interpret.

13. And it came to pass, as he interpreted to us, so it was; me he restored unto mine office, and him he hanged.

14. **Then Pharaoh sent and called Joseph, and they brought him hastily out of the dungeon: and he shaved himself, and changed his raiment, and came in unto Pharaoh.**

15. **And Pharaoh said unto Joseph, I have dreamed a dream, and there is none that can interpret it**: and I have heard say of thee, that thou canst understand a dream to interpret it.

16. **And Joseph answered Pharaoh, saying, It is not in me: God shall give Pharaoh an answer of peace.**

17. And Pharaoh said unto Joseph, In my dream, behold, I stood upon the bank of the river:

18. And, behold, there came up out of the river seven kine, fatfleshed and well favoured; and they fed in a meadow:

19. And, behold, seven other kine came up after them, poor and very ill favoured and leanfleshed, such as I never saw in all the land of Egypt for badness:

20. And the lean and the ill favoured kine did eat up the first seven fat kine:

21. And when they had eaten them up, it could not be known that they had eaten them; but they were still ill favoured, as at the beginning. So I awoke.

22. And I saw in my dream, and, behold, seven ears came up in one stalk, full and good:

23. And, behold, seven ears, withered, thin, and blasted with the east wind, sprung up after them:

24. And the thin ears devoured the seven good ears: and I told this unto the magicians; but there was none that could declare it to me.

25. **And Joseph said unto Pharaoh, The dream of Pharaoh is one: God hath shewed Pharaoh what he is about to do.**

26. **The seven good kine are seven years; and the seven good ears are seven years: the dream is one.**

27. And the seven thin and ill favoured kine that came up after them are seven years; and the seven empty ears blasted with the east wind shall be seven years of famine.

28. This is the thing which I have spoken unto Pharaoh: What God is about to do he sheweth unto Pharaoh.

29. Behold, there come seven years of great plenty throughout all the land of Egypt:

30. And there shall arise after them seven years of famine; and all the plenty shall be forgotten in the land of Egypt; and the famine shall consume the land;

31. And the plenty shall not be known in the land by reason of that famine following; for it shall be very grievous.

32. And for that the dream was doubled unto Pharaoh twice; it is because the thing is established by God, and God will shortly bring it to pass.

33. Now therefore let Pharaoh look out a man discreet and wise, and set him over the land of Egypt.

34. Let Pharaoh do this, and let him appoint officers over the land, **and take up the fifth part of the land of Egypt in the seven plenteous years.**

35. And let them gather all the food of those good years that come, and lay up corn under the hand of Pharaoh, and let them keep food in the cities.

36. And that food shall be for store to the land against the seven years of famine, which shall be in the land of Egypt; that the land perish not through the famine.

37. And the thing was good in the eyes of Pharaoh, and in the eyes of all his servants.

38. And Pharaoh said unto his servants, Can we find such a one as this is, a man in whom the Spirit of God is?

39. And Pharaoh said unto Joseph, Forasmuch as God hath shewed thee all this, there is none so discreet and wise as thou art:

40. Thou shalt be over my house, and according unto thy word shall all my people be ruled: only in the throne will I be greater than thou.

41. And Pharaoh said unto Joseph, See, I have set thee over all the land of Egypt.

42. And Pharaoh took off his ring from his hand, and put it upon Joseph's hand, and arrayed him in vestures of fine linen, and put a gold chain about his neck;

43. And he made him to ride in the second chariot which he had; and they cried before him, Bow the knee: and he made him ruler over all the land of Egypt.

44. And Pharaoh said unto Joseph, I am Pharaoh, and without thee shall no man lift up his hand or foot in all the land of Egypt.

45. And Pharaoh called Joseph's name Zaphnath-paaneah; and he gave him to wife Asenath the daughter of Poti-pherah priest of On. And Joseph went out over all the land of Egypt.

46. And Joseph was thirty years old when he stood before Pharaoh king of Egypt. And Joseph went out from the presence of Pharaoh, and went throughout all the land of Egypt.

47. And in the seven plenteous years the earth brought forth by handfuls.

48. And he gathered up all the food of the seven years, which were in the land of Egypt, and laid up the food in the cities: the food of the field, which was round about every city, laid he up in the same.

49. And Joseph gathered corn as the sand of the sea, very much, until he left numbering; for it was without number.

50. And unto Joseph were born two sons before the years of famine came, which Asenath the daughter of Poti-pherah priest of On bare unto him.

51. And Joseph called the name of the firstborn Manasseh: For God, said he, hath made me forget all my toil, and all my father's house.

52. And the name of the second called he Ephraim: For God hath caused me to be fruitful in the land of my affliction.

53. And the seven years of plenteousness, that was in the land of Egypt, were ended.

54. And the seven years of dearth began to come, according as Joseph had said: and the dearth was in all lands; but in all the land of Egypt there was bread.

55. And when all the land of Egypt was famished, the people cried to Pharaoh for bread: and Pharaoh said unto all the Egyptians, Go unto Joseph; what he saith to you, do.

56. And the famine was over all the face of the earth: and Joseph opened all the storehouses, and sold unto the Egyptians; and the famine waxed sore in the land of Egypt.

57. And all countries came into Egypt to Joseph for to buy corn; because that the famine was so sore in all lands.

COMMENTARY

In the Qur'an:

1. Pharaoh had only one dream.

2. A former prisoner, Pharaoh's servant, came to Joseph in prison and asked for the interpretation. Joseph gave the interpretation to the servant.

3. Pharaoh requested to see Joseph, but he asked about his accusers. All the women testify of his innocence, and Aziz's wife admitted her false accusation against Joseph.

4. Pharaoh finally ordered them to bring Joseph before him. Joseph offered himself to be the "Chief Executive" in Egypt.

In the Bible:

1. Pharaoh had two dreams.

2. The chief butler recalled Joseph's ability to interpret dreams. Joseph was brought before Pharaoh and gave him not only the interpretations of both dreams but also advice.

3. Potiphar's wife was not mentioned since the time that she had caused Joseph to be imprisoned, nor were any "other women" mentioned, as in the qur'anic story, who desired Joseph.

4. Pharaoh himself decided to give authority over the land to Joseph, so that he could help to organize preparation for the future famine.

THE QUR'AN

"Joseph and his Brothers"

Sura 12

Yusuf

58. And Yusuf's brothers came and went in to him, and he knew them, while they did not recognize him.

59. And when he furnished them with their provision, he said: **Bring to me a brother of yours from your father; do you not see that I give full measure and that I am the best of hosts?**

60. But if you do not bring him to me, you shall have no measure (of corn) from me, nor shall you come near me.

61. They said: We will strive to make his father yield in respect of him, and we are sure to do (it).

62. And he said to his servants: Put their money into their bags that they may recognize it when they go back to their family, so that they may come back.

63. So when they returned to their father, they said: **O our father, the measure is withheld from us, therefore send with us our brother, (so that) we may get the measure, and we will most surely guard him.** **64.** He said: **I cannot trust in you with respect to him, except as I trusted in you with respect to his brother before**; but Allah is the best Keeper, and He is the most Merciful of the merciful ones.

65. And when they opened their goods, they found their money returned to them. They said: O our father! what (more) can we desire? This is our property returned to us, and we will bring corn for our family and guard our brother, and will have in addition the measure of a camel (load); this is an easy measure.

66. He said: **I will by no means send him with you until you give me a firm covenant in Allah's name that you will most certainly bring him back to me, unless you are completely surrounded. And when they gave him their covenant, he said: Allah is the One in Whom trust is placed as regards what we say.**

67. And he said: O my sons! do not (all) enter by one gate and enter by different gates and I cannot avail you aught against Allah; judgment is only Allah's; on Him do I rely, and on Him let those who are reliant rely.

68. And when they had entered as their father had bidden them, it did not avail them aught against Allah, but (it was only) a desire in the soul of Yaqoub which he satisfied; and surely he was possessed of knowledge because We had given him knowledge, but most people do not know.

69. And when they went in to Yusuf. he lodged his brother with himself, saying: I am your brother, therefore grieve not at what they do.

70. So when he furnished them with their provisions, (someone) placed the drinking cup in his brother's bag. Then a crier cried out: O caravan! you are most surely thieves.

71. They said while they were facing them: What is it that you miss?

72. They said: We miss the king's drinking cup, and he who shall bring it shall have a camel-load and I am responsible for it.

73. They said: By Allah! you know for certain that we have not come to make mischief in the land, and we are not thieves.

74. They said: But what shall be the requital of this, if you are liars?

75. They said: The requital of this is that the person in whose bag it is found shall himself be (held for) the satisfaction thereof; thus do we punish the wrongdoers.

76. So he began with their sacks before the sack of his brother, then he brought it out from his brother's sack. Thus did We plan for the sake of Yusuf; it was not (lawful) that he should take his brother under the king's law unless Allah pleased; We raise the degrees of whomsoever We please, and above every one possessed of knowledge is the All-knowing one.

77. They said: If he steal, a brother of his did indeed steal before; but Yusuf kept it secret in his heart and did not disclose it to them. He said: You are in an evil condition and Allah knows best what you state.

78. They said: O chief! he has a father, a very old man, therefore retain one of us in his stead; surely we see you to be of the doers of good.

79. He said: Allah protect us that we should seize other than him with whom we found our property, for then most surely we would be unjust.

80. Then when they despaired of him, they retired, conferring privately together. The eldest of them said: Do you not know that your father took from you a covenant in Allah's name, and how you fell short of your duty with respect to Yusuf before? Therefore I will by no means depart from this land until my father permits me or Allah decides for me, and He is the best of the judges:

81. Go back to your father and say: O our father! surely your son committed theft, and we do not bear witness except to what we have known, and we could not keep watch over the unseen:

82. And inquire in the town in which we were and the caravan with which we proceeded, and most surely we are truthful.

83. He (Yaqoub) said: Nay, your souls have made a matter light for you, so patience is good; maybe Allah will bring them all together to me; surely He is the Knowing, the Wise.

84. And he turned away from them, and said: O my sorrow for Yusuf! and his eyes became white on account of the grief, and he was a repressor (of grief).

85. They said: By Allah! you will not cease to remember Yusuf until you are a prey to constant disease or (until) you are of those who perish.

86. He said: I only complain of my grief and sorrow to Allah, and I know from Allah what you do not know.

87. O my sons! Go and inquire respecting Yusuf and his brother, and despair not of Allah's mercy; surely none despairs of Allah's mercy except the unbelieving people.

88. So when they came in to him, they said: O chief! distress has afflicted us and our family and we have brought scanty money, so give us full measure and be charitable to us; surely Allah rewards the charitable.

89. He said: Do you know how you treated Yusuf and his brother when you were ignorant?

90. They said: Are you indeed Yusuf? He said: I am Yusuf and this is my brother; Allah has indeed been gracious to us; surely he who guards (against evil) and is patient (is rewarded) for surely Allah does not waste the reward of those who do good.

91. They said: By Allah! now has Allah certainly chosen you over us, and we were certainly sinners.

THE BIBLE

"Joseph and his Brothers"

Genesis

Chapter 42

1. Now when Jacob saw that there was corn in Egypt, Jacob said unto his sons, Why do ye look one upon another?

2. And he said, Behold, I have heard that there is corn in Egypt: get you down thither, and buy for us from thence; that we may live, and not die.

3. And Joseph's ten brethren went down to buy corn in Egypt.

4. But Benjamin, Joseph's brother, Jacob sent not with his brethren; for he said, Lest peradventure mischief befall him.

5. And the sons of Israel came to buy corn among those that came: for the famine was in the land of Canaan.

6. And Joseph was the governor over the land, and he it was that sold to all the people of the land: and Joseph's brethren came, and bowed down themselves before him with their faces to the earth.

7. And Joseph saw his brethren, and he knew them, but made himself strange unto them, and spake roughly unto them; and he said unto them, Whence come ye? And they said, From the land of Canaan to buy food.

8. And Joseph knew his brethren, but they knew not him.

9. And Joseph remembered the dreams which he dreamed of them, and said unto them, Ye are spies; to see the nakedness of the land ye are come.

10. And they said unto him, Nay, my lord, but to buy food are thy servants come.

11. We are all one man's sons; we are true men, thy servants are no spies.

12. And he said unto them, Nay, but to see the nakedness of the land ye are come.

13. And they said, Thy servants are twelve brethren, the sons of one man in the land of Canaan; and, behold, the youngest is this day with our father, and one is not.

14. And Joseph said unto them, That is it that I spake unto you, saying, Ye are spies:

15. Hereby ye shall be proved: By the life of Pharaoh ye shall not go forth hence, except your youngest brother come hither.

16. Send one of you, and let him fetch your brother, and ye shall be kept in prison, that your words may be proved, whether there be any truth in you: or else by the life of Pharaoh surely ye are spies.

17. And he put them all together into ward three days.

18. And Joseph said unto them the third day, This do, and live; for I fear God:

19. If ye be true men, let one of your brethren be bound in the house of your prison: go ye, carry corn for the famine of your houses:

20. But bring your youngest brother unto me; so shall your words be verified, and ye shall not die. And they did so.

21. And they said one to another, We are verily guilty concerning our brother, in that we saw the anguish of his soul, when he besought us, and we would not hear; therefore is this distress come upon us.

22. And Reuben answered them, saying, Spake I not unto you, saying, Do not sin against the child; and ye would not hear? therefore, behold, also his blood is required.

23. And they knew not that Joseph understood them; for he spake unto them by an interpreter.

24. **And he turned himself about from them, and wept; and returned to them again, and communed with them, and took from them Simeon, and bound him before their eyes.**

25. Then Joseph commanded to fill their sacks with corn, **and to restore every man's money into his sack,** and to give them provision for the way: and thus did he unto them.

26. And they laded their asses with the corn, and departed thence.

27. **And as one of them opened his sack to give his ass provender in the inn, he espied his money; for, behold, it was in his sack's mouth.**

28. **And he said unto his brethren, My money is restored; and, lo, it is even in my sack: and their heart failed them, and they were afraid, saying one to another, What is this that God hath done unto us?**

29. And they came unto Jacob their father unto the land of Canaan, and told him all that befell unto them; saying,

30. The man, who is the lord of the land, spake roughly to us, and took us for spies of the country.

31. And we said unto him, We are true men; we are no spies:

32. We be twelve brethren, sons of our father; one is not, and the youngest is this day with our father in the land of Canaan.

33. And the man, the lord of the country, said unto us, Hereby shall I know that ye are true men; leave one of your brethren here with me, and take food for the famine of your households, and be gone:

34. And bring your youngest brother unto me: then shall I know that ye are no spies, but that ye are true men: so will I deliver you your brother, and ye shall traffick in the land.

35. **And it came to pass as they emptied their sacks, that, behold, every man's bundle of money was in his sack: and when both they and their father saw the bundles of money, they were afraid.**

36. And Jacob their father said unto them, **Me have ye bereaved of my children: Joseph is not, and Simeon is not, and ye will take Benjamin away: all these things are against me.**

37. And Reuben spake unto his father, saying, Slay my two sons, if I bring him not to thee: deliver him into my hand, and I will bring him to thee again.

38. And he said, **My son shall not go down with you; for his brother is dead, and he is left alon**e: if mischief befall him by the way in the which ye go, then shall ye bring down my gray hairs with sorrow to the grave.

Genesis

Chapter 43

1. And the famine was sore in the land.

2. And it came to pass, when they had eaten up the corn which they had brought out of Egypt, their father said unto them, Go again, buy us a little food.

3. And Judah spake unto him, saying, The man did solemnly protest unto us, saying, Ye shall not see my face, except your brother be with you.

4. If thou wilt send our brother with us, we will go down and buy thee food:

5. But if thou wilt not send him, we will not go down: for the man said unto us, Ye shall not see my face, except your brother be with you.

6. And Israel said, Wherefore dealt ye so ill with me, as to tell the man whether ye had yet a brother?

7. And they said, The man asked us straitly of our state, and of our kindred, saying, Is your father yet alive? have ye another brother? and we told him according to the tenor of these words: could we certainly know that he would say, Bring your brother down?

8. And Judah said unto Israel his father, Send the lad with me, and we will arise and go; that we may live, and not die, both we, and thou, and also our little ones.

9. I will be surety for him; of my hand shalt thou require him: if I bring him not unto thee, and set him before thee, then let me bear the blame for ever:

10. For except we had lingered, surely now we had returned this second time.

11. And their father Israel said unto them, If it must be so now, do this; take of the best fruits in the land in your vessels, and carry down the man a present, a little balm, and a little honey, spices, and myrrh, nuts, and almonds:

12. And take double money in your hand; and the money that was brought again in the mouth of your sacks, carry it again in your hand; peradventure it was an oversight:

13. Take also your brother, and arise, go again unto the man:

14. And God Almighty give you mercy before the man, that he may send away your other brother, and Benjamin. If I be bereaved of my children, I am bereaved.

15. And the men took that present, and they took double money in their hand, and Benjamin; and rose up, and went down to Egypt, and stood before Joseph.

16. And when Joseph saw Benjamin with them, he said to the ruler of his house, Bring these men home, and slay, and make ready; for these men shall dine with me at noon.

17. And the man did as Joseph bade; and the man brought the men into Joseph's house.

18. And the men were afraid, because they were brought into Joseph's house; and they said, **Because of the money that was returned in our sacks at the first time are we brought in; that he may seek occasion against us, and fall upon us, and take us for bondmen, and our asses.**

19. And they came near to the steward of Joseph's house, and they communed with him at the door of the house,

20. And said, O sir, we came indeed down at the first time to buy food:

21. And it came to pass, when we came to the inn, that we opened our sacks, and, behold, every man's money was in the mouth of his sack, our money in full weight: and we have brought it again in our hand.

22. And other money have we brought down in our hands to buy food: we cannot tell who put our money in our sacks.

23. And he said, Peace be to you, fear not: your God, and the God of your father, hath given you treasure in your sacks: I had your money. And he brought Simeon out unto them.

24. And the man brought the men into Joseph's house, and gave them water, and they washed their feet; and he gave their asses provender.

25. And they made ready the present against Joseph came at noon: for they heard that they should eat bread there.

26. And when Joseph came home, they brought him the present which was in their hand into the house, and bowed themselves to him to the earth.

27. And he asked them of their welfare, and said, Is your father well, the old man of whom ye spake? Is he yet alive?

28. And they answered, Thy servant our father is in good health, he is yet alive. And they bowed down their heads, and made obeisance.

29. And he lifted up his eyes, and saw his brother Benjamin, his mother's son, and said, Is this your younger brother, of whom ye spake unto me? And he said, God be gracious unto thee, my son.

30. And Joseph made haste; for his bowels did yearn upon his brother: and he sought where to weep; **and he entered into his chamber, and wept there.**

31. And he washed his face, and went out, and refrained himself, and said, Set on bread.

32. And they set on for him by himself, and for them by themselves, and for the Egyptians, which did eat with him, by themselves: because the Egyptians might not eat bread with the Hebrews; for that is an abomination unto the Egyptians.

33. And they sat before him, the firstborn according to his birthright, and the youngest according to his youth: and the men marvelled one at another.

34. And he took and sent messes unto them from before him: but Benjamin's mess was five times so much as any of theirs. And they drank, and were merry with him.

Genesis

Chapter 44

1. And he commanded the steward of his house, saying, Fill the men's sacks with food, as much as they can carry, and put every man's money in his sack's mouth.

2. And put my cup, the silver cup, in the sack's mouth of the youngest, and his corn money. And he did according to the word that Joseph had spoken.

3. As soon as the morning was light, the men were sent away, they and their asses.

4. And when they were gone out of the city, and not yet far off, Joseph said unto his steward, Up, follow after the men; and when thou dost overtake them, say unto them, Wherefore have ye rewarded evil for good?

5. Is not this it in which my lord drinketh, and whereby indeed he divineth? ye have done evil in so doing.

6. And he overtook them, and he spake unto them these same words.

7. And they said unto him, Wherefore saith my lord these words? God forbid that thy servants should do according to this thing:

8. Behold, the money, which we found in our sacks' mouths, we brought again unto thee out of the land of Canaan: how then should we steal out of thy lord's house silver or gold?

9. With whomsoever of thy servants it be found, both let him die, and we also will be my lord's bondmen.

10. And he said, Now also let it be according unto your words; he with whom it is found shall be my servant; and ye shall be blameless.

11. Then they speedily took down every man his sack to the ground, and opened every man his sack.

12. And he searched, and began at the eldest, and left at the youngest: and the cup was found in Benjamin's sack.

13. Then they rent their clothes, and laded every man his ass, and returned to the city.

14. And Judah and his brethren came to Joseph's house; for he was yet there: and they fell before him on the ground.

15. And Joseph said unto them, What deed is this that ye have done? wot ye not that such a man as I can certainly divine?

16. And Judah said, What shall we say unto my lord? what shall we speak? or how shall we clear ourselves? God hath found out the iniquity of thy servants: behold, we are my lord's servants, both we, and he also with whom the cup is found.

17. And he said, God forbid that I should do so: **but the man in whose hand the cup is found, he shall be my servant; and as for you, get you up in peace unto your father**.

18. Then Judah came near unto him, and said, Oh my lord, let thy servant, I pray thee, speak a word in my lord's ears, and let not thine anger burn against thy servant: for thou art even as Pharaoh.

19. My lord asked his servants, saying, Have ye a father, or a brother?

20. And we said unto my lord, We have a father, an old man, and a child of his old age, a little one; and his brother is dead, and he alone is left of his mother, and his father loveth him.

21. And thou saidst unto thy servants, Bring him down unto me, that I may set mine eyes upon him.

22. And we said unto my lord, **The lad cannot leave his father: for if he should leave his father, his father would die.**

23. And thou saidst unto thy servants, Except your youngest brother come down with you, ye shall see my face no more.

24. And it came to pass when we came up unto thy servant my father, we told him the words of my lord.

25. And our father said, Go again, and buy us a little food.

26. And we said, We cannot go down: if our youngest brother be with us, then will we go down: for we may not see the man's face, except our youngest brother be with us.

27. And thy servant my father said unto us, Ye know that my wife bare me two sons:

28. And the one went out from me, and I said, Surely he is torn in pieces; and I saw him not since:

29. And if ye take this also from me, and mischief befall him, ye shall bring down my gray hairs with sorrow to the grave.

30. Now therefore when I come to thy servant my father, and the lad be not with us; seeing that his life is bound up in the lad's life;

31. It shall come to pass, **when he seeth that the lad is not with us, that he will die: and thy servants shall bring down the gray hairs of thy servant our father with sorrow to the grave**.

32. For thy servant became surety for the lad unto my father, saying, If I bring him not unto thee, then I shall bear the blame to my father for ever.

33. Now therefore, **I pray thee, let thy servant abide instead of the lad a bondman to my lord; and let the lad go up with his brethren.**

34. For how shall I go up to my father, and the lad be not with me? lest peradventure I see the evil that shall come on my father.

Genesis

Chapter 45

1. Then Joseph could not refrain himself before all them that stood by him; and he cried, Cause every man to go out from me. And there stood no man with him, while Joseph made himself known unto his brethren.

2. And he wept aloud: and the Egyptians and the house of Pharaoh heard.

3. And Joseph said unto his brethren, I am Joseph; doth my father yet live? And his brethren could not answer him; for they were troubled at his presence.

4. And Joseph said unto his brethren, Come near to me, I pray you. And they came near. And he said, I am Joseph your brother, whom ye sold into Egypt.

5. Now therefore be not grieved, nor angry with yourselves, that ye sold me hither: for God did send me before you to preserve life.

6. For these two years hath the famine been in the land: and yet there are five years, in the which there shall neither be earing nor harvest.

7. And God sent me before you to preserve you a posterity in the earth, and to save your lives by a great deliverance.

8. So now it was not you that sent me hither, but God: and he hath made me a father to Pharaoh, and lord of all his house, and a ruler throughout all the land of Egypt.

9. Haste **ye, and go up to my father, and say unto him, Thus saith thy son Joseph, God hath made me lord of all Egypt: come down unto me, tarry not:**

10. And thou shalt dwell in the land of Goshen, and thou shalt be near unto me, thou, and thy children, and thy children's children, and thy flocks, and thy herds, and all that thou hast:

11. And there will I nourish thee; for yet there are five years of famine; lest thou, and thy household, and all that thou hast, come to poverty.

12. And, behold, your eyes see, and the eyes of my brother Benjamin, that it is my mouth that speaketh unto you.

13. And ye shall tell my father of all my glory in Egypt, and of all that ye have seen; and ye shall haste and bring down my father hither.

14. And he fell upon his brother Benjamin's neck, and wept; and Benjamin wept upon his neck.

15. Moreover he kissed all his brethren, and wept upon them: and after that his brethren talked with him.

16. And the fame thereof was heard in Pharaoh's house, saying, Joseph's brethren are come: and it pleased Pharaoh well, and his servants.

17. And Pharaoh said unto Joseph, Say unto thy brethren, This do ye; lade your beasts, and go, get you unto the land of Canaan;

18. And take your father and your households, and come unto me: and I will give you the good of the land of Egypt, and ye shall eat the fat of the land.

19. Now thou art commanded, this do ye; take you wagons out of the land of Egypt for your little ones, and for your wives, and bring your father, and come.

20. Also regard not your stuff; for the good of all the land of Egypt is yours.

21. And the children of Israel did so: and Joseph gave them wagons, according to the commandment of Pharaoh, and gave them provision for the way.

22. To all of them he gave each man changes of raiment; but to Benjamin he gave three hundred pieces of silver, and five changes of raiment.

23. And to his father he sent after this manner; ten asses laden with the good things of Egypt, and ten she asses laden with corn and bread and meat for his father by the way.

24. So he sent his brethren away, and they departed: and he said unto them, See that ye fall not out by the way.

COMMENTARY

In the Qur'an:

1. Joseph asked his brothers to bring to him their youngest brother; otherwise, he would not trade with them in the future.

2. After having opened their bags, his brothers found their stock-in-trade and happily decided that they would use it again.

3. After the brothers swore to protect their youngest brother, Jacob agreed to let them travel to Egypt together.

4. After having met with his full brother, Joseph revealed to him his true identity.

5. Joseph released all his brothers to go back to Canaan and he put his personal golden cup into his youngest brother's bag. (at that point this brother already knew that the ruler of Egypt was his brother Joseph, but did not tell this news to anyone, keeping it as a surprise).

6. Joseph ordered that his brother be imprisoned in Egypt for his supposed act of stealing the golden cup. The brothers asked to let their brother go free and begged Joseph to allow any other brother to be imprisoned instead but Joseph rejected this offer. Then the oldest brother requested that the others tell Jacob about the unfortunate event of the theft of the cup.

7. Jacob still believed that Joseph was alive and asked the brothers to find out Joseph's fate and fate of the brother that was left behind in Egypt.

8. The brothers came back to Egypt to ask Joseph for mercy and to ask him to give them grain abundantly. Joseph asked them what they knew about fate of Joseph and his full brother. They suddenly recognized Joseph and asked for his forgiveness.

In the Bible:

1. Joseph asked his brothers about the youngest one, Benjamin, and accused them of spying in Egypt. They offered to prove otherwise by bringing Benjamin to Egypt. Joseph imprisoned Simeon as a token to ensure their return.

2. After opening their bags and finding their money returned to them, the brothers were afraid that if they go back to Egypt they would be accused of theft. They mentioned this "miracle" to Joseph's servant on their next visit. The servant assured them that he himself had received their money from their previous trip.

3. Jacob did not want to let Benjamin travel to Egypt so the brothers had to stay in Canaan until they had no more food. At that point, Jacob was forced to let Benjamin travel with them.

4. When Joseph recognized Benjamin, he did not disclose his identity.

5. In order to test his brothers' loyalty, he had hidden his personal golden cup in Benjamin's bag. It was terrible news for all, including Benjamin.

6. Joseph ordered Benjamin be imprisoned while the rest were allowed to return home freely. But his brothers stood by Benjamin, and Judah (who had plotted to kill Joseph many years back) was willing to be imprisoned instead of the younger brother.

7. None of the brothers returned to their father with bad news. For many years, Jacob (Israel) believed that his beloved son Joseph was dead.

8. When Joseph saw his brothers' act of self-sacrifice, he revealed his true identity to them. That was a big and pleasant surprise for all the brothers, including Benjamin. Then he invited them to fetch his father Jacob to come and live all together in Egypt.

THE QUR'AN

"Joseph and his Father"

Sura 12

Yusuf

93. Take this my shirt and cast it on my father's face, he will (again) be able to see, and come to me with all your families.

94. And when the caravan had departed, their father said: Most surely I perceive the greatness of Yusuf, unless you pronounce me to be weak in judgment.

95. They said: By Allah, you are most surely in your old error.

96. So when the bearer of good news came he cast it on his face, so forthwith he regained his sight. He said: Did I not say to you that I know from Allah what you do not know?

97. They said: O our father! ask forgiveness of our faults for us, surely we were sinners.

98. He said: I will ask for you forgiveness from my Lord; surely He is the Forgiving, the Merciful.

99. Then when they came in to Yusuf, he took his parents to lodge with him and said: Enter safe into Egypt, if Allah please.

100. And he raised his parents upon the throne and they fell down in prostration before him, and he said: O my father! this is the significance of my vision of old; my Lord has indeed made it to be true; and He was indeed kind to me when He brought me forth from the prison and brought you from the desert after the Shaitan had sown dissensions between me and my brothers, surely my Lord is benignant to whom He pleases; surely He is the Knowing, the Wise.

101. My Lord! Thou hast given me of the kingdom and taught me of the interpretation of sayings: Originator of the heavens and the earth! Thou art my guardian in this world and the hereafter; make me die a muslim and join me with the good.

102. This is of the announcements relating to the unseen (which) We reveal to you, and you were not with them when they resolved upon their affair, and they were devising plans.

103. And most men will not believe though you desire it eagerly.

104. And you do not ask them for a reward for this; it is nothing but a reminder for all mankind.

105. And how many a sign in the heavens and the earth which they pass by, yet they turn aside from it.

106. And most of them do not believe in Allah without associating others (with Him).

107. Do they then feel secure that there may come to them an extensive chastisement from Allah or (that) the hour may come to them suddenly while they do not perceive?

108. Say: This is my way: I call to Allah, I and those who follow me being certain, and glory be to Allah, and I am not one of the polytheists.

109. And We have not sent before you but men from (among) the people of the towns, to whom We sent revelations. Have they not then travelled in the land and seen what was the end of those before them? And certainly the abode of the hereafter is best for those who guard (against evil); do you not then understand?

110. Until when the apostles despaired and the people became sure that they were indeed told a lie, Our help came to them and whom We pleased was delivered; and Our punishment is not averted from the guilty people.

111. In their histories there is certainly a **lesson for men of understanding**. It is not a narrative which could be forged, but a verification of what is before it and a **distinct explanation of all things** and a guide and a mercy to a people who believe.

THE BIBLE

"Joseph and his Father"

Genesis

Chapter 45

25. And they went up out of Egypt, and came into the land of Canaan unto Jacob their father,

26. And told him, saying, Joseph is yet alive, and he is governor over all the land of Egypt. And Jacob's heart fainted, *for he believed them not.*

27. And they told him all the words of Joseph, which he had said unto them: and when he saw the wagons which Joseph had sent to carry him, the spirit of Jacob their father revived:

28. And Israel said, It is enough; Joseph my son is yet alive: I will go and see him before I die.

Genesis

Chapter 46

1. And Israel took his journey with all that he had, and came to Beer-sheba, and offered sacrifices unto the God of his father Isaac.

2. And God spake unto Israel in the visions of the night, and said, Jacob, Jacob. And he said, Here am I.

3. And he said, **I am God, the God of thy father: fear not to go down into Egypt; for I will there make of thee a great nation:**

4. I will go down with thee into Egypt; and I will also surely bring thee up again: **and Joseph shall put his hand upon thine eyes.**

COMMENTARY

In the Qur'an:

1. Joseph sent brothers to bring his shirt to Jacob in order to heal his father Jacob's eyesight.

2. After receiving news about Joseph, Jacob reminded his sons that he never believed that Joseph was dead. The sons asked for forgiveness from their father and he promised to pray for them.

3. The brothers bowed down before Joseph and he reminded his father about the dream that he dreamed long ago.

4. The Qur'an mentions that Joseph's story is "... *certainly a lesson for men of understanding. It is not a narrative which could be forged, but a verification of what is before it and a distinct explanation of all things and a guide and a mercy to a people who believe.*"

In the Bible:

1. Joseph asked his brothers to go back to Jacob and to bring him and all their families to Egypt to live. There is no mention of his shirt to be used to heal his father's eyesight. We read in **Genesis 48 : 9-11**

   And Joseph said unto his father, They are my sons, whom God hath given me in this place. And he said, Bring them, I pray thee, unto me, and I will bless them. Now the eyes of Israel were dim for age, so that he could not see. And he brought them near unto him; and he kissed them, and embraced them. And Israel said unto Joseph, I had not thought to see thy face: and, lo, God hath shewed me also thy seed.

2. Even after his sons told Jacob that Joseph was alive and well in Egypt, Jacob (Israel) did not believe them until he heard all the words from Joseph and saw all the wagons laden with gifts that Joseph sent to him.

3. Joseph doesn't remind his brothers about his old dream.

4. Question: which is the real story about Joseph, the one in the Bible? Or is the one in the Qur'an "*…a tale invented…*"? For they are quite different from each other.

Chapter Six

MOSES

The Qur'an

"The Birth of Moses"

Sura 28
The Narratives

7. And We revealed to Musa's mothers, saying: Give him suck, then when you fear for him, cast him into the river and do not fear nor grieve; surely We will bring him back to you and make him one of the apostles.

8. And Firon's family took him up that he might be an enemy and a grief for them; surely Firon and Haman and their hosts were wrongdoers.

9. And Firon's wife said: A refreshment of the eye to me and to you; do not slay him; maybe he will be useful to us, or we may take him for a son; and they did not perceive.

10. And the heart of Musa's mother was free (from anxiety) she would have almost disclosed it had We not strengthened her heart so that she might be of the believers.

11. And she said to his sister: Follow him up. So she watched him from a distance while they did not perceive,

12. And We ordained that he refused to suck any foster mother before, so she said: Shall I point out to you the people of a house who will take care of him for you, and they will be benevolent to him?

13. So We gave him back to his mother that her eye might be refreshed, and that she might not grieve, and that she might know that the promise of Allah is true, but most of them do not know.

14. And when he attained his maturity and became full grown, We granted him wisdom and knowledge; and thus do We reward those who do good (to others).

THE BIBLE

"The Birth of Moses"

Exodus

Chapter 2

1. And there went a man of the house of Levi, and took to wife a daughter of Levi.

2. And the woman conceived, and bare a son: and when she saw him that he was a goodly child, she hid him three months.

3. And when she could not longer hide him, she took for him an ark of bulrushes, and daubed it with slime and with pitch, and put the child therein; and she laid it in the flags by the river's brink.

4. And his sister stood afar off, to wit what would be done to him.

5. And the **daughter of Pharaoh** came down to wash herself at the river; and her maidens walked along by the river's side; and when she saw the ark among the flags, she sent her maid to fetch it.

6. And when she had opened it, she saw the child: and, behold, the babe wept. And she had compassion on him, and said, This is one of the Hebrews' children.

7. Then said his sister to Pharaoh's daughter, Shall I go and call to thee a nurse of the Hebrew women, that she may nurse the child for thee?

8. And Pharaoh's daughter said to her, Go. And the maid went and called the child's mother.

9. And Pharaoh's daughter said unto her, **Take this child away, and nurse it for me, and I will give thee thy wages. And the woman took the child, and nursed it.**

10. And the child grew, and she brought him unto Pharaoh's daughter, and he became her son. And she called his name Moses: and she said, Because I drew him out of the water.

Acts

Chapter 7

15. So Jacob went down into Egypt, and died, he, and our fathers,

16. And were carried over into Sychem, and laid in the sepulchre that Abraham bought for a sum of money of the sons of Emmor the father of Sychem.

17. But when the time of the promise drew nigh, which God had sworn to Abraham, the people grew and multiplied in Egypt,

18. Till another king arose, which knew not Joseph.

19. The same dealt subtilly with our kindred, and evil entreated our fathers, so that they cast out their young children, to the end they might not live.

20. In which time Moses was born, and was exceeding fair, and nourished up in his father's house **three months**:

21. And when he was cast out, **Pharaoh's daughter took him up, and nourished him for her own son.**

22. And Moses was learned in all the wisdom of the Egyptians, and was mighty in words and in deeds.

Hebrews

Chapter 11

23. By faith Moses, when he was born, was hid **three months** of his parents, because they saw he was a proper child; and they were not afraid of the king's commandment.

24. By faith Moses, when he was come to years, refused to be called the son of **Pharaoh's daughter**;

COMMENTARY

In the Qur'an:

1. God warned the mother of Moses about his future as a prophet and directed her to save her baby's life by casting him into the river.

2. The mother of Moses was about to *"disclose his (case)"*, but God *"strengthened her heart"* and she sent Moses' sister to follow him.

3. Pharaoh's people picked him up from the water and the *"wife of Pharaoh"* asked them not to kill the baby, but to let her adopt him.

4. Baby Moses *"refused suck at first"*, according to divine arrangement, until his sister showed up and offered the *"wife of Pharaoh"* to find a nursing mother for Moses from among the Jews.

In the Bible:

1. The mother of Moses *"saw him that he was a goodly child, she hid him three months."* It was her decision.

2. She decided to preserve him by placing Moses into a well-protected basket and put it into the river, while Miriam, the sister of Moses, watched over him to see what would happen.

3. The *"daughter of Pharaoh"* came to the river, saw the basket and ordered her maiden to fetch it. When she saw the crying baby, *"she had compassion on him, and said, This is one of the Hebrews' children"*. She decided to adopt the baby.

4. Moses' sister came unto her and offered to find a nurse for the baby. The *"daughter of Pharaoh"* ordered Moses' own mother to nurse the baby herself and offered a good payment for her job.

THE QUR'AN

"The Sin of Moses and his Escape from Egypt"

Sura 28

The Narratives

15. And he went into the city at a time of unvigilance on the part of its people, **so he found therein two men fighting, one being of his party and the other of his foes, and he who was of his party cried out to him for help against him who was of his enemies, so Musa struck him with his fist and killed him.** He said: This is on account of the Shaitan's doing; surely he is an enemy, openly leading astray.

16. He said: **My Lord! surely I have done harm to myself, so do Thou protect me. So He protected him**; surely He is the Forgiving, the Merciful.

17. He said: **My Lord! because Thou hast bestowed a favor on me, I shall never be a backer of the guilty.**

18. And he was in the city, fearing, awaiting, when lo! he who had asked his assistance the day before was crying out to him for aid. Musa said to him: You are most surely one erring manifestly.

19. So when he desired to seize him who was an enemy to them both, he said: O Musa! do you intend to kill me as you killed a person yesterday? You desire nothing but that you should be a tyrant in the land, and you do not desire to be of those who act aright.

20. And a man came running from the remotest part of the city. He said: **O Musa! surely the chiefs are consulting together to slay you, therefore depart (at once);** surely I am of those who wish well to you.

21. So he went forth therefrom, fearing, awaiting, (and) he said: **My Lord! deliver me from the unjust people**.

22. And when he turned his face towards Madyan, he said: Maybe my Lord will guide me in the right path.

23. And when he came to the water of Madyan, he found on it a group of men watering, and he found besides them **two women keeping back (their flocks)**. He said: What is the matter with you? They said: **We cannot water until the shepherds take away (their sheep) from the water, and our father is a very old man.**

24. So **he watered (their sheep) for them**, then went back to the shade and said: My Lord! surely I stand in need of whatever good Thou mayest send down to me.

25. Then one of the two women came to him walking bashfully. She said: My father invites you that he may give you the reward of your having watered for us. So when he came to him and gave to him the account, he said: Fear not, you are secure from the unjust people.

26. Said one of them: O my father! employ him, surely the best of those that you can employ is the strong man, the faithful one.

27. He said: I desire to marry one of these two daughters of mine to you on condition that you should serve me for eight years; but if you complete ten, it will be of your own free will, and I do not wish to be hard to you; if Allah please, you will find me one of the good.

28. He said: This shall be (an agreement) between me and you; **whichever of the two terms I fulfill, there shall be no wrongdoing to me;** and Allah is a witness of what we say.

THE BIBLE

"The Sin of Moses and His Escape From Egypt"

Exodus

Chapter 2

11. And it came to pass in those days, when Moses was grown, that **he went out unto his brethren, and looked on their burdens: and he spied an Egyptian smiting an Hebrew, one of his brethren.**

12. And he looked this way and that way, **and when he saw that there was no man, he slew the Egyptian, and hid him in the sand.**

13. And when he went out the second day, behold, **two men of the Hebrews strove together: and he said to him that did the wrong, Wherefore smitest thou thy fellow?**

14. And he said, **Who made thee a prince and a judge over us? intendest thou to kill me, as thou killedst the Egyptian? And Moses feared, and said, Surely this thing is known.**

15. Now when Pharaoh heard this thing, he sought to slay Moses. But Moses fled from the face of Pharaoh, and dwelt in the land of Midian: and he sat down by a well.

16. Now the **priest of Midian had seven daughters:** and **they came and drew water**, and filled the troughs to water their father's flock.

17. And the shepherds came and drove them away: but Moses stood up and helped them, and watered their flock.

18. And when they came to Reuel their father, he said, How is it that ye are come so soon to day?

19. And they said, An Egyptian delivered us out of the hand of the shepherds, and also drew water enough for us, and watered the flock.

20. And he said unto his daughters, And where is he? why is it that ye have left the man? call him, that he may eat bread.

21. And Moses was content to dwell with the man: and he gave Moses Zipporah his daughter.

22. And she bare him a son, and he called his name Gershom: for he said, I have been a stranger in a strange land.

COMMENTARY

In the Qur'an:

1. Moses was walking nearby when one of his fellow Jews asked for his help in a fight.

2. The same person asked Moses for help to fight an Egyptian *"who was an enemy to both of them…"*

3. Moses rushed to hold the enemy down. He was accused of intending to kill this Egyptian as he had killed another the day before and eventually to *"become a powerful violent man in the land."*

4. Moses came to the well and saw shepherds that were watering their flock and *"**two women** who were keeping back (their flocks)"*. When he discovered the women's dilemma, he helped them to water their flocks.

5. The father of these women offered Moses the job to shepherd his flocks for eight to ten years, and to marry one of his daughters. Moses agreed with him.

In the Bible:

1. Moses *"looked on their burdens: and he spied an Egyptian smiting an Hebrew, one of his brethren. 12 And he looked this way and that way, and when he saw that there was no man, he slew the Egyptian, and hid him in the sand."* He did not indicate remorse for his action.

2. The next day Moses saw two different Hebrews fighting with each other. He tried to reason with them to stop the fight.

3. He was accused by one of the Hebrews not to be *"a prince and a judge over us? intendest thou to kill me, as thou killedst the Egyptian?"*.

4. Moses came to the well and saw **seven** daughters of *"the priest of Midian"*. Later other shepherds came and forced the girls to withdraw their flocks from the well, but *"Moses stood up and helped them, and watered their flock"*.

5. Their father offered Moses the position of shepherd and later give him one of his daughters as a wife, but did not set any time frame of service as a payment for marriage. The idea of a "time frame of service" comes from the story of **Jacob and Laban**, not the story of Moses:

Genesis 29:16-20

16. *And Laban had two daughters: the name of the elder was Leah, and the name of the younger was Rachel.*

17. *Leah was tender eyed; but Rachel was beautiful and well favoured.*

18. *And Jacob loved Rachel; and said,* **I will serve thee seven years for Rachel thy younger daughter.**

19. *And Laban said, It is better that I give her to thee, than that I should give her to another man: abide with me.*

20. **And Jacob served seven years for Rachel;** *and they seemed unto him but a few days, for the love he had to her.*

THE QUR'AN

"Moses and the Burning Bush"

Sura 20

Ta Ha

9. And has the story of Musa come to you?

10. When he saw fire, he said to his family: Stop, for surely I see a fire, haply I may bring to you therefrom a live coal or find a guidance at the fire.

11. So when he came to it, a voice was uttered: O Musa:

12. Surely I am your Lord, **therefore put off your shoes; surely you are in the sacred valley, Tuwa,**

13. And I have chosen you, so listen to what is revealed:

14. Surely I am Allah, there is no god but I, therefore serve Me and keep up prayer for My remembrance:

15. Surely the hour is coming-- I am about to make it manifest-- so that every soul may be rewarded as it strives:

16. Therefore let not him who believes not in it and follows his low desires turn you away from it so that you should perish;

17. And what is this in your right hand, O Musa!

18. He said: This is my staff: I recline on it and I beat the leaves with it to make them fall upon my sheep, and I have other uses for it.

19. He said: Cast it down, O Musa!

20. So he cast it down; and lo! it was a serpent running.

21. He said: Take hold of it and fear not; We will restore it to its former state:

22. And press your hand to your side, it shall come out white without evil: another sign:

23. That We may show you of Our greater signs:

24. Go to Firon, surely he has exceeded all limits.

25. He said: O my Lord! Expand my breast for me,

26. And make my affair easy to me,

27. And loose the knot from my tongue,

28. (That) they may understand my word;

29. And give to me an aider from my family:

30. Haroun, my brother,

31. Strengthen my back by him,

32. And associate him (with me) in my affair,

35. Surely, Thou art seeing us.

36. He said: You are indeed granted your petition, O Musa And certainly We bestowed on you a favor at another time;

Sura 27

The Ant

7. When Musa said to his family: Surely I see fire; I will bring to you from it some news, or I will bring to you therefrom a burning firebrand so that you may warm yourselves.

8. So when he came to it a voice was uttered saying: Blessed is Whoever is in the fire and whatever is about it; and glory be to Allah, the Lord of the worlds;

9. O Musa! surely I am Allah, the Mighty, the Wise;

10. And cast down your staff. So when he saw it in motion as if it were a serpent, he turned back retreating and did not return: O Musa! fear not; surely the apostles shall not fear in My presence;

11. Neither he who has been unjust, then he does good instead after evil, for surely I am the Forgiving, the Merciful:

12. And enter your hand into the opening of your bosom, it shall come forth white without evil; **among nine signs to Firon and his people, surely they are a transgressing people.**

Sura 28

The Narratives

29. So when Musa had fulfilled the term, and he journeyed with his family, he perceived on this side of the mountain a fire. He said to his family: Wait, I have seen a fire, maybe I will bring to you from it some news or a brand of fire, so that you may warm yourselves.

30. And when he came to it, a voice was uttered from the right side of the valley in the blessed spot of the bush, saying: O Musa! surely I am Allah, the Lord of the worlds.

31. And saying: Cast down your staff. So when he saw it in motion as if it were a serpent, he turned back retreating, and did not return. O Musa! come forward and fear not; surely you are of those who are secure;

32. Enter your hand into the opening of your bosom, it will come forth white without evil, and draw your hand to yourself to ward off fear: so these two shall be two arguments from your Lord to Firon and his chiefs, surely they are a transgressing people.

33. He said: My Lord! surely I killed one of them, so I fear lest they should slay me;

34. And my brother, Haroun, he is more eloquent of tongue than I, therefore send him with me as an aider, verifying me: surely I fear that they would reject me.

35. He said: We will strengthen your arm with your brother, and We will give you both an authority, so that they shall not reach you; (go) with Our signs; you two and those who follow you shall be uppermost.

THE BIBLE

"Moses and the Burning Bush"

Exodus

Chapter 3

1. Now Moses kept the flock of Jethro his father in law, the priest of Midian: and he led the flock to the backside of the desert, and came to the mountain of God, even to Horeb.

2. And the angel of the LORD appeared unto him in a flame of fire out of the midst of a bush: and he looked, and, behold, the bush burned with fire, and the bush was not consumed.

3. And Moses said, I will now turn aside, and see this great sight, why the bush is not burnt.

4. And when the LORD saw that he turned aside to see, God called unto him out of the midst of the bush, and said, Moses, Moses. And he said, Here am I.

5. And he said, Draw not nigh hither: put off thy shoes from off thy feet, for the place whereon thou standest is holy ground.

6. Moreover he said, **I am the God of thy father, the God of Abraham, the God of Isaac, and the God of Jacob. And Moses hid his face; for he was afraid to look upon God.**

7. And the LORD said, I have surely seen the affliction of my people which are in Egypt, and have heard their cry by reason of their taskmasters; for I know their sorrows;

8. And I am come down to deliver them out of the hand of the Egyptians, and to bring them up out of that land unto a good land and a large, unto a land flowing with milk and honey; unto the place of the Canaanites, and the Hittites, and the Amorites, and the Perizzites, and the Hivites, and the Jebusites.

9. Now therefore, behold, the cry of the children of Israel is come unto me: and I have also seen the oppression wherewith the Egyptians oppress them.

10. Come now therefore, and I will send thee unto Pharaoh, that thou mayest bring forth my people the children of Israel out of Egypt.

11. And Moses said unto God, Who am I, that I should go unto Pharaoh, **and that I should bring forth the children of Israel out of Egypt?**

12. And he said, Certainly I will be with thee; and this shall be a token unto thee, that I have sent thee: When thou hast brought forth the people out of Egypt, ye shall serve God upon this mountain.

13. And Moses said unto God, Behold, when I come unto the children of Israel, and shall say unto them, The God of your fathers hath sent me unto you; and they shall say to me, What is his name? what shall I say unto them?

14. And God said unto Moses, I AM THAT I AM: and he said, Thus shalt thou say unto the children of Israel, I AM hath sent me unto you.

15. And God said moreover unto Moses, **Thus shalt thou say unto the children of Israel, The LORD God of your fathers, the God of Abraham, the God of Isaac, and the God of Jacob, hath sent me unto you: this is my name for ever, and this is my memorial unto all generations.**

16. Go, and gather the elders of Israel together, and say unto them, The LORD God of your fathers, the God of Abraham, of Isaac, and of Jacob, appeared unto me, saying, I have surely visited you, and seen that which is done to you in Egypt:

17. And I have said, I will bring you up out of the affliction of Egypt unto the land of the Canaanites, and the Hittites, and the Amorites, and the Perizzites, and the Hivites, and the Jebusites, unto a land flowing with milk and honey.

18. And they shall hearken to thy voice: **and thou shalt come, thou and the elders of Israel, unto the king of Egypt, and ye shall say unto him, The LORD God of the Hebrews hath met with us: and now let us go, we beseech thee, three days' journey into the wilderness, that we may sacrifice to the LORD our God.**

19. And I am sure that the king of Egypt will not let you go, no, not by a mighty hand.

20. And I will stretch out my hand, and smite Egypt with all my wonders which I will do in the midst thereof: and after that he will let you go.

21. And I will give this people favour in the sight of the Egyptians: and it shall come to pass, that, when ye go, ye shall not go empty:

22. But every woman shall borrow of her neighbour, and of her that sojourneth in her house, jewels of silver, and jewels of gold, and raiment: and ye shall put them upon your sons, and upon your daughters; and ye shall spoil the Egyptians.

Exodus

Chapter 4

1. And Moses answered and said, **But, behold, they will not believe me, nor hearken unto my voice: for they will say, The LORD hath not appeared unto thee.**

2. And the LORD said unto him, What is that in thine hand? And he said, A rod.

3. And he said, Cast it on the ground. And he cast it on the ground, and it became a serpent; and Moses fled from before it.

4. And the LORD said unto Moses, Put forth thine hand, and take it by the tail. And he put forth his hand, and caught it, and it became a rod in his hand:

5. That they may believe that the LORD God of their fathers, the God of Abraham, the God of Isaac, and the God of Jacob, hath appeared unto thee.

6. And the LORD said furthermore unto him, Put now thine hand into thy bosom. And he put his hand into his bosom: and when he took it out, behold, his hand was leprous as snow.

7. And he said, Put thine hand into thy bosom again. And he put his hand into his bosom again; and plucked it out of his bosom, and, behold, it was turned again as his other flesh.

8. And it shall come to pass, if they will not believe thee, neither hearken to the voice of the first sign, that they will believe the voice of the latter sign.

9. And it shall come to pass, if they will not believe also these two signs, neither hearken unto thy voice, that thou shalt take of the water of the river, and pour it upon the dry land: and the water which thou takest out of the river shall become blood upon the dry land.

10. And Moses said unto the LORD, O my Lord, I am not eloquent, neither heretofore, nor since thou hast spoken unto thy servant: but I am slow of speech, and of a slow tongue.

11 And the LORD said unto him, Who hath made man's mouth? or who maketh the dumb, or deaf, or the seeing, or the blind? have not I the LORD?

12 Now therefore go, and I will be with thy mouth, and teach thee what thou shalt say.

13 And he said, O my Lord, send, I pray thee, by the hand of him whom thou wilt send.

14. And the anger of the LORD was kindled against Moses, and he said, Is not Aaron the Levite thy brother? I know that he can speak well. And also, behold, he cometh forth to meet thee: and when he seeth thee, he will be glad in his heart.

15. And thou shalt speak unto him, and put words in his mouth: and I will be with thy mouth, and with his mouth, and will teach you what ye shall do.

16. And he shall be thy spokesman unto the people: and he shall be, even he shall be to thee instead of a mouth, and thou shalt be to him instead of God.

17. And thou shalt take this rod in thine hand, wherewith thou shalt do signs.

18. And Moses went and returned to Jethro his father in law, and said unto him, Let me go, I pray thee, and return unto my brethren which are in Egypt, and see whether they be yet alive. And Jethro said to Moses, Go in peace.

19. And the LORD said unto Moses in Midian, Go, return into Egypt: for all the men are dead which sought thy life.

20. And Moses took his wife and his sons, and set them upon an ass, and he returned to the land of Egypt: and Moses took the rod of God in his hand.

21. And the LORD said unto Moses, When thou goest to return into Egypt, see that thou do all those wonders before Pharaoh, which I have put in thine hand: but I will harden his heart, that he shall not let the people go.

22. And thou shalt say unto Pharaoh, Thus saith the LORD, Israel is my son, even my firstborn:

23. And I say unto thee, Let my son go, that he may serve me: and if thou refuse to let him go, behold, I will slay thy son, even thy firstborn.

27. And the LORD said to Aaron, Go into the wilderness to meet Moses. And he went, and met him in the mount of God, and kissed him.

28. And Moses told Aaron all the words of the LORD who had sent him, and all the signs which he had commanded him.

29. And Moses and Aaron went and gathered together all the elders of the children of Israel:

30. And Aaron spake all the words which the LORD had spoken unto Moses, and did the signs in the sight of the people.

31. And the people believed: and when they heard that the LORD had visited the children of Israel, and that he had looked upon their affliction, then they bowed their heads and worshipped.

COMMENTARY:

In the Qur'an:

1. Musa saw a fire from his tent and told his family; he decided right away that he would get guidance by visiting the site of the fire.

2. A voice told Musa that he was in the **sacred Tuva Valley**.

3. Musa asked Allah to give Arun a task also, to which Allah agreed.

4. Allah told Musa that there would be **nine** signs for Pharaoh.

In the Bible:

1. Moses was alone with his flock when he saw the burning bush.

2. Moses was on **Horeb, the mountain of God.**

3. Moses asked God to choose another man instead of him. God offered him his brother Aaron as his helper.

4. God sent **ten** signs (plagues) to punish Egypt.

THE QUR'AN

"Moses and Pharaoh"

Sura 7

The Elevated Places

103. Then we raised after them Musa with Our communications to Firon and his chiefs, but they disbelieved in them; consider then what was the end of the mischief makers.

104. And Musa said: O Firon! surely I am an apostle from the Lord of the worlds:

105. (I am) worthy of not saying anything about Allah except the truth: **I have come to you indeed with clear proof from your Lord, therefore send with me the children of Israel**

106. He said: **If you have come with a sign, then bring it, if you are of the truthful ones.**

107. So he threw his rod, then lo! it was a clear serpent.

108. And he drew forth his hand, and lo! it was white to the beholders.

109. The chiefs of Firon's people said: most surely this is an enchanter possessed of knowledge:

110. He intends to turn you out of your land. What counsel do you then give?

111. They said: Put him off and his brother, and send collectors into the cities:

112. That they may bring to you every enchanter possessed of knowledge.

113. And the enchanters came to Firon (and) said: We must surely have a reward if we are the prevailing ones.

114. He said: Yes, and you shall certainly be of those who are near (to me).

115. They said: O Musa! will you cast, or shall we be the first to cast?

116. He said: Cast. So when they cast, they deceived the people's eyes and frightened them, and they produced a mighty enchantment.

117. And We revealed to Musa, saying: Cast your rod; then lo! it devoured the lies they told.

118. So the truth was established, and what they did became null.

119. Thus they were vanquished there, and they went back abased.

120. And the enchanters were thrown down, prostrating (themselves).

121. They said: We believe in the Lord of the worlds,

122. The Lord of Musa and Haroun.

123. Firon said: Do you believe in Him before I have given you permission? Surely this is a plot which you have secretly devised in this city, that you may turn out of it its people, but you shall know:

124. 1 will certainly cut off your hands and your feet on opposite sides, then will I crucify you all together.

125. They said: Surely to our Lord shall we go back:

Sura 10

Jonah

84. And Musa said: O my people! if you believe in Allah, then rely on Him (alone) if you submit (to Allah).

85. So they said: On Allah we rely: O our Lord! make us not subject to the persecution of the unjust people:

86. And do Thou deliver us by Thy mercy from the unbelieving people.

87. And We revealed to Musa and his brother, saying: **Take for your people houses to abide in Egypt and make your houses places of worship and keep up prayer and give good news to the believers.**

88. And Musa said: Our Lord! surely Thou hast given to Firon and his chiefs finery and riches in this world's life, to this end, our Lord, that they lead (people) astray from Thy way: **Our Lord! destroy their riches and harden their hearts so that they believe not until they see the painful punishment.**

89. He said: The prayer of you both has indeed been accepted, therefore continue in the right way and do not follow the path of those who do not know.

90. And We made the children of Israel to pass through the sea, then Firon and his hosts followed them for oppression and tyranny; until when drowning overtook him, **he said: I believe that there is no god but He in Whom the children of Israel believe and I am of those who submit.**

91. What! Now! Moreover, indeed, you disobeyed before and you were of the mischief-makers.

92. But We will this day deliver you with your body that you may be a sign to those after you, and most surely, the majority of the people are heedless to Our communications.

Sura 11

The Holy Prophet

96. And certainly We sent Musa with Our communications and a clear authority,

97. To Firon and his chiefs, but they followed the bidding of Firon, and Firon's bidding was not right-directing.

98. He shall lead his people on the resurrection day, and bring them down to the fire; and evil the place to which they are brought.

99. And they are overtaken by curse in this (world), and on the resurrection day, evil the gift which shall be given.

Sura 17

The Children of Israel

101. And certainly **We gave Musa nine clear signs**; so ask the children of Israel. When he came to them, Firon said to him: Most surely I deem you, O Musa, to be a man deprived of reason.

Sura 20

Ta Ha

65. They said: O Musa! will you cast, or shall we be the first who cast down?

66. He said: Nay! cast down. then lo! their cords and their rods-- it was imaged to him on account of their magic as if they were running.

67. So Musa conceived in his mind a fear.

68. We said: Fear not, surely you shall be the uppermost,

69. And cast down what is in your right hand; it shall devour what they have wrought; they have wrought only the plan of a magician, and the magician shall not be successful wheresoever he may come from.

70. And the magicians were cast down making obeisance; they said: We believe in the Lord of Haroun and Musa.

71. (Firon) said: You believe in him before I give you leave; most surely he is the chief of you who taught you enchantment, therefore I will certainly cut off your hands and your feet on opposite sides, and I will certainly crucify you on the trunks of the palm trees, and certainly you will come to know which of us is the more severe and the more abiding in chastising.

72. They said: We do not prefer you to what has come to us of clear arguments and to He Who made us, therefore decide what you are going to decide; you can only decide about this world's life.

Sura 26

The Poets

38. So the magicians were gathered together at the appointed time on the fixed day,

39. And it was said to the people: Will you gather together?

40. Haply we may follow the magicians, if they are the vanquishers.

41. And when the magicians came, they said to Firon: Shall we get a reward if we are the vanquishers?

42. He said: Yes, and surely you will then be of those who are made near.

43. Musa said to them: Cast what you are going to cast.

44. So they cast down their cords and their rods and said: By Firon's power, we shall most surely be victorious.

45. Then Musa cast down his staff and lo! it swallowed up the lies they told.

46. And the magicians were thrown down prostrate;

47. They said: We believe in the Lord of the worlds:

48. The Lord of Musa and Haroun.

49. Said he: You believe in him before I give you permission; most surely he is the chief of you who taught you the magic, so you shall know: certainly I will cut off your hands and your feet on opposite sides, and certainly I will crucify you all.

50. They said: No harm; surely to our Lord we go back;

51. Surely we hope that our Lord will forgive us our wrongs because we are the first of the believers.

Sura 28

The Narratives

4. Surely **Firon** exalted himself in the land and made its people into parties, weakening one party from among them; **he slaughtered their sons and let their women live;** surely he was one of the mischiefmakers.

5. And We desired to bestow a favor upon those who were deemed weak in the land, and to make them the Imams, and to make them the heirs,

6. And to grant them power in the land, and to **make Firon and Haman** and their hosts see from them what they feared.

7. And **We revealed to Musa's mother**, saying: **Give him suck, then when you fear for him, cast him into the river** and do not fear nor grieve; surely We will bring him back to you and make him one of the apostles.

8. And Firon's family took him up that he might be an enemy and a grief for them; **surely Firon and Haman** and their hosts were wrongdoers.

36. So when Musa came to them with Our clear signs, they said: This is nothing but forged enchantment, and we never heard of it amongst our fathers of old.

37. And Musa said: My Lord knows best who comes with guidance from Him, and whose shall be the good end of the abode; surely the unjust shall not be successful.

38. **And Firon said**: O chiefs! I do not know of any god for you besides myself; therefore kindle a fire for me, **O Haman,** for brick, **then prepare for me a lofty building so that I may obtain knowledge of Musa's God**, and most surely I think him to be one of the liars.

39. And he was unjustly proud in the land, he and his hosts, and they deemed that they would not be brought back to Us.

Sura 29

The Spider

39. And (We destroyed) **Qaroun** and **Firon and Haman**; and certainly Musa came to them with clear arguments, but they behaved haughtily in the land; yet they could not outstrip (Us).

Sura 40

The Believer

36. And Firon said: **O Haman! build for me a tower that I may attain the means of access,**

37. **The means of access to the heavens, then reach the God of Musa, and I surely think him to be a liar**. And thus the evil of his deed was made fairseeming to Firon, and he was turned away from the way; and the struggle of Firon was not (to end) in aught but destruction.

THE BIBLE

"Moses and Pharaoh"

Exodus

Chapter 5

1. And afterward Moses and Aaron went in, and told Pharaoh, Thus saith the LORD God of Israel, Let my people go, that they may hold a feast unto me in the wilderness.

2. And Pharaoh said, Who is the LORD, that I should obey his voice to let Israel go? **I know not the LORD, neither will I let Israel go.**
3. And they said, The God of the Hebrews hath met with us: let us go, we pray thee, three days' journey into the desert, and sacrifice unto the LORD our God; lest he fall upon us with pestilence, or with the sword.

Exodus

Chapter 7

10. And Moses and Aaron went in unto Pharaoh, and they did so as the LORD had commanded: **and Aaron cast down his rod before Pharaoh, and before his servants, and it became a serpent.**
11. Then Pharaoh also called the wise men and the sorcerers: now the magicians of Egypt, they also did in like manner with their enchantments.
12. For they cast down every man his rod, and they became serpents: but Aaron's rod swallowed up their rods.
13. And he hardened Pharaoh's heart, that he hearkened not unto them; as the LORD had said.

Genesis

Chapter 11

1. And the whole earth was of one language, and of one speech.
2. And it came to pass, as they journeyed from the east, that they found a plain in the land of Shinar; and they dwelt there.
3. And they said one to another, Go to, let us make brick, and burn them throughly. And they had brick for stone, and slime had they for morter.
4. And they said, Go to, let us build us a city and a tower, whose top may reach unto heaven; and let us make us a name, lest we be scattered abroad upon the face of the whole earth.
5. And the LORD came down to see the city and the tower, which the children of men builded.
6. And the LORD said, Behold, the people is one, and they have all one language; and this they begin to do: and now nothing will be restrained from them, which they have imagined to do.
7. Go to, let us go down, and there confound their language, that they may not understand one another's speech.

8. So the LORD scattered them abroad from thence upon the face of all the earth: and they left off to build the city.

9. Therefore is the name of it called Babel; because the LORD did there confound the language of all the earth: and from thence did the LORD scatter them abroad upon the face of all the earth.

COMMENTARY:

In the Qur'an:

1. Moses said to Pharaoh *"... I have come to you indeed with clear proof from **your Lord**, therefore send with me the children of Israel..."* referring to Allah as Pharaoh's God.

2. Moses cast down his rod himself.

3. Some enchanters possessed knowledge and became believers in God.

4. God asked Moses, *"Take for your people houses to abide in Egypt and make your houses places of worship and keep up prayer and give good news to the believers".*

5. Moses showed nine signs to Pharaoh.

6. Pharaoh ordered the building of a *"...lofty palace The ways and means of (reaching) the heavens, and that I may mount up to the god of Moses..."*

7. Haman (Qaroun) was in a high position in Pharaoh's kingdom. It looks like he, Haman (Qaroun) and his master were already in position before Moses was born and during the time that Moses approached Pharaoh to allow the Israelites to depart the land of Egypt. Haman (Qaroun) was about to execute (twice, at different times) Pharaoh's order to "reduce" the Israelites' population.

In the Bible:

1. Moses never tried to convince Pharaoh that the Egyptians and the Israelites have the same one God.

2. Aaron, not Moses, cast the rod down.

121

3. There is no indication that anyone amongst Pharaoh's servants became believers (in Allah or God).

4. God ordered the Israelites to put the blood of a lamb on the door posts of their homes for the salvation of first-borns in the family and as a sign of deliverance from slavery (Passover).

5. God sent ten plagues to punish Pharaoh and Egypt.

6. It was not Pharaoh, but a group of people long before him who had decided to:

    > "...build us a city and a tower, whose top may reach unto heaven;..."
    > "Therefore is the name of it called Babel; because the LORD did there confound the language of all the earth: and from thence did the LORD scatter them abroad upon the face of all the earth."**(Genesis. 11: 4, 9)**

    Moses lived about 1500 BC. This event occurred about ten generations earlier, in the place now known as Babylon and the tower was called the tower of Babel.

7. The person called Haman existed in the time period after the Babylonian captivity of the remnant of Israel in the sixth century BC, long after Moses died on earth. Haman was an Agagite, living in Persia, who was an official in King Ahasuerus' court. Haman did indeed seek to destroy all the nation of Israel who were living throughout the Persian empire because of one Jew named Mordecai:

    > *1. After these things did king Ahasuerus promote* **Haman the son of Hammedatha** *the Agagite, and advanced him, and set his seat above all the princes that were with him.*
    > *2. And all the king's servants, that were in the king's gate, bowed, and reverenced Haman: for the king had so commanded concerning him. But Mordecai bowed not, nor did him reverence.*
    > *3. Then the king's servants, which were in the king's gate, said unto Mordecai, Why transgressest thou the king's commandment?*

4. Now it came to pass, when they spake daily unto him, and he hearkened not unto them, that they told Haman, to see whether Mordecai's matters would stand: for he had told them that he was a Jew.

*5. And when Haman saw that Mordecai bowed not, nor did him reverence, then **was Haman full of wrath.***

*6. And he thought scorn to lay hands on Mordecai alone; for they had shewed him the people of Mordecai: wherefore **Haman sought to destroy all the Jews that were throughout the whole kingdom of Ahasuerus,** even the people of Mordecai.."***(Esther 3:1-6)**

The Qur'an confuses two different stories that are separated by about a thousand years. Haman would have to have been more than one hundred years old by the time Moses, at the age of eighty, had asked Pharaoh to let his people go. Haman was in the first Pharaoh's office before Moses was born, and was still working in the second Pharaoh's court (the first Pharaoh's son) at the time Moses approached the second Pharaoh with God's request.

THE QUR'AN
"Pharaoh Threatens to Kill Moses"

Sura 40

The Believer

23. And certainly **We sent Musa** with Our communications and clear authority,

24. To **Firon** and **Haman** and **Qaroun,** but they said: A lying magician.

25. So when he brought to them the truth from Us, **they said: Slay the sons of those who believe with him and keep their women alive; and the struggle of the unbelievers will only come to a state of perdition.**

26. And Firon said: Let me alone that I may slay Musa and let him call upon his Lord; surely I fear that he will change your religion or that he will make mischief to appear in the land.

27. And Musa said: Surely I take refuge with my Lord and-- your Lord from every proud one who does not believe in the day of reckoning.

28. And a believing man of Firon's people who hid his faith said: **What! will you slay a man because he says: My Lord is Allah, and indeed he has brought to you clear arguments from your Lord? And if he be a liar, on him will be his lie, and if he be truthful, there will befall you some of that which he threatens you (with); surely Allah does not guide him who is extravagant, a liar:**

29. O my people! yours is the kingdom this day, being masters in the land, but who will help us against the punishment of Allah if it come to us? Firon said: I do not show you aught but that which I see (myself), and I do not make you follow any but the right way.

The Bible

"Pharaoh Threatens to Kill Moses"

Exodus

Chapter 1

1. Now these are the names of the children of Israel, which came into Egypt; every man and his household came with Jacob.

2. Reuben, Simeon, Levi, and Judah,

3. Issachar, Zebulun, and Benjamin,

4. Dan, and Naphtali, Gad, and Asher.

5. And all the souls that came out of the loins of Jacob were seventy souls: for Joseph was in Egypt already.

6. And Joseph died, and all his brethren, and all that generation.

7. And the children of Israel were fruitful, and increased abundantly, and multiplied, and waxed exceeding mighty; and the land was filled with them.

8. Now there arose up a new king over Egypt, which knew not Joseph.

9. And he said unto his people, Behold, the people of the children of Israel are more and mightier than we:

10. Come on, let us deal wisely with them; lest they multiply, and it come to pass, that, when there falleth out any war, they join also unto our enemies, and fight against us, and so get them up out of the land.

11. Therefore they did set over them taskmasters to afflict them with their burdens. And they built for Pharaoh treasure cities, Pithom and Raamses.

12. But the more they afflicted them, the more they multiplied and grew. And they were grieved because of the children of Israel.

13. And the Egyptians made the children of Israel to serve with rigour:

14. And they made their lives bitter with hard bondage, in morter, and in brick, and in all manner of service in the field: all their service, wherein they made them serve, was with rigour.

15. And the king of Egypt spake to the Hebrew midwives, of which the name of the one was Shiphrah, and the name of the other Puah:

16. And he said, When ye do the office of a midwife to the Hebrew women, and see them upon the stools; if it be a son, then ye shall kill him: but if it be a daughter, then she shall live.

17. But the midwives feared God, and did not as the king of Egypt commanded them, but saved the men children alive.

18. And the king of Egypt called for the midwives, and said unto them, Why have ye done this thing, and have saved the men children alive?

19. And the midwives said unto Pharaoh, Because the Hebrew women are not as the Egyptian women; for they are lively, and are delivered ere the midwives come in unto them.

20. Therefore God dealt well with the midwives: and the people multiplied, and waxed very mighty.

21. And it came to pass, because the midwives feared God, that he made them houses.

22. And Pharaoh charged all his people, saying, Every son that is born ye shall cast into the river, and every daughter ye shall save alive.

Exodus

Chapter 2

1. And there went a man of the house of Levi, and took to wife a daughter of Levi.

2. And the woman conceived, and bare a son: and when she saw him that he was a goodly child, **she hid him three months.**

3. And when she could not longer hide him, she took for him an ark of bulrushes, and daubed it with slime and with pitch, and put the child therein; and she laid it in the flags by the river's brink.

COMMENTARY:

In the Qur'an:

1. Pharaoh decided to *"…Slay the sons of those who believe with him (Moses), and keep alive their females"*, in order to prevent Moses from changing the Egyptians' religion or from making trouble in Egypt.

2. Some of the Egyptians in Pharaoh's court were believers in God and rejected his order to kill Moses.

In the Bible:

1. This is a story of the beginning of Israel as a nation in the land of Egypt. Pharaoh was concerned about their increasing population. In order to reduce their numbers he first burdened them with heavy labor, and later gave an order for midwives to kill every male child and to keep only females at their birth. When it did not stop their increase, Pharaoh gave a direct order to his people: *"Every son that is born ye shall cast into the river, and every daughter ye shall save alive."* At this point we learn about the baby Moses and the reason he was put into the basket to sail in the Nile River's waters.

2. Later in the Bible, when Moses came to Pharaoh saying: *"… Let my people go…"* there is no indication of any of Pharaoh's servants opposing neither Pharaoh's orders nor having been believers in the Hebrews' God.

CONCLUSION

The Qur'an mixes into one account two stories which actually take place about eighty years apart from each other.

THE QUR'AN

"Moses Divides the Red Sea"

Sura 26

The Poets

61. So when the two hosts saw each other, the companions of Musa cried out: Most surely we are being overtaken.

62. He said: By no means; surely my Lord is with me: He will show me a way out.

63. Then We revealed to Musa: **Strike the sea with your staff.** So it had cloven asunder, and each part was like a huge mound.

THE BIBLE

"Moses Divides the Red Sea"

Exodus

Chapter 14

10. And when Pharaoh drew nigh, the children of Israel lifted up their eyes, and, behold, the Egyptians marched after them; and they were sore afraid: and the children of Israel cried out unto the LORD.

11. And they said unto Moses, Because there were no graves in Egypt, hast thou taken us away to die in the wilderness? wherefore hast thou dealt thus with us, to carry us forth out of Egypt?

12. Is not this the word that we did tell thee in Egypt, saying, Let us alone, that we may serve the Egyptians? For it had been better for us to serve the Egyptians, than that we should die in the wilderness.

13. And Moses said unto the people, Fear ye not, stand still, and see the salvation of the LORD, which he will shew to you to day: for the Egyptians whom ye have seen to day, ye shall see them again no more for ever.

14. The LORD shall fight for you, and ye shall hold your peace.

15. And the LORD said unto Moses, Wherefore criest thou unto me? speak unto the children of Israel, that they go forward:

16. But lift thou up thy rod, and stretch out thine hand over the sea, and divide it: and the children of Israel shall go on dry ground through the midst of the sea.

COMMENTARY:

In the Qur'an:

1. God told Moses to **"Strike the sea with thy rod."**

In the Bible:

1. God told Moses to **"Lift up your rod, and stretch out your hand over the sea."**

THE QUR'AN

"Moses Smites the Rock"

Sura 2

The Cow

60. And when Musa prayed for drink for his people, We said: **Strike the rock with your staff So there gushed from it twelve springs; each tribe knew its drinking place**: Eat and drink of the provisions of Allah and do not act corruptly in the land, making mischief.

Sura 7

The Elevated Places

160. And We divided them into twelve tribes, as nations; and We revealed to Musa when his people asked him for water: **Strike the rock with your staff, so out flowed from it twelve springs; each tribe knew its drinking place**; and We made the clouds to give shade over them and We sent to them manna and quails: Eat of the good things We have given you. And they did not do Us any harm, but they did injustice to their own souls.

THE BIBLE

"Moses Smites the Rock"

Exodus

Chapter 15

1. Then sang Moses and the children of Israel this song unto the LORD, and spake, saying, I will sing unto the LORD, for he hath triumphed gloriously: the horse and his rider hath he thrown into the sea.

27. And they came to Elim, where were twelve wells of water, and threescore and ten palm trees: and they encamped there by the waters.

Exodus

Chapter 17

1. And all the congregation of the children of Israel journeyed from **the wilderness of Sin**, after their journeys, according to the commandment of the LORD, and pitched in **Rephidim:** and there was no water for the people to drink.

2. Wherefore the people did chide with Moses, and said, **Give us water that we may drink.** And Moses said unto them, Why chide ye with me? wherefore do ye tempt the LORD?

3. And the people thirsted there for water; **and the people murmured against Moses**, and said, Wherefore is this that thou hast brought us up out of Egypt, to kill us and our children and our cattle with thirst?

4. And Moses cried unto the LORD, saying, What shall I do unto this people? they be almost ready to stone me.

5. And the LORD said unto Moses, Go on before the people, and take with thee of the elders of Israel; and thy rod, wherewith thou smotest the river, take in thine hand, and go.

6. Behold, I will stand before thee there upon the rock in Horeb; and thou shalt smite the rock, and there shall come water out of it, that the people may drink. And Moses did so in the sight of the elders of Israel.

7. And he called the name of the place Massah, and Meribah, because of the chiding of the children of Israel, and because they tempted the LORD, saying, Is the LORD among us, or not?

Numbers

Chapter 20

1. Then came the children of Israel, even the whole congregation, into **the desert of Zin** in the first month: and the people abode **in Kadesh**; and Miriam died there, and was buried there.

2. And there was no water for the congregation: and they gathered themselves together against Moses and against Aaron.

3. And the people chode with Moses, and spake, saying, Would God that we had died when our brethren died before the LORD!

4. And why have ye brought up the congregation of the LORD into this wilderness, that we and our cattle should die there?

5. And wherefore have ye made us to come up out of Egypt, to bring us in unto this evil place? it is no place of seed, or of figs, or of vines, or of pomegranates; neither is there any water to drink.

6. And Moses and Aaron went from the presence of the assembly unto the door of the tabernacle of the congregation, and they fell upon their faces: and the glory of the LORD appeared unto them.

7. And the LORD spake unto Moses, saying,

8. Take the rod, and gather thou the assembly together, thou, and Aaron thy brother, **and speak ye unto the rock before their eyes; and it shall give forth his water**, and thou shalt bring forth to them water out of the rock: so thou shalt give the congregation and their beasts drink.

9. And Moses took the rod from before the LORD, as he commanded him.

10. And Moses and Aaron gathered the congregation together before the rock, and he said unto them, Hear now, ye rebels; must we fetch you water out of this rock?

11. And Moses lifted up his hand, and **with his rod he smote the rock twice: and the water came out abundantly,** and the congregation drank, and their beasts also.

12. And the LORD spake unto Moses and Aaron, Because ye believed me not, to sanctify me in the eyes of the children of Israel,

therefore ye shall not bring this congregation into the land which I have given them.

13. This is the water of Meribah; because the children of Israel strove with the LORD, and he was sanctified in them.

COMMENTARY:

In the Qur'an:

Here it speaks about one event as Musa (Moses), through Allah's help, brought 12 springs of water from the rock.

In the Bible:

We find three separate events. Twelve springs already existed in the oasis in Elim, and twice Moses brought a single spring of water from the rock, but the second time he struck the rock with the rod, instead of speaking to it. For that sin, Moses did not enter into the Promised Land: "*... Because ye believed me not, to sanctify me in the eyes of the children of Israel, therefore ye shall not bring this congregation into the land which I have given them.*"

THE QUR'AN

"The People of Israel Ask to See God"

Sura 2

The Cow

55. And when you said: O Musa! **we will not believe in you until we see Allah manifestly,** so the **punishment overtook you while you looked on.**

56. Then We raised you up after your death that you may give thanks.

Sura 4

The Women

153. The followers of the Book ask you to bring down to them a book from heaven; so indeed they demanded of Musa a greater thing than that, for they said: **Show us Allah manifestly; so the lightning overtook them on account of their injustice**. Then they took the calf (for a god), after clear signs had come to them, but We pardoned this; and We gave to Musa clear authority.

THE BIBLE

"The People of Israel Ask to See God"

Exodus

Chapter 20

18. And **all the people saw the thunderings, and the lightnings**, and the noise of the trumpet, and the mountain smoking: and **when the people saw it, they removed, and stood afar off.**
19. And they said unto Moses, Speak thou with us, and we will hear: but let not God speak with us, lest we die.
20. And Moses said unto the people, Fear not: for God is come to prove you, and that his fear may be before your faces, that ye sin not..

COMMENTARY:

In the Qur'an:

The Israelites wanted to see God before they would believe Moses. There followed a death and resurrection of the unbelievers so that they may be grateful to God.

In the Bible:

The people of Israel *"...removed, and stood afar off."* and refused to hear from God directly: *"...Speak thou with us, and we will hear: but let not God speak with us, lest we die..."*. There was no death and resurrection of unbelievers followed by praising of God.

THE QUR'AN

"Moses and the Golden Calf"

Sura 20

Ta Ha

83. And what caused you to hasten from your people, O Musa?

84. He said: They are here on my track and I hastened on to Thee, my Lord, that Thou mightest be pleased.

85. He said: So surely We have tried your people after you, and **the Samiri has led them astray**.

86. So Musa returned to his people wrathful, sorrowing. Said he: O my people! did not your Lord promise you a goodly promise: did then the time seem long to you, or did you wish that displeasure from your Lord should be due to you, so that you broke (your) promise to me?

87. They said: We did not break (our) promise to you of our own accord, but we were made to bear the burdens of the ornaments of the people, then we made a casting of them, **and thus did the Samiri suggest.**

88. So he brought forth for them a calf, a (mere) body, which had a mooing sound, so they said: This is your god and the god of Musa, but he forgot.

89. What! could they not see that it did not return to them a reply, and (that) it did not control any harm or benefit for them?

90. And certainly Haroun had said to them before: O my people! you are only tried by it, and surely your Lord is the Beneficent God, therefore follow me and obey my order.

91. They said: We will by no means cease to keep to its worship until Musa returns to us.

92. (Musa) said: O Haroun! what prevented you, when you saw them going astray,

93. So that you did not follow me? Did you then disobey my order?

94. He said: O son of my mother! seize me not by my beard nor by my head; surely I was afraid lest you should say: You have caused a division among the children of Israel and not waited for my word.

95. He said: **What was then your object, O Samiri?**

96. He said: **I saw (Jibreel) what they did not see, so I took a handful (of the dust) from the footsteps of the messenger, then I threw it in the casting; thus did my soul commend to me**
97. He said: Be gone then, surely for you it will be in this life to say, Touch (me) not; and surely there is a threat for you, which shall not be made to fail to you, and look at your god to whose worship you kept (so long); we will certainly burn it, then **we will certainly scatter it a (wide) scattering in the sea.**

Sura 2

The Cattle

54. And when Musa said to his people: O my people! you have surely been unjust to yourselves by taking the calf (for a god), therefore turn to your Creator (penitently), **so kill your people (yourselves), that is best for you with your Creator**: so He turned to you (mercifully), for surely He is the Oft-returning (to mercy), the Merciful.

THE BIBLE

"Moses and the Golden Calf"

Exodus

Chapter 32

1. And when the people saw that Moses delayed to come down out of the mount, **the people gathered themselves together unto Aaron, and said unto him, Up, make us gods,** which shall go before us; for as for this Moses, the man that brought us up out of the land of Egypt, we wot not what is become of him.
2. And Aaron said unto them, Break off the golden earrings, which are in the ears of your wives, of your sons, and of your daughters, and bring them unto me.
3. And all the people brake off the golden earrings which were in their ears, and brought them unto Aaron.
4. And he received them at their hand, and fashioned it with a graving tool, after he had made it a molten calf: and they said, These be thy gods, O Israel, which brought thee up out of the land of Egypt.

5. And when Aaron saw it, he built an altar before it; and Aaron made proclamation, and said, Tomorrow is a feast to the LORD.

6. And they rose up early on the morrow, and offered burnt offerings, and brought peace offerings; and the people sat down to eat and to drink, and rose up to play.

7. And the LORD said unto Moses, Go, get thee down; for thy people, which thou broughtest out of the land of Egypt, have corrupted themselves:

8. They have turned aside quickly out of the way which I commanded them: they have made them a molten calf, and have worshipped it, and have sacrificed thereunto, and said, These be thy gods, O Israel, which have brought thee up out of the land of Egypt.

9. And the LORD said unto Moses, I have seen this people, and, behold, it is a stiffnecked people:

10. Now therefore let me alone, **that my wrath may wax hot against them, and that I may consume them: and I will make of thee a great nation.**

11. And Moses besought the LORD his God, and said, LORD, why doth thy wrath wax hot against thy people, which thou hast brought forth out of the land of Egypt with great power, and with a mighty hand?

12. Wherefore should the Egyptians speak, and say, For mischief did he bring them out, to slay them in the mountains, and to consume them from the face of the earth? Turn from thy fierce wrath, and repent of this evil against thy people.

13. Remember Abraham, Isaac, and Israel, thy servants, to whom thou swarest by thine own self, and saidst unto them, I will multiply your seed as the stars of heaven, and all this land that I have spoken of will I give unto your seed, and they shall inherit it for ever.

14. And the LORD repented of the evil which he thought to do unto his people.

15. And Moses turned, and went down from the mount, and the two tables of the testimony were in his hand: the tables were written on both their sides; on the one side and on the other were they written.

16. And the tables were the work of God, and the writing was the writing of God, graven upon the tables.

17. And when Joshua heard the noise of the people as they shouted, he said unto Moses, There is a noise of war in the camp.

135

18. And he said, It is not the voice of them that shout for mastery, neither is it the voice of them that cry for being overcome: but the noise of them that sing do I hear.

19. And it came to pass, as soon as he came nigh unto the camp, that he saw the calf, and the dancing: and Moses' anger waxed hot, and he cast the tables out of his hands, and brake them beneath the mount.

20. And he took the calf which they had made, and burnt it in the fire, and ground it to powder, and strawed it upon the water, and made the children of Israel drink of it.

21. And Moses said unto Aaron, What did this people unto thee, that thou hast brought so great a sin upon them?

22. And Aaron said, Let not the anger of my lord wax hot: thou knowest the people, that they are set on mischief.

23. For they said unto me, Make us gods, which shall go before us: for as for this Moses, the man that brought us up out of the land of Egypt, we wot not what is become of him.

24. And I said unto them, Whosoever hath any gold, let them break it off. So they gave it me: then I cast it into the fire, and there came out this calf.

25. And when Moses saw that the people were naked; (for Aaron had made them naked unto their shame among their enemies:)

26. Then Moses stood in the gate of the camp, and said, **Who is on the LORD's side? let him come unto me. And all the sons of Levi gathered themselves together unto him**.

27. And he said unto them, Thus saith the LORD God of Israel, **Put every man his sword by his side, and go in and out from gate to gate throughout the camp, and slay every man his brother, and every man his companion, and every man his neighbour.**

28. And the children of Levi did according to the word of Moses: **and there fell of the people that day about three thousand men**.

29. For Moses had said, Consecrate yourselves to day to the LORD, even every man upon his son, and upon his brother; that he may bestow upon you a blessing this day.

30. And it came to pass on the morrow, that Moses said unto the people, Ye have sinned a great sin: and now I will go up unto the LORD; peradventure I shall make an atonement for your sin.

31. And Moses returned unto the LORD, and said, Oh, this people have sinned a great sin, and have made them gods of gold.

32. Yet now, if thou wilt forgive their sin--; and if not, blot me, I pray thee, out of thy book which thou hast written.

33. And the LORD said unto Moses, Whosoever hath sinned against me, him will I blot out of my book.

34. Therefore now go, lead the people unto the place of which I have spoken unto thee: behold, mine Angel shall go before thee: nevertheless in the day when I visit I will visit their sin upon them.

35. And the LORD plagued the people, because they made the calf, which Aaron made.

COMMENTARY:

In the Qur'an:

1. The nation of Israel was seduced by the so-called Samiri, who actually formed the idol of the golden calf.

2. Aaron tried unsuccessfully to prevent the people from idol worship.

3. Moses asks the unjust people to commit suicide because of their sin.

4. Moses *"... scattering in the sea..."* the golden calf.

In the Bible:

1. Aaron was asked by the people to make a god for them and he created it himself out of gold jewellery.

2. Aaron was responsible for this act of idolatry. As a result of it, Moses broke the stone tablets, and the tribe of Levi slew with the sword about three thousand men as punishment.

3. God sent a plague among the people.

4. Moses *"...took the calf which they had made, and burnt it in the fire, and ground it to powder, and strawed it upon the water, and made the children of Israel drink of it...."*

THE QUR'AN

"Moses Sees the Glory of God"

Sura 7

The Elevated Places

143. And when Musa came at Our appointed time and his Lord spoke to him, he said: **My Lord! Show me (Thyself), so that I may look upon Thee. He said: You cannot (bear to) see Me but look at the mountain, if it remains firm in its place, then will you see Me; but when his Lord manifested His glory to the mountain He made it crumble and Musa fell down in a swoon;** then when he recovered, he said: Glory be to Thee, I turn to Thee, and I am the first of the believers.

THE BIBLE

"Moses Sees the Glory of God"

Exodus

Chapter 33

17. And the LORD said unto Moses, I will do this thing also that thou hast spoken: for thou hast found grace in my sight, and I know thee by name.

18. And he said, I beseech thee, shew me thy glory.

19. And he said, I will make all my goodness pass before thee, and I will proclaim the name of the LORD before thee; and will be gracious to whom I will be gracious, and will shew mercy on whom I will shew mercy.

20. And he said, Thou canst not see my face: for there shall no man see me, and live.

21. And the LORD said, Behold, there is a place by me, and thou shalt stand upon a rock:

22. And it shall come to pass, while my glory passeth by, that I will put thee in a clift of the rock, and will cover thee with my hand while I pass by:

23. And I will take away mine hand, and thou shalt see my back parts: but my face shall not be seen.

COMMENTARY:

In the Qur'an:

1. God showed His glory by *destroying a mountain* in front of Moses.

In the Bible:

1. Moses was instructed *to hide himself in the rock* and God's hand covered him so that he saw only the back of God's glory.

THE QUR'AN

"The Failure of Israel to Enter the Land and its Consequences"

Sura 5

The Dinner Table

20. And when Musa said to his people: O my people! remember the favor of Allah upon you when He raised prophets among you and made you kings and gave you what He had not given to any other among the nations.

21. O my people! enter the holy land which Allah has prescribed for you and turn not on your backs for then you will turn back losers.

22. They said: O Musa! surely there is a strong race in it, and we will on no account enter it until they go out from it, so if they go out from it, then surely we will enter.

23. Two men of those who feared, upon both of whom Allah had bestowed a favor, said: Enter upon them by the gate, for when you have entered it you shall surely be victorious, and on Allah should you rely if you are believers.

24. They said: O Musa! we shall never enter it so long as they are in it; go therefore you and your Lord, then fight you both surely we will here sit down.

25. He said: My Lord! Surely I have no control (upon any) but my own self and my brother; *therefore make a separation between us and the nation of transgressors.*

26. He said: So it shall surely be forbidden to them for forty years, they shall wander about in the land, therefore do not grieve for the nation of transgressors.

THE BIBLE

"The Failure of Israel to Enter the Land and its Consequences"

Numbers

Chapter 13

1. And the LORD spake unto Moses, saying,

2. Send thou men, that they may search the land of Canaan, which I give unto the children of Israel: of every tribe of their fathers shall ye send a man, every one a ruler among them.

28. Nevertheless the people be strong that dwell in the land, and the cities are walled, and very great: and moreover we saw the children of Anak there.

30. And Caleb stilled the people before Moses, and said**, Let us go up at once, and possess it; for we are well able to overcome it.**

31. But the men that went up with him said, We be not able to go up against the people; for they are stronger than we.

32. And they brought up an evil report of the land which they had searched unto the children of Israel, saying, The land, through which we have gone to search it, is a land that eateth up the inhabitants thereof; and all the people that we saw in it are men of a great stature.

Numbers

Chapter 14

1. And all the congregation lifted up their voice, and cried; and the people wept that night.

2. And all the children of Israel murmured against Moses and against Aaron: and the whole congregation said unto them, Would God that we had died in the land of Egypt! or would God we had died in this wilderness!

3. And wherefore hath the LORD brought us unto this land, to fall by the sword, that our wives and our children should be a prey? were it not better for us to return into Egypt?

4. And they said one to another, Let us make a captain, and let us return into Egypt.

5. Then Moses and Aaron fell on their faces before all the assembly of the congregation of the children of Israel.

6. And Joshua the son of Nun, and Caleb the son of Jephunneh, which were of them that searched the land, rent their clothes:

7. And they spake unto all the company of the children of Israel, saying, The land, which we passed through to search it, is an exceeding good land.

8. If the LORD delight in us, then he will bring us into this land, and give it us; a land which floweth with milk and honey.

9. Only rebel not ye against the LORD, neither fear ye the people of the land; for they are bread for us: their defence is departed from them, and the LORD is with us: fear them not.

10. But all the congregation bade stone them with stones. And the glory of the LORD appeared in the tabernacle of the congregation before all the children of Israel.

11. And the LORD said unto Moses, **How long will this people provoke me? and how long will it be ere they believe me,** for all the signs which I have shewed among them?

12. **I will smite them with the pestilence, and disinherit them, and will make of thee a greater nation and mightier than they.**

13. And Moses said unto the LORD, Then the Egyptians shall hear it, (for thou broughtest up this people in thy might from among them;)

14. And they will tell it to the inhabitants of this land: for they have heard that thou LORD art among this people, that thou LORD art seen face to face, and that thy cloud standeth over them, and that thou goest before them, by day time in a pillar of a cloud, and in a pillar of fire by night.

15. Now if thou shalt kill all this people as one man, then the nations which have heard the fame of thee will speak, saying,

16. Because the LORD was not able to bring this people into the land which he sware unto them, therefore he hath slain them in the wilderness.

19. Pardon, I beseech thee, the iniquity of this people according unto the greatness of thy mercy, and as thou hast forgiven this people, from Egypt even until now.

20. And the LORD said, **I have pardoned according to thy word:**

21. But as truly as I live, all the earth shall be filled with the glory of the LORD.

22. Because all those men which have seen my glory, and my miracles, which I did in Egypt and in the wilderness, and have tempted me now these ten times, and have not hearkened to my voice;

23. Surely they shall not see the land which I sware unto their fathers, neither shall any of them that provoked me see it:

29. Your carcases shall fall in this wilderness; and all that were numbered of you, according to your whole number, from twenty years old and upward, which have murmured against me,

33. And your children shall wander in the wilderness forty years, and bear your whoredoms, until your carcases be wasted in the wilderness.

34. After the number of the days in which ye searched the land, even forty days, each day for a year, shall ye bear your iniquities, even forty years, and ye shall know my breach of promise.

COMMENTARY

In the Qur'an:

1. Moses tried to distance himself and his brother from the rest of the people who disbelieved. Moreover, he spoke to God against them.

In the Bible:

1. Moses, in spite of being hated by the others, continued to intercede for them before God and asked Him to spare the lives of the Israelites.

THE QUR'AN

"The Rebellion of Korah"

Sura 28

The Narratives

76. Surely Qaroun was of the people of Musa, but he rebelled against them, and We had given him of the treasures, so much so that his hoards of wealth would certainly weigh down a company of men possessed of great strength. **When his people said to him: Do not exult, surely Allah does not love the exultant;**

77. And seek by means of what Allah has given you the future abode, and do not neglect your portion of this world, and do good (to others) as Allah has done good to you, and do not seek to make mischief in the land, surely Allah does not love the mischief-makers.

78. He said: I have been given this only on account of the knowledge I have. Did he not know that Allah had destroyed before him of the generations those who were mightier in strength than he and greater in assemblage? And the guilty shall not be asked about their faults.

79. So he went forth to his people in his finery. Those who desire this world's life said: O would that we had the like of what Qaroun is given; most surely he is possessed of mighty good fortune.

80. And those who were given the knowledge said: Woe to you! Allah's reward is better for him who believes and does good, and none is made to receive this except the patient.

81. Thus We made the earth to swallow up him and his abode; so he had no body of helpers to assist him against Allah nor was he of those who can defend themselves.

82. And those who yearned for his place only the day before began to say: Ah! (know) that Allah amplifies and straitens the means of subsistence for whom He pleases of His servants; had not Allah been gracious to us, He would most surely have abased us; ah! (know) that the ungrateful are never successful.

THE BIBLE

"The Rebellion of Korah"

Numbers

Chapter 16

1. Now Korah, the son of Izhar, the son of Kohath, the son of Levi, and Dathan and Abiram, the sons of Eliab, and On, the son of Peleth, sons of Reuben, took men:

2. And they rose up before Moses, with certain of the children of Israel, two hundred and fifty princes of the assembly, famous in the congregation, men of renown:

3. And they gathered themselves together against Moses and against Aaron, and said unto them, Ye take too much upon you, seeing all the congregation are holy, every one of them, and the LORD is among them: **wherefore then lift ye up yourselves above the congregation of the LORD?**

4. And when Moses heard it, he fell upon his face:

5. And he spake unto Korah and unto all his company, saying, Even to morrow the LORD will shew who are his, and who is holy; and will cause him to come near unto him: even him whom he hath chosen will he cause to come near unto him.

6. This do; Take you censers, Korah, and all his company;

7. And put fire therein, and put incense in them before the LORD to morrow: and it shall be that the man whom the LORD doth choose, he shall be holy: ye take too much upon you, ye sons of Levi.

8. And Moses said unto Korah, Hear, I pray you, ye sons of Levi:

9. Seemeth it but a small thing unto you, that the God of Israel hath separated you from the congregation of Israel, to bring you near to himself to do the service of the tabernacle of the LORD, and to stand before the congregation to minister unto them?

10. And he hath brought thee near to him, and all thy brethren the sons of Levi with thee: and seek ye the priesthood also?

11. For which cause both thou and all thy company are gathered together against the LORD: and what is Aaron, that ye murmur against him?

12. And Moses sent to call Dathan and Abiram, the sons of Eliab: which said, We will not come up:

13. Is it a small thing that thou hast brought us up out of a land that floweth with milk and honey, to kill us in the wilderness, except thou make thyself altogether a prince over us?

14. Moreover thou hast not brought us into a land that floweth with milk and honey, or given us inheritance of fields and vineyards: wilt thou put out the eyes of these men? we will not come up.

15. And Moses was very wroth, and said unto the LORD, Respect not thou their offering: I have not taken one ass from them, neither have I hurt one of them.

16. And Moses said unto Korah, Be thou and all thy company before the LORD, thou, and they, and Aaron,   tomorrow:

17. **And take every man his censer, and put incense in them, and bring ye before the LORD every man his censer, two hundred and fifty censers; thou also, and Aaron, each of you his censer.**

18. And they took every man his censer, and put fire in them, and laid incense thereon, and stood in the door of the tabernacle of the congregation with Moses and Aaron.

19. And Korah gathered all the congregation against them unto the door of the tabernacle of the congregation: and the glory of the LORD appeared unto all the congregation.

20. And the LORD spake unto Moses and unto Aaron, saying,

21. Separate yourselves from among this congregation, that I may consume them in a moment.

22. And they fell upon their faces, and said, O God, the God of the spirits of all flesh, shall one man sin, and wilt thou be wroth with all the congregation?

23. And the LORD spake unto Moses, saying,

24. Speak unto the congregation, saying, Get you up from about the tabernacle of Korah, Dathan, and Abiram.

25. And Moses rose up and went unto Dathan and Abiram; and the elders of Israel followed him.

26. And he spake unto the congregation, saying, **Depart, I pray you, from the tents of these wicked men, and touch nothing of theirs, lest ye be consumed in all their sins.**

27. So they gat up from the tabernacle of Korah, Dathan, and Abiram, on every side: **and Dathan and Abiram came out, and stood in the door of their tents, and their wives, and their sons, and their little children.**

28. And Moses said, Hereby ye shall know that the LORD hath sent me to do all these works; for I have not done them of mine own mind.

29. If these men die the common death of all men, or if they be visited after the visitation of all men; then the LORD hath not sent me.

30. But if the LORD make a new thing, and the earth open her mouth, and swallow them up, with all that appertain unto them, and they go down quick into the pit; then ye shall understand that these men have provoked the LORD.

31. And it came to pass, as he had made an end of speaking all these words, that the ground clave asunder that was under them:

32. And the earth opened her mouth, and swallowed them up, and their houses, **and all the men that appertained unto Korah, and all their goods.**

33. They, and all that appertained to them, went down alive into the pit, and the earth closed upon them: and they perished from among the congregation.

34. And all Israel that were round about them fled at the cry of them: for they said, Lest the earth swallow us up also.

35. And there came out a fire from the LORD, and consumed the two hundred and fifty men that offered incense.

36. And the LORD spake unto Moses, saying,

37. Speak unto Eleazar the son of Aaron the priest, that he take up the censers out of the burning, and scatter thou the fire yonder; for they are hallowed.

38. The censers of these sinners against their own souls, let them make them broad plates for a covering of the altar: for they offered them before the LORD, therefore they are hallowed: and they shall be a sign unto the children of Israel.

39. And Eleazar the priest took the brasen censers, wherewith they that were burnt had offered; and they were made broad plates for a covering of the altar:

40. To be a memorial unto the children of Israel, that no stranger, which is not of the seed of Aaron, come near to offer incense before the LORD; that he be not as Korah, and as his company: as the LORD said to him by the hand of Moses.

41. But on the morrow all the congregation of the children of Israel murmured against Moses and against Aaron, saying, Ye have killed the people of the LORD.

42. And it came to pass, when the congregation was gathered against Moses and against Aaron, that they looked toward the tabernacle of the congregation: and, behold, the cloud covered it, and the glory of the LORD appeared.

43. And Moses and Aaron came before the tabernacle of the congregation.

44. And the LORD spake unto Moses, saying,

45. Get you up from among this congregation, that I may consume them as in a moment. And they fell upon their faces.

46. And Moses said unto Aaron, Take a censer, and put fire therein from off the altar, and put on incense, and go quickly unto the congregation, and make an atonement for them: for there is wrath gone out from the LORD; the plague is begun.

47. And Aaron took as Moses commanded, and ran into the midst of the congregation; and, behold, the plague was begun among the people: and he put on incense, and made an atonement for the people.

48. And he stood between the dead and the living; and the plague was stayed.

49. Now they that died in the plague were fourteen thousand and seven hundred, beside them that died about the matter of Korah.

50. And Aaron returned unto Moses unto the door of the tabernacle of the congregation: and the plague was stayed.

COMMENTARY:

In the Qur'an:

1. Korah was rich and proud.
2. His own people tried to restrain him and show that God was the only source of Korah's wealth.
3. Korah insisted that all his riches were from himself, and some of the people praised him.
4. The wise people still argued with Korah's statement.
5. God opened the earth and destroyed Korah and his house.
6. The people who had praised Korah the day before finally praised God and acknowledged His power over everything.

In the Bible:

1. Korah, Dathan, Abiram and two hundred and fifty *"...princes of the assembly, famous in the congregation, men of renown..."* rebelled against Moses and Aaron, accusing them of egotism, by lifting *"... up yourselves above the congregation of the LORD..."*. Moses prayed to God and announced that the next day the Lord would show whom He put in leadership over Israel.

2. Moses tried to quell the rebellion of Korah by reminding him that he was already chosen by God as a Levite to have special service in the Tabernacle.

3. Moses asked Dathan and Abiram be included in the negotiations, but they refused, accusing Moses of forcing them to leave the good land of Egypt in order to wander in the desert.

4. Moses asked all the remaining people to move away from the tents of Korah, Dathan and Abiram, and promised an unusual destruction for them.

5. God opened the earth and destroyed Korah, Dathan, Abiram and their houses along with 250 others.

6. The next day, the people accused Moses of murdering Korah and his supporters. God sent a plague and an additional 14,700 were killed for their support of this rebellion.

Chapter Seven

DAVID

THE QUR'AN

"Gideon, Saul and David"

Sura 2

The Cow

246. Have you not considered the chiefs of the children of Israel after Musa, when they said to a prophet of theirs: **Raise up for us a king (that) we may fight in the way of Allah.** He said: May it not be that you would not fight if fighting is ordained for you? They said: And what reasons have we that we should not fight in the way of Allah, and we have indeed been compelled to abandon our homes and our children. But when fighting was ordained for them, they turned back, except a few of them, and Allah knows the unjust.

247. And their prophet said to them: Surely Allah has raised **Talut (Saul)** to be a king over you. They said: How can he hold kingship over us while we have a greater right to kingship than he, and he has not been granted an abundance of wealth? He said: Surely Allah has chosen him in preference to you, and He has increased him abundantly in knowledge and physique, and Allah grants His kingdom to whom He pleases, and Allah is Amplegiving, Knowing.

248. And the prophet said to them: Surely the sign of His kingdom is, **that there shall come to you the chest in which there is tranquillity from your Lord and residue of the relics of what the children of Musa and the children of Haroun have left, the angels bearing it;** most surely there is a sign in this for those who believe.

249. So when **Talut (Saul)** departed with the forces, **he said: Surely Allah will try you with a river; whoever then drinks from it, he is not of me, and whoever does not taste of it, he is surely of me, except he who takes with his hand as much of it as fills the hand; but with the exception of a few of them they drank from it.** So when he had crossed it, he and those who believed with him, they said: We have today no power against **Jalut (Goliath)** and his forces. Those who were sure that they would meet their Lord said: How often has a small party vanquished a numerous host by Allah's permission, and Allah is with the patient.

250. And when they went out against **Jalut (Goliath)**and his forces they said: **Our Lord, pour down upon us patience, and make our steps firm and assist us against the unbelieving people.**

251. So they put them to flight by Allah's permission. And Dawood (David) slew Jalut (Goliath), and Allah gave him kingdom and wisdom, and taught him of what He pleased. And were it not for Allah's repelling some men with others, the earth would certainly be in a state of disorder; but Allah is Gracious to the creatures.

252. These are the communications of Allah: We recite them to you with truth; and most surely you are (one) of the apostles.

THE BIBLE

"Gideon, Saul and David"

Judges

Chapter 6

1. And the children of Israel did evil in the sight of the LORD: and the LORD delivered them into the hand of Midian seven years.

2. And the hand of Midian prevailed against Israel: and because of the Midianites the children of Israel made them the dens which are in the mountains, and caves, and strong holds.

11. And there came an angel of the LORD, and sat under an oak which was in Ophrah, that pertained unto Joash the Abi-ezrite: and his son Gideon threshed wheat by the winepress, to hide it from the Midianites.

14. And the LORD looked upon him, and said, **Go in this thy might, and thou shalt save Israel from the hand of the Midianites: have not I sent thee?**

15. And he said unto him, Oh my Lord, wherewith shall I save Israel? **behold, my family is poor in Manasseh, and I am the least in my father's house.**

16. And the LORD said unto him, Surely I will be with thee, and thou shalt smite the Midianites as one man.

34. But the Spirit of the LORD came upon Gideon, and he blew a trumpet; and Abi-ezer was gathered after him.

Judges

Chapter 7

1. Then Jerubbaal, who is Gideon, and all the people that were with him, rose up early, and pitched beside the well of Harod: so that the host of the Midianites were on the north side of them, by the hill of Moreh, in the valley.

2. And the LORD said unto Gideon, The people that are with thee are too many for me to give the Midianites into their hands, lest Israel vaunt themselves against me, saying, Mine own hand hath saved me.

3. Now therefore go to, proclaim in the ears of the people, saying, **Whosoever is fearful and afraid, let him return and depart early from mount Gilead.** And there returned of the people twenty and two thousand; **and there remained ten thousand.**

4. And the LORD said unto Gideon, The people are yet too many; bring them down unto the water, and I will try them for thee there: and it shall be, that of whom I say unto thee, This shall go with thee, the same shall go with thee; and of whomsoever I say unto thee, This shall not go with thee, the same shall not go.

5. So he brought down the people unto the water: and the **LORD said unto Gideon, Every one that lappeth of the water with his tongue, as a dog lappeth, him shalt thou set by himself; likewise every one that boweth down upon his knees to drink.**

6. And the number of them that lapped, putting their hand to their mouth, were three hundred men: but all the rest of the people bowed down upon their knees to drink water.

7. And the LORD said unto Gideon, **By the three hundred men that lapped will I save you, and deliver the Midianites into thine hand**: and let all the other people go every man unto his place.

16. And he divided the three hundred men into three companies, and he put a trumpet in every man's hand, with empty pitchers, and lamps within the pitchers.

20. And the three companies blew the trumpets, and brake the pitchers, and held the lamps in their left hands, and the trumpets in their right hands to blow withal: and they cried, The sword of the LORD, and of Gideon.

25. And they took two princes of the Midianites, Oreb and Zeeb; and they slew Oreb upon the rock Oreb, and Zeeb they slew at the winepress of Zeeb, and pursued Midian, and brought the heads of Oreb and Zeeb to Gideon on the other side Jordan.

Judges

Chapter 8

22. Then the men of Israel said unto Gideon, Rule thou over us, both thou, and thy son, and thy son's son also: for thou hast delivered us from the hand of Midian.

23. And Gideon said unto them, I will not rule over you, neither shall my son rule over you: the LORD shall rule over you.

First Samuel

Chapter 8

1. And it came to pass, when Samuel was old, that he made his sons judges over Israel.

2. Now the name of his firstborn was Joel; and the name of his second, Abiah: they were judges in Beer-sheba.

3. And his sons walked not in his ways, but turned aside after lucre, and took bribes, and perverted judgment.

4. Then all the elders of Israel gathered themselves together, and came to Samuel unto Ramah,

5. And said unto him, **Behold, thou art old, and thy sons walk not in thy ways: now make us a king to judge us like all the nations.**

6. But the thing displeased Samuel, when they said, Give us a king to judge us. And Samuel prayed unto the LORD.

7. And the LORD said unto Samuel, Hearken unto the voice of the people in all that they say unto thee: for they have not rejected thee, but they have rejected me, that I should not reign over them.

8. According to all the works which they have done since the day that I brought them up out of Egypt even unto this day, wherewith they have forsaken me, and served other gods, so do they also unto thee.

First Samuel

Chapter 9

27. And as they were going down to the end of the city, **Samuel said to Saul,** Bid the servant pass on before us, (and he passed on,) but stand thou still a while, that I may shew thee the word of God.

First Samuel

Chapter 10

1. Then Samuel took a vial of oil, and poured it upon his head, and kissed him, and said, Is it not because the LORD hath anointed thee to be captain over his inheritance?

17. And Samuel called the people together unto the LORD to Mizpeh;

18. And said unto the children of Israel, Thus saith the LORD God of Israel, I brought up Israel out of Egypt, and delivered you out of the hand of the Egyptians, and out of the hand of all kingdoms, and of them that oppressed you:

19. And ye have this day rejected your God, who himself saved you out of all your adversities and your tribulations; and ye have said unto him, Nay, but set a king over us. Now therefore present yourselves before the LORD by your tribes, and by your thousands.

20. And when Samuel had caused all the tribes of Israel to come near, the tribe of Benjamin was taken.

21. When he had caused the tribe of Benjamin to come near by their families, the family of Matri was taken, and Saul the son of Kish was taken: and when they sought him, he could not be found.

22. Therefore they inquired of the LORD further, if the man should yet come thither. And the LORD answered, Behold, he hath hid himself among the stuff.

23. And they ran and fetched him thence: and when he stood among the people, he was higher than any of the people from his shoulders and upward.

24. And Samuel said to all the people, See ye him whom the LORD hath chosen, that there is none like him among all the people? And all the people shouted, and said, God save the king.

25. Then Samuel told the people the manner of the kingdom, and wrote it in a book, and laid it up before the LORD. And Samuel sent all the people away, every man to his house.

26. And Saul also went home to Gibeah; and there went with him a band of men, whose hearts God had touched.

27. But the children of Belial said, How shall this man save us? And they despised him, and brought him no presents. But he held his peace.

First Samuel

Chapter 17

1. Now the Philistines gathered together their armies to battle, and were gathered together at Shochoh, which belongeth to Judah, and pitched between Shochoh and Azekah, in Ephes-dammim.

2. And Saul and the men of Israel were gathered together, and pitched by the valley of Elah, and set the battle in array against the Philistines.

3. And the Philistines stood on a mountain on the one side, and Israel stood on a mountain on the other side: and there was a valley between them.

4. And there went out a champion out of the camp of the Philistines, named Goliath, of Gath, whose height was six cubits and a span.

8. And he stood and cried unto the armies of Israel, and said unto them, Why are ye come out to set your battle in array? am not I a Philistine, and ye servants to Saul? choose you a man for you, and let him come down to me.

9. If he be able to fight with me, and to kill me, then will we be your servants: but if I prevail against him, and kill him, then shall ye be our servants, and serve us.

11. When Saul and all Israel heard those words of the Philistine, they were dismayed, and greatly afraid.

24. And all the men of Israel, when they saw the man, fled from him, and were sore afraid.

26. And David spake to the men that stood by him, saying, What shall be done to the man that killeth this Philistine, and taketh away the reproach from Israel? for who is this uncircumcised Philistine, that he should defy the armies of the living God?

44. And the Philistine said to David, Come to me, and I will give thy flesh unto the fowls of the air, and to the beasts of the field.

45. Then said David to the Philistine, Thou comest to me with a sword, and with a spear, and with a shield: but I come to thee in the name of the LORD of hosts, the God of the armies of Israel, whom thou hast defied.

46. This day will the LORD deliver thee into mine hand; and I will smite thee, and take thine head from thee; and I will give the carcases of the host of the Philistines this day unto the fowls of the

air, and to the wild beasts of the earth; that all the earth may know that there is a God in Israel.

49. And David put his hand in his bag, and took thence a stone, and slang it, and smote the Philistine in his forehead, that the stone sunk into his forehead; and he fell upon his face to the earth.

50. So David prevailed over the Philistine with a sling and with a stone, and smote the Philistine, and slew him; but there was no sword in the hand of David.

51. Therefore David ran, and stood upon the Philistine, and took his sword, and drew it out of the sheath thereof, and slew him, and cut off his head therewith. And when the Philistines saw their champion was dead, they fled.

COMMENTARY

In the Qur'an:

1. Here is a story about Talut (King Saul).

2. Only these who *"...did not..."* drink from the river were chosen.

3. Only one reason is mentioned for the Israelites asking for a king: **Raise up for us a king (that) we may fight in the way of Allah.** The Qur'an omits the name of the prophet for whom they asked.

4. The sign that was to prove that Talut (Saul) was appointed by God to rule Israel was a chest: *"...Surely the sign of His kingdom is, that there shall come to you the chest in which there is tranquillity from your Lord and residue of the relics of what the children of Musa and the children of Haroun have left, the angels bearing it; most surely there is a sign in this for those who believe..."*

5. The Israelites asked God to grant them victory over the Philistines: *"...Our Lord, pour down upon us patience, and make our steps firm and assist us against the unbelieving people..."*

In the Bible:

1. Here are two stories about two battles of Israel which happened more than 200 years apart. (see **Judges 8:28, 9:22, 10:3, 10:8, 12:7, 12:9, 12:11, 12:14, 13:1, 15:20, 1 Samuel 7:15**). One battle took place under the command of Gideon against the

Midianites; another was under the command of King Saul against the **Philistines**.

2. These who "…*lappeth of the water with his tongue, as a dog lappeth…*" were chosen to fight in **Gideon's** army, not Saul's. **(Judges 7:1-7).**

3. The Bible gives a different reason why the people of Israel had asked for a king: *"Behold, you are old and your sons do not walk in your ways; now appoint for us a king to govern us like all the nations."* The Bible also says that asking for a king was a major sin of the Israelites. The Bible names Samuel as one of the greatest prophets of Israel.

4. In the Bible there is such a story of a "chest" (the Ark of the Covenant), but before Saul became king, when Samuel was young, the Israelites were defeated by the Philistines and this special "chest" was not in their possession:

1 Samuel 4:10-11

"…10. And the Philistines fought, and Israel was smitten, and they fled every man into his tent: and there was a very great slaughter; for there fell of Israel thirty thousand footmen. 11. And the ark of God was taken:"

The Ark brought great trouble to its captors:

1 Samuel 5: 6

"But the hand of the LORD was heavy upon them of Ashdod, and he destroyed them, and smote them with emerods, even Ashdod and the coasts thereof."

So, the Philistines decided to get rid of the Ark:

1 Samuel 6:11, 12

"11. And they laid the ark of the LORD upon the cart, and the coffer with the mice of gold and the images of their emerods.

12. And the kine took the straight way to the way of Beth-shemesh, and went along the highway, lowing as they went, and turned not aside to the right hand or to the left; and the lords of the Philistines went after them unto the border of Beth-shemesh.".

As a result, the Ark of the Covenant was miraculously delivered back to Israel by God.

5. It was David, not the Israelites, who spoke these prophetic words: *"...Thou comest to me with a sword, and with a spear, and with a shield: but I come to thee in the name of the LORD of hosts, the God of the armies of Israel, whom thou hast defied. This day will the LORD deliver thee into mine hand; and I will smite thee, and take thine head from thee; and I will give the carcases of the host of the Philistines this day unto the fowls of the air, and to the wild beasts of the earth; that all the earth may know that there is a God in Israel...".*

THE QUR'AN

"David and Bathsheba"

Sura 38

Suad

21. And has there come to you the story of the litigants, when they made an entry into the private chamber by ascending over the walls?
22. When they entered in upon Dawood and **he was frightened at them, they said: Fear not; two litigants, of whom one has acted wrongfully towards the other, therefore decide between us with justice, and do not act unjustly, and guide us to the right way.**
23. Surely this is my brother; **he has ninety-nine ewes and I have a single ewe; but he said: Make it over to me, and he has prevailed against me in discourse.**
24. He said: Surely he has been unjust to you in demanding your ewe (to add) to his own ewes; and most surely most of the partners act wrongfully towards one another, save those who believe and do good, and very few are they; **and Dawood was sure that We had tried him, so he sought the protection of his Lord and he fell down bowing and turned time after time (to Him).**

25. Therefore We rectified for him this, and most surely he had a nearness to Us and an excellent resort.

26. O Dawood! surely We have made you a ruler in the land; so **judge between men with justice and do not follow desire**, lest it should lead you astray from the path of Allah; (as for) those who go astray from the path of Allah, they shall surely have a severe punishment because they forgot the day of reckoning.

THE BIBLE

"David and Bathsheba"

Second Samuel

Chapter 11

1. And it came to pass, after the year was expired, at the time when kings go forth to battle, that David sent Joab, and his servants with him, and all Israel; and they destroyed the children of Ammon, and besieged Rabbah. But David tarried still at Jerusalem.

2. And it came to pass in an eveningtide, that **David arose from off his bed**, and walked upon the roof of the king's house: **and from the roof he saw a woman washing herself; and the woman was very beautiful to look upon.**

3. And David sent and inquired after the woman. And one said, Is not this **Bath-sheba, the daughter of Eliam, the wife of Uriah the Hittite?**

. **And David sent messengers, and took her; and she came in unto him, and he lay with her; for she was purified from her uncleanness: and she returned unto her house.**

5. **And the woman conceived, and sent and told David, and said, I am with child.**

6. And David sent to Joab, saying, Send me Uriah the Hittite. And Joab sent Uriah to David.

7 And when Uriah was come unto him, David demanded of him how Joab did, and how the people did, and how the war prospered.

8. **And David said to Uriah, Go down to thy house, and wash thy feet. And Uriah departed out of the king's house, and there followed him a mess of meat from the king.**

9. But Uriah slept at the door of the king's house with all the servants of his lord, and went not down to his house.

10. And when they had told David, saying, Uriah went not down unto his house, **David said unto Uriah, Camest thou not from thy journey? why then didst thou not go down unto thine house?**

11. And Uriah said unto David, The ark, and Israel, and Judah, abide in tents; and my lord Joab, and the servants of my lord, are encamped in the open fields; shall I then go into mine house, to eat and to drink, and to lie with my wife? as thou livest, and as thy soul liveth, I will not do this thing.

12. And David said to Uriah, Tarry here to day also, and tomorrow I will let thee depart. So Uriah abode in Jerusalem that day, and the morrow.

13. And when David had called him, he did eat and drink before him; and he made him drunk: and at even he went out to lie on his bed with the servants of his lord, but went not down to his house.

14. And it came to pass in the morning, that David wrote a letter to Joab, and sent it by the hand of Uriah.

15. And he wrote in the letter, saying, Set ye Uriah in the forefront of the hottest battle, and retire ye from him, that he may be smitten, and die.

16. And it came to pass, when Joab observed the city, that he assigned Uriah unto a place where he knew that valiant men were.

17. And the men of the city went out, and fought with Joab: and there fell some of the people of the servants of David; and Uriah the Hittite died also.

18. Then Joab sent and told David all the things concerning the war;

19. And charged the messenger, saying, When thou hast made an end of telling the matters of the war unto the king,

20. And if so be that the king's wrath arise, and he say unto thee, Wherefore approached ye so nigh unto the city when ye did fight? knew ye not that they would shoot from the wall?

21. Who smote Abimelech the son of Jerubbesheth? did not a woman cast a piece of a millstone upon him from the wall, that he died in Thebez? why went ye nigh the wall? then say thou, Thy servant Uriah the Hittite is dead also.

22. So the messenger went, and came and shewed David all that Joab had sent him for.

23. And the messenger said unto David, Surely the men prevailed against us, and came out unto us into the field, and we were upon them even unto the entering of the gate.

24. And the shooters shot from off the wall upon thy servants; and some of the king's servants be dead, **and thy servant Uriah the Hittite is dead also.**

25. Then David said unto the messenger, Thus shalt thou say unto Joab, Let not this thing displease thee, for the sword devoureth one as well as another: make thy battle more strong against the city, and overthrow it: and encourage thou him.

26. And when the wife of Uriah heard that Uriah her husband was dead, she mourned for her husband.

27. And when the mourning was past, David sent and fetched her to his house, and she became his wife, and bare him a son. But the thing that David had done displeased the LORD.

Second Samuel

Chapter 12

1. And the LORD sent Nathan unto David. **And he came unto him, and said unto him, There were two men in one city; the one rich, and the other poor.**

2.The rich man had exceeding many flocks and herds:

3. But the poor man had nothing, save one little ewe lamb, which he had bought and nourished up: and it grew up together with him, and with his children; it did eat of his own meat, and drank of his own cup, and lay in his bosom, and was unto him as a daughter.

4. And there came a traveller unto the rich man, and he spared to take of his own flock and of his own herd, to dress for the wayfaring man that was come unto him; but took the poor man's lamb, and dressed it for the man that was come to him.

5 And David's anger was greatly kindled against the man; and he said to Nathan, As the LORD liveth, the man that hath done this thing shall surely die:

6. And he shall restore the lamb fourfold, because he did this thing, and because he had no pity.

7. And Nathan said to David, Thou art the man. Thus saith the LORD God of Israel, I anointed thee king over Israel, and I delivered thee out of the hand of Saul;

8. And I gave thee thy master's house, and thy master's wives into thy bosom, and gave thee the house of Israel and of Judah; and if that had been too little, I would moreover have given unto thee such and such things.

9. Wherefore hast thou despised the commandment of the LORD, to do evil in his sight? thou hast killed Uriah the Hittite with the sword, and hast taken his wife to be thy wife, and hast slain him with the sword of the children of Ammon.

10. Now therefore the sword shall never depart from thine house; because thou hast despised me, and hast taken the wife of Uriah the Hittite to be thy wife.

11. Thus saith the LORD, Behold, I will raise up evil against thee out of thine own house, and I will take thy wives before thine eyes, and give them unto thy neighbour, and he shall lie with thy wives in the sight of this sun.

12. For thou didst it secretly: but I will do this thing before all Israel, and before the sun.

13. And David said unto Nathan, I have sinned against the LORD. And Nathan said unto David, The LORD also hath put away thy sin; thou shalt not die.

14. Howbeit, because by this deed thou hast given great occasion to the enemies of the LORD to blaspheme, the child also that is born unto thee shall surely die.

15. And Nathan departed unto his house. **And the LORD struck the child that Uriah's wife bare unto David, and it was very sick.**

16. David therefore besought God for the child; and David fasted, and went in, and lay all night upon the earth.

17. And the elders of his house arose, and went to him, to raise him up from the earth: but he would not, neither did he eat bread with them.

18. And it came to pass on the seventh day, that the child died. And the servants of David feared to tell him that the child was dead: for they said, Behold, while the child was yet alive, we spake unto him, and he would not hearken unto our voice: how will he then vex himself, if we tell him that the child is dead?

19. But when David saw that his servants whispered, David perceived that the child was dead: therefore David said unto his servants, Is the child dead? And they said, He is dead.

20. Then David arose from the earth, and washed, and anointed himself, and changed his apparel, and came into the house of the LORD, and worshipped: then he came to his own house; and when he required, they set bread before him, and he did eat.

21. Then said his servants unto him, What thing is this that thou hast done? thou didst fast and weep for the child, while it was alive; but when the child was dead, thou didst rise and eat bread.

22. And he said, While the child was yet alive, I fasted and wept: for I said, Who can tell whether GOD will be gracious to me, that the child may live?

23. But now he is dead, wherefore should I fast? can I bring him back again? I shall go to him, but he shall not return to me.

24. And David comforted Bath-sheba his wife, and went in unto her, and lay with her: and she bare a son, and he called his name Solomon: and the LORD loved him.

COMMENTARY

In the Qur'an:

1. Two disputants suddenly came before David, somehow having sneaked past unnoticed by palace guards. They asked David to settle their dispute.

2. David listened to their story and made the right judgment. When he realized that he was actually being tested by God he asked for forgiveness (for something wrong he had done).

3. God forgave him and rewarded him with *"...a beautiful place of (Final) Return..."*.

In the Bible:

1. David saw a beautiful woman, and in spite of the fact that she was married, he slept with her. After she became pregnant, he tried to do everything in order to let her husband lie with her so this sin of adultery would not be known after she gave birth to the child.

163

But when his plan failed, he sent a letter to his army general, Joab, with an order to place Bath-Sheba's husband in the front lines so that he would be killed by his enemies' hands. David committed the sin of adultery, and in order to cover it, he plotted another sin – murder. He did not repent, but he took Bath-Sheba for his wife after the murder of her husband Uriah and she gave birth to a baby. God sent the prophet Nathan to confront David by asking David to judge a story of a poor man wronged by a rich man.

2. David became very angry and pronounced a death penalty for the abuser. Nathan accused David of his double sin. David repented.

3. God forgave David by not killing him, but exacted consequences for what he had done by allowing the baby that was conceived of their adulterous union to die:

> *"...Now therefore the sword shall never depart from thine house...",*
>
> *"...Behold, I will raise up evil against thee out of thine own house, and I will take thy wives before thine eyes, and give them unto thy neighbour, and he shall lie with thy wives in the sight of this sun. For thou didst it secretly: but I will do this thing before all Israel, and before the sun...",*
>
> *"...the child also that is born unto thee shall surely die...".*

Chapter Eight

SOLOMON

THE QUR'AN

"The Wisdom of Solomon"

Sura 27

The Ant

15. And certainly We gave knowledge to Dawood and Sulaiman, and they both said: Praise be to Allah, Who has made us to excel many of His believing servants.

16. And Sulaiman was Dawood's heir, and he said: O men! we have been taught the language of birds, and we have been given all things; most surely this is manifest grace.

17. And his hosts of the jinn and the men and the birds were gathered to him, and they were formed into groups.

18. Until when they came to the valley of the Naml, a Namlite said: **O Naml! enter your houses, (that) Sulaiman and his hosts may not crush you while they do not know.**

19. So he smiled, wondering at her word, and said: My Lord! grant me that I should be grateful for Thy favor which Thou hast bestowed on me and on my parents, and that I should do good such as Thou art pleased with, and make me enter, by Thy mercy, into Thy servants, the good ones.

Sura 34

The Saba

12. And (We made) the wind (subservient) to Sulaiman, which made a month's journey in the morning and a month's journey m the evening, and We made a fountain of molten copper to flow out for him, and of the jinn there were those who worked before him by the command of his Lord; and whoever turned aside from Our command from among them, We made him taste of the punishment of burning.

13. They made for him what he pleased of fortresses and images, and bowls (large) as watering-troughs and cooking-pots that will not move from their place; give thanks, O family of Dawood! and very few of My servants are grateful.

14. But when We decreed death for him, naught showed them his death but a creature of the earth that ate away his staff; and when

it fell down, the jinn came to know plainly that if they had known the unseen, they would not have tarried in abasing torment.

Sura 38
Suad

36. Then **We made the wind subservient to him**; it made his command to run gently wherever he desired,
37. And the shaitans, every builder and diver,
38. And others fettered in chains.
39. This is Our free gift, therefore give freely or withhold, without reckoning.
40. And most surely he had a nearness to Us and an excellent resort.

THE BIBLE
"The Wisdom of Solomon"
First Kings
Chapter 3

3. And Solomon loved the LORD, walking in the statutes of David his father: only he sacrificed and burnt incense in high places.
4. And the king went to Gibeon to sacrifice there; for that was the great high place: a thousand burnt offerings did Solomon offer upon that altar.
5. In Gibeon the LORD appeared to Solomon in a dream by night: and God said, Ask what I shall give thee.
6. And Solomon said, Thou hast shewed unto thy servant David my father great mercy, according as he walked before thee in truth, and in righteousness, and in uprightness of heart with thee; and thou hast kept for him this great kindness, that thou hast given him a son to sit on his throne, as it is this day.
7. And now, O LORD my God, thou hast made thy servant king instead of David my father: **and I am but a little child**: I know not how to go out or come in.
8. And thy servant is in the midst of thy people which thou hast chosen, a great people, that cannot be numbered nor counted for multitude.

9. Give therefore thy servant an understanding heart to judge thy people, that I may discern between good and bad: for who is able to judge this thy so great a people?

10. And the speech pleased the Lord, that Solomon had asked this thing.

11. And God said unto him, Because thou hast asked this thing, and hast not asked for thyself long life; neither hast asked riches for thyself, nor hast asked the life of thine enemies; but hast asked for thyself understanding to discern judgment;

12. Behold, I have done according to thy words: lo, I have given thee a wise and an understanding heart; so that there was none like thee before thee, neither after thee shall any arise like unto thee.

13. And I have also given thee that which thou hast not asked, both riches, and honour: so that there shall not be any among the kings like unto thee all thy days.

14. And if thou wilt walk in my ways, to keep my statutes and my commandments, as thy father David did walk, then I will lengthen thy days.

First Kings

Chapter 4

29. And God gave Solomon wisdom and understanding exceeding much, and largeness of heart, even as the sand that is on the sea shore.

30. And Solomon's wisdom excelled the wisdom of all the children of the east country, and all the wisdom of Egypt.

31. For he was wiser than all men; than Ethan the Ezrahite, and Heman, and Chalcol, and Darda, the sons of Mahol: and his fame was in all nations round about.

32. And he spake three thousand proverbs: and his songs were a thousand and five.

33. And he spake of trees, from the cedar tree that is in Lebanon even unto the hyssop that springeth out of the wall: he spake also of beasts, and of fowl, and of creeping things, and of fishes.

34. And there came of all people to hear the wisdom of Solomon, from all kings of the earth, which had heard of his wisdom.

First Kings

Chapter 5

1. And **Hiram king of Tyre sent his servants unto Solomon**; for he had heard that they had anointed him king in the room of his father: for Hiram was ever a lover of David.

13. And king Solomon raised a levy out of all Israel; and the levy was thirty thousand men.

14. And he sent them to Lebanon ten thousand a month by courses: a month they were in Lebanon, and two months at home: and Adoniram was over the levy.

15. And Solomon had threescore and ten thousand that bare burdens, and fourscore thousand hewers in the mountains;

16. Beside the chief of Solomon's officers which were over the work, three thousand and three hundred, which ruled over the people that wrought in the work.

17. And the king commanded, and they brought great stones, costly stones, and hewed stones, to lay the foundation of the house.

18. And Solomon's builders and Hiram's builders did hew them, and the stonesquarers: so they prepared timber and stones to build the house.

First Kings

Chapter 6

1. And it came to pass in the four hundred and eightieth year after the children of Israel were come out of the land of Egypt, **in the fourth year of Solomon's reign over Israel, in the month Zif, which is the second month, that he began to build the house of the LORD.**

14. So Solomon built the house, and finished it.

37. In the fourth year was the foundation of the house of the LORD laid, in the month Zif:

38. And in the eleventh year, in the month Bul, which is the eighth month, was the house finished throughout all the parts thereof, and according to all the fashion of it. So was he seven years in building it.

First Kings

Chapter 7

1. But Solomon was building his own house thirteen years, and he finished all his house.

13. And king Solomon sent and fetched Hiram out of Tyre.

14. He was a widow's son of the tribe of Naphtali, and his father was a man of Tyre, a worker in brass: and he was filled with wisdom, and understanding, **and cunning to work all works in brass. And he came to king Solomon, and wrought all his work.**

First Kings

Chapter 8

1. Then Solomon assembled the elders of Israel, and all the heads of the tribes, the chief of the fathers of the children of Israel, unto king Solomon in Jerusalem, that they might bring up the ark of the covenant of the LORD out of the city of David, which is Zion.

10. And it came to pass, when the priests were come out of the holy place, that the cloud filled the house of the LORD,

11. So that the priests could not stand to minister because of the cloud: for the glory of the LORD had filled the house of the LORD.

12. Then spake Solomon, The LORD said that he would dwell in thick darkness.

13. I have surely built thee an house to dwell in, a settled place for thee to abide in for ever.

COMMENTARY

In the Qur'an:

1. God enabled Solomon to understand the language of birds. The ants knew Solomon by sight as well as Israelites, and were able to recognize him while he was riding a horse nearby.

2. Jinns and birds were working as servants for Solomon. The wind was under his command as well.

3. When Solomon died, the Jinns did not realize this and kept working for a man already dead. (Perhaps they were finishing the building of

the Temple while Solomon was already dead without knowing that fact, otherwise they might have stopped working).

In the Bible:

1. God made Solomon the wisest man on earth but there is no mention of any supernatural ability to understand the language of animals.

2. Many Israelites and Lebanese were working for Solomon but only for the purpose of building the Temple. No Jinns were ever mentioned in the Bible and birds were not servants of Solomon either. The wind was under the command of Jesus only (**Luke 8:22-25**), not Solomon.

3. The Bible is very clear in timing: Solomon started building the Temple in the fourth year of his reign and finished it in the eleventh year. It took seven years in total to build. Solomon was king for forty years (**1 Kings 11:42**). Therefore, he completed building the Temple near the beginning of his reign.

THE QUR'AN

"Solomon and the Queen of Sheba"

Sura 27

The Ant

20. And he *(Solomon)* **reviewed the birds, then said: How is it I see not the hoopoe or is it that he is of the absentees?**

21. I will most certainly punish him with a severe punishment, or kill him, or he shall bring to me a clear plea.

22. And he tarried not long, then said: I comprehend that which you do not comprehend **and I have brought to you a sure information from Sheba.**

23. Surely I found a woman ruling over them, and she has been given abundance and she has a mighty throne:

24. I found her and her people adoring the sun instead of Allah, and the Shaitan has made their deeds fair-seeming to them and thus turned them from the way, so they do not go aright

25. That they do not make obeisance to Allah, Who brings forth what is hidden in the heavens and the earth and knows what you hide and what you make manifest:

26. Allah, there is no god but He: He is the Lord of mighty power.

27. He said: We will see whether you have told the truth or whether you are of the liars:

28. Take this my letter and hand it over to them, then turn away from them and see what (answer) they return.

29. She said: O chief! surely an honorable letter has been delivered to me

30. Surely it is from Sulaiman, and surely it is in the name of Allah, the Beneficent, the Merciful;

31. Saying: exalt not yourselves against me and come to me in submission.

32. She said: O chiefs! give me advice respecting my affair: I never decide an affair until you are in my presence.

33. They said: We are possessors of strength and possessors of mighty prowess, and the command is yours, therefore see what you will command.

34. She said: Surely the kings, when they enter a town, ruin it and make the noblest of its people to be low, and thus they (always) do;

35. And surely I am going to send a present to them, and shall wait to see what (answer) do the messengers bring back.

36. So when he came to Sulaiman, he said: What! will you help me with wealth? But what Allah has given me is better than what He has given you. Nay, you are exultant because of your present;

37. Go back to them, so we will most certainly come to them with hosts which they shall have no power to oppose, and we will most certainly expel them from there in abasement, and they shall be in a state of ignominy.

38. He said: O chiefs! Which of you can bring to me her throne before they come to me in submission?

39. One audacious among the jinn said: I will bring it to you before you rise up from your place; and most surely I am strong (and) trusty for it.

40. One who had the knowledge of the Book said: **I will bring it to you in the twinkling of an eye. Then when he saw it settled beside him, he said: This is of the grace of my Lord that He may try me whether I am grateful or ungrateful; and whoever is grateful, he**

is grateful only for his own soul, and whoever is ungrateful, then surely my Lord is Self-sufficient, Honored.

41. He said: **Alter her throne for her, we will see whether she follows the right way or is of those who do not go aright.**

42. So when she came, it was said: **Is your throne like this? She said: It is as it were the same, and we were given the knowledge before it, and we were submissive.**

43. And what she worshipped besides Allah prevented her, surely she was of an unbelieving people.

44. It was said to her: **Enter the palace; but when she saw it she deemed it to be a great expanse of water, and bared her legs. He said: Surely it is a palace made smooth with glass. She said: My Lord! surely I have been unjust to myself, and I submit with Sulaiman to Allah, the Lord of the worlds.**

THE BIBLE

"Solomon and the Queen of Sheba"

First Kings

Chapter 10

1. And when the queen of Sheba heard of the fame of Solomon concerning the name of the LORD, she came to prove him with hard questions.

2. And she came to Jerusalem with a very great train, with camels that bare spices, and very much gold, and precious stones: and when she was come to Solomon, she communed with him of all that was in her heart.

3. And Solomon told her all her questions: there was not any thing hid from the king, which he told her not.

4. And when the queen of Sheba had seen all Solomon's wisdom, and the house that he had built,

5. And the meat of his table, and the sitting of his servants, and the attendance of his ministers, and their apparel, and his cupbearers, and his ascent by which he went up unto the house of the LORD; there was no more spirit in her.

6. And she said to the king, It was a true report that I heard in mine own land of thy acts and of thy wisdom.

7. Howbeit I believed not the words, until I came, and mine eyes had seen it: and, behold, the half was not told me: thy wisdom and prosperity exceedeth the fame which I heard.

8. Happy are thy men, happy are these thy servants, which stand continually before thee, and that hear thy wisdom.

9. Blessed be the LORD thy God, which delighted in thee, to set thee on the throne of Israel: because the LORD loved Israel for ever, therefore made he thee king, to do judgment and justice.

10. And she gave the king an hundred and twenty talents of gold, and of spices very great store, and precious stones: there came no more such abundance of spices as these which the queen of Sheba gave to king Solomon.

11. And the navy also of Hiram, that brought gold from Ophir, brought in from Ophir great plenty of almug trees, and precious stones.

12. And the king made of the almug trees pillars for the house of the LORD, and for the king's house, harps also and psalteries for singers: there came no such almug trees, nor were seen unto this day.

13. And king Solomon gave unto the queen of Sheba all her desire, whatsoever she asked, beside that which Solomon gave her of his royal bounty. So she turned and went to her own country, she and her servants.

COMMENTARY

In the Qur'an:

1. Solomon had heard about the Queen of Sheba from the hoopoe bird, a creature with unusual intellect with whom he had a long conversation.

2. The Queen of Sheba sent ambassadors with gifts, but Solomon rejected these gifts.

3. Solomon ordered Jinn to steal the throne of the queen and it was brought to Solomon's presence instantaneously. Solomon wanted to test whether she would recognize her throne after it was transformed by Jinn. When she came to Jerusalem, she did recognize it.

4. When she entered the Palace she uncovered her legs, thereby disgracing herself and she submitted herself remorsefully to God.

In the Bible:

1. The Queen of Sheba had heard about the wisdom of Solomon and decided to come to see for herself if it was true.

2. The Queen personally brought Solomon costly gifts, to which Solomon responded with gifts in return. She "...*gave the king a hundred and twenty talents of gold, and a very great quantity of spices, and precious stones. And King Solomon gave to the queen of Sheba all that she desired, whatever she asked besides what was given her by the bounty of King Solomon. So she turned and went back to her own land, with her servants...*"

3. No trials or tests of faith were given to the Queen by Solomon. Rather "...*Solomon answered all her questions; there was nothing hidden from the king which he could not explain to her...*".

4. The Queen praised the Lord after seeing the order and manner of the House of God and the services of the priests.

Chapter Nine

JONAH

THE QUR'AN

"The Adventure of Jonah"

Sura 37

The Rangers

139. And Yunus was most surely of the apostles.

140. When he ran away to a ship completely laden,

141. So he shared (with them), but was of those who are cast off.

142. So the fish swallowed him while he did that for which he blamed himself

143. But had it not been that he was of those who glorify (Us),

144. He would certainly have tarried in its belly to the day when they are raised.

145. Then We cast him on to the vacant surface of the earth while he was sick.

146. And We caused to grow up for him a gourdplant.

147. And We sent him to a hundred thousand, rather they exceeded.

148. And they believed, so We gave them provision till a time.

THE BIBLE

"The Adventure of Jonah"

Jonah

Chapter 1

1. Now the word of the LORD came unto Jonah the son of Amittai, saying,

2. Arise, go to Nineveh, that great city, and cry against it; for their wickedness is come up before me.

3. But Jonah rose up to flee unto Tarshish from the presence of the LORD, and went down to Joppa; and he found a ship going to Tarshish: so he paid the fare thereof, and went down into it, to go with them unto Tarshish from the presence of the LORD.

4. But the LORD sent out a great wind into the sea, and there was a mighty tempest in the sea, so that the ship was like to be broken.

5. Then the mariners were afraid, and cried every man unto his god, and cast forth the wares that were in the ship into the sea, to lighten it of them. But Jonah was gone down into the sides of the ship; and he lay, and was fast asleep.

6. So the shipmaster came to him, and said unto him, What meanest thou, O sleeper? **arise, call upon thy God, if so be that God will think upon us, that we perish not.**

7. And they said every one to his fellow, Come, and let us cast lots, that we may know for whose cause this evil is upon us. So they cast lots, and the lot fell upon Jonah.

11. Then said they unto him, What shall we do unto thee, that the sea may be calm unto us? for the sea wrought, and was tempestuous.

12. And he said unto them, Take me up, and cast me forth into the sea; so shall the sea be calm unto you: for I know that for my sake this great tempest is upon you.

17. Now the LORD had prepared a great fish to swallow up Jonah. And Jonah was in the belly of the fish three days and three nights.

Jonah

Chapter 2

1. Then Jonah prayed unto the LORD his God out of the fish's belly,

2. And said, I cried by reason of mine affliction unto the LORD, and he heard me; out of the belly of hell cried I, and thou heardest my voice.

3. For thou hadst cast me into the deep, in the midst of the seas; and the floods compassed me about: all thy billows and thy waves passed over me.

4. Then I said, I am cast out of thy sight; yet I will look again toward thy holy temple.

9. But I will sacrifice unto thee with the voice of thanksgiving; I will pay that that I have vowed. Salvation is of the LORD.

10. And the LORD spake unto the fish, and it vomited out Jonah upon the dry land.

Jonah

Chapter 3

1. And the word of the LORD came unto Jonah the second time, saying,

2. Arise, go unto Nineveh, that great city, and preach unto it the preaching that I bid thee.

3. So Jonah arose, and went unto Nineveh, according to the word of the LORD. Now Nineveh was an exceeding great city of three days' journey.
4. And Jonah began to enter into the city a day's journey, and he cried, and said, Yet forty days, and Nineveh shall be overthrown.
5. So the people of Nineveh believed God, and proclaimed a fast, and put on sackcloth, from the greatest of them even to the least of them.
10. And God saw their works, that they turned from their evil way; and God repented of the evil, that he had said that he would do unto them; and he did it not.

Jonah

Chapter 4

1. But it displeased Jonah exceedingly, and he was very angry.
2. And he prayed unto the LORD, and said, I pray thee, O LORD, was not this my saying, when I was yet in my country? Therefore I fled before unto Tarshish: for I knew that thou art a gracious God, and merciful, slow to anger, and of great kindness, and repentest thee of the evil.
3. Therefore now, O LORD, take, I beseech thee, my life from me; for it is better for me to die than to live.
4. Then said the LORD, Doest thou well to be angry?
5. So Jonah went out of the city, and sat on the east side of the city, and there made him a booth, and sat under it in the shadow, till he might see what would become of the city.
6. And the LORD God prepared a gourd, and made it to come up over Jonah, that it might be a shadow over his head, to deliver him from his grief. So Jonah was exceeding glad of the gourd.
7. But God prepared a worm when the morning rose the next day, and it smote the gourd that it withered.
8. And it came to pass, when the sun did arise, that God prepared a vehement east wind; **and the sun beat upon the head of Jonah, that he fainted, and wished in himself to die, and said, It is better for me to die than to live.**
9. And God said to Jonah, Doest thou well to be angry for the gourd? And he said, I do well to be angry, even unto death.
10. Then said the LORD, Thou hast had pity on the gourd, for the which thou hast not laboured, neither madest it grow; which came up in a night, and perished in a night:

11. And should not I spare Nineveh, that great city, wherein are more than sixscore thousand persons that cannot discern between their right hand and their left hand; and also much cattle?

COMMENTARY

In the Qur'an:

1. This is a very "simplified" story of Jonah, who fled to a ship, agreed to cast lots, was condemned, was swallowed by a big fish, repented and survived his ordeal.

2. After Jonah was cast ashore, God caused a plant to grow above him to restore his physical health (*as I can understand it from reading the previous ayat, Jonah was "...in a state of sickness..."*). God then sent Jonah to preach to multitudes of people, who accepted Jonah's words.

In the Bible:

1. God sent Jonah with a specific mission to preach a message of salvation to the city of Nineveh, but Jonah fled to a ship sailing in the opposite direction. God directed a powerful storm against the ship in order for Jonah to understand his sin against God. Realizing that the storm was the consequence of his disobedience to God's command, Jonah asked the sailors to throw him into the sea in order to save them and the ship from the wrath of God. A big fish swallowed Jonah and he spent three days and nights in the belly of this fish. Finally he repented and agreed to fulfill God's mission to go to Nineveh.

2. He came to the city and preached about the coming destruction unless all the people there would repent before God. But Jonah really wanted God to destroy this city, and he found a spot on the top of the hill to watch God's wrath take place on Nineveh. As he sat, waiting, God caused a plant to grow over him to provide him with shade. After a short time God sent a worm to destroy this plant. Jonah was so upset over the destruction of the plant that he wished death for himself. God explained to his prophet that the lives of thousands of people, including wicked gentiles, were as valuable to God as that plant was to Jonah.

Chapter Ten

EZEKIEL

The Qur'an

"Ezekiel and the Dry Bones"

Sura 2

The Cow

259. Or the like of him (Uzair) who passed by a town, and it had fallen down upon its roofs; he said: When will Allah give it life after its death? **So Allah caused him to die for a hundred years, then raised him to life.** He said: How long have you tarried? He said: I have tarried a day, or a part of a day. Said He: Nay! you have tarried a hundred years; then look at your food and drink-- years have not passed over it; and look at your ass; and that **We may make you a sign to men, and look at the bones, how We set them together, then clothed them with flesh; so when it became clear to him, he said: I know that Allah has power over all things.**

The Bible

"Ezekiel and the Dry Bones"

Ezekiel

Chapter 37

1. The hand of the LORD was upon me, and carried me out in the spirit of the LORD, and set me down in the midst of the valley which was full of bones,

2. And caused me to pass by them round about: and, behold, there were very many in the open valley; and, lo, they were very dry.

3. And he said unto me, Son of man, can these bones live? And I answered, O Lord GOD, thou knowest.

4. Again he said unto me, Prophesy upon these bones, and say unto them, O ye dry bones, hear the word of the LORD.

5. Thus saith the Lord GOD unto these bones; Behold, I will cause breath to enter into you, and ye shall live:

6. And I will lay sinews upon you, and will bring up flesh upon you, and cover you with skin, and put breath in you, and ye shall live; and ye shall know that I am the LORD.

7. So I prophesied as I was commanded: and as I prophesied, there was a noise, and behold a shaking, and the bones came together, bone to his bone.

8. And when I beheld, lo, the sinews and the flesh came up upon them, and the skin covered them above: but there was no breath in them.

9. Then said he unto me, Prophesy unto the wind, prophesy, son of man, and say to the wind, Thus saith the Lord GOD; Come from the four winds, O breath, and breathe upon these slain, that they may live.

10. So I prophesied as he commanded me, and the breath came into them, and they lived, and stood up upon their feet, an exceeding great army.

11. Then he said unto me, Son of man, these bones are the whole house of Israel: behold, they say, Our bones are dried, and our hope is lost: we are cut off for our parts.

12. Therefore prophesy and say unto them, Thus saith the Lord GOD; Behold, O my people, I will open your graves, and cause you to come up out of your graves, and bring you into the land of Israel.

13. And ye shall know that I am the LORD, when I have opened your graves, O my people, and brought you up out of your graves,

14. And shall put my spirit in you, and ye shall live, **and I shall place you in your own land: then shall ye know that I the LORD have spoken it, and performed it, saith the LORD.**

21. And say unto them, Thus saith the Lord GOD; Behold, I will take the children of Israel from among the heathen, whither they be gone, and will gather them on every side, and bring them into their own land:

22. And I will make them one nation in the land upon the mountains of Israel; and one king shall be king to them all: and they shall be no more two nations, neither shall they be divided into two kingdoms any more at all:

23. Neither shall they defile themselves any more with their idols, nor with their detestable things, nor with any of their transgressions:

but I will save them out of all their dwellingplaces, wherein they have sinned, **and will cleanse them: so shall they be my people, and I will be their God.**

24. And David my servant shall be king over them; and they all shall have one shepherd: they shall also walk in my judgments, and observe my statutes, and do them.

25. And they shall dwell in the land that I have given unto Jacob my servant, wherein your fathers have dwelt; and they shall dwell therein, even they, and their children, and their children's children for ever: and my servant David shall be their prince for ever.

26. Moreover I will make a covenant of peace with them; **it shall be an everlasting covenant with them:** and I will place them, and multiply them, and will set my sanctuary in the midst of them for evermore.

27. My tabernacle also shall be with them: yea, I will be their God, and they shall be my people.

28. And the heathen shall know that I the LORD do sanctify Israel, when my sanctuary shall be in the midst of them for evermore.

COMMENTARY

In the Qur'an:

1. This is a story of a traveler who died and was resurrected by Allah as a sign that Allah has the power to bring life even to the bones of people dead long ago.

In the Bible:

1. The prophet Ezekiel was not killed by God, but was asked to **prophesy** to dry bones so that they would once again became living people. It was a sign **not** to show the ability of God to resurrect the dead, but to show that the nation of Israel would be brought back to the land of Israel in future and would be sanctified and restored by God as reminder to all nations. King David will be *"...their prince for ever..."* and God will keep His covenants with them forever.

Chapter Eleven

GOD'S PEOPLE

THE QUR'AN

"The Relationship Between God and His People"

Sura 5

The Dinner Table

18. And the Jews and the Christians say: We are the sons of Allah and His beloved ones. Say: Why does He then chastise you for your faults? Nay, you are mortals from among those whom He has created, He forgives whom He pleases and chastises whom He pleases; and Allah's is the kingdom of the heavens and the earth and what is between them, and to Him is the eventual coming.

19. O followers of the Book! indeed Our Apostle has come to you explaining to you after a cessation of the (mission of the) apostles, lest you say: There came not to us a giver of good news or a warner, so indeed there has come to you a giver of good news and a warner; and Allah has power over all things.

THE BIBLE

"The Relationship Between God and His People"

Proverbs

Chapter 3

11. My son, **despise not the chastening of the LORD; neither be weary of his correction**:

12. For whom the LORD loveth he correcteth; even as a **father the son in whom he delighteth.**

Proverbs

Chapter 13

24. He that spareth his rod hateth his son: **but he that loveth him chasteneth him betimes.**

Jeremiah

Chapter 31

18. I have surely heard Ephraim bemoaning himself thus; **Thou hast chastised me, and I was chastised, as a bullock unaccustomed to the yoke: turn thou me, and I shall be turned; for thou art the LORD my God.**

19. Surely after that I was turned, I repented; and after that I was instructed, I smote upon my thigh: I was ashamed, yea, even confounded, because I did bear the reproach of my youth.

20. Is Ephraim my dear son? is he a pleasant child? for since I spake against him, I do earnestly remember him still: therefore my bowels are troubled for him; I will surely have mercy upon him, saith the LORD.

Hebrews

Chapter 12

6. For whom the Lord loveth he chasteneth, and scourgeth every son whom he receiveth.

7. If ye endure chastening, God dealeth with you as with sons; for what son is he whom the father chasteneth not?

8. But if ye be without chastisement, whereof all are partakers, then are ye bastards, and not sons.

9. Furthermore we have had fathers of our flesh which corrected us, and we gave them reverence: **shall we not much rather be in subjection unto the Father of spirits, and live?**

10. For they verily for a few days chastened us after their own pleasure; but he for our profit, that we might be partakers of his holiness.

Revelation

Chapter 3

19. As many as I love, I rebuke and chasten: be zealous therefore, and repent.

20. Behold, I stand at the door, and knock: if any man hear my voice, and open the door, I will come in to him, and will sup with him, and he with me.

COMMENTARY

In the Qur'an:

1. God would not chastise His people (believers).

In the Bible:

1. God chastises ONLY His own people in order to turn us away from our sins towards a close relationship with Him. In much the same way, as parents we punish our own children and not the children of neighbours.

Chapter Twelve

JESUS

The Qur'an

"The Birth and Life of Mary"

Sura 3

The Family of Imran

33. Surely Allah chose Adam and Nuh and the descendants of Ibrahim **and the descendants of *Imran*** above the nations.

34. Offspring one of the other; and Allah is Hearing, Knowing.

35. When **a woman of Imran** said: My Lord! surely I vow to Thee what is in my womb, to be devoted (to Thy service); accept therefore from me, surely Thou art the Hearing, the Knowing.

36. So when she brought forth, she said: My Lord! Surely I have brought it forth a female-- and Allah knew best what she brought forth-- and the male is not like the female, and **I have named it Marium,** and I commend her and her offspring into Thy protection from the accursed Shaitan.

37. So her Lord accepted her with a good acceptance and made her grow up a good growing, and gave her into the charge of Zakariya; whenever Zakariya entered the sanctuary to (see) her, he found with her food. He said: O Marium! whence comes this to you? She said: It is from Allah. Surely Allah gives to whom He pleases without measure.

Sura 19

Marium

22. So she conceived him; then withdrew herself with him to a remote place.

27. And she came to her people with him, carrying him (with her). They said: O Marium! surely you have done a strange thing.

28. O sister of Haroun! your father was not a bad man, nor, was your mother an unchaste woman.

29. But she pointed to him. They said: How should we speak to one who was a child in the cradle?

Sura 66

The Prohibition

12. And Marium, the daughter of Imran, who guarded her chastity, so We breathed into her of Our inspiration and she accepted the truth of the words of her Lord and His books, and she was of, the obedient ones.

THE NON-CANONIC GOSPELS

"The Birth and Life of Mary"

Infancy Gospel of James, or Protovangelium

I. I In the histories of the twelve tribes of Israel it is written that there was one *Ioacim*, exceeding rich: and he offered his gifts twofold, saying: That which is of my superfluity shall be for the whole people, and that which is for my forgiveness shall be for tile Lord, for a propitiation unto me.

IV. 1 And behold an angel of the Lord appeared, saying unto her: Anna, Anna, the Lord hath hearkened unto thy prayer, and thou shalt conceive and bear, and thy seed shall be spoken of in the whole world. And Anna said: As the Lord my God liveth, if I bring forth either male or female, I will bring it for a gift unto the Lord my God, and it shall be ministering unto him all the days of its life.

VI. 1 And day by day the child waxed strong, and when she was six months old her mother stood her upon the ground to try if she would stand; and she walked seven steps and returned unto her bosom. And she caught her up, saying: As the Lord my God liveth, thou shalt walk no more upon this ground, **until I bring thee into the temple of the Lord. And she made a sanctuary in her bed chamber and suffered nothing common or unclean to pass through it. And she called for the daughters of the Hebrews that were undefiled, and they carried her hither and thither**.

VIII. 1 And her parents gat them down marveling, and praising the Lord God because the child was not turned away backward.

And Mary **was in the temple of the Lord** as a dove that is nurtured: and **she received food from the hand of an angel**.

"The Birth and Life of Mary"

The Gospel of the Nativity of Mary

CHAP. 1 - **The blessed and glorious ever-virgin Mary**, sprung from the royal stock and family of David, born in the city of Nazareth, **was brought up at Jerusalem in the temple of the Lord.**

CHAP. 3 - …Accordingly thy wife Anna will bring forth a daughter to thee, and thou shall call her name Mary: she shall be, as you have vowed, consecrated to the Lord from her infancy, and **she shall be filled with the Holy Spirit, even from her mother's womb. She shall neither eat nor drink any unclean thing, nor shall she spend her life among the crowds of the people without, but in the temple of the Lord, that it may not be possible either to say, or so much as to suspect, any evil concerning her. Therefore, when she has grown up, just as she herself shall be miraculously born of a barren woman, so in an incomparable manner she, a virgin, shall bring forth the Son of the Most High, who shall be called Jesus,** and who, according to the etymology of His name, shall be the Saviour of all nations. And this shall be the sign to thee of those things which I announce: When thou shalt come to the Golden gate in Jerusalem, thou shalt there meet Anna thy wife, who, lately anxious from the delay of thy return, will then rejoice at the sight of thee. Having thus spoken, the angel departed from him.

CHAP. 6 - And when the circle of three years had rolled round, and the time of her weaning was fulfilled, they brought the virgin to the temple of the Lord with offerings. Now there were round the temple, according to the fifteen Psalms of Degrees,[1] fifteen steps going up; for, on account of the temple having been built on a mountain, the altar of burnt-offering, which stood outside, could not be reached except by steps. On one of these, then, her parents placed the little girl, the blessed virgin Mary. And when they were putting off the clothes which they had worn on the journey, and were putting on, as was usual, others that were neater and cleaner, the virgin of the Lord went up all the steps, one after the other, without the help of any one leading her or lifting her, in such a manner that, in this respect at least, you would think that she had already attained full age. For already the Lord in the infancy of His virgin wrought a great thing, and by the indication of this miracle foreshowed how great she was to be. Therefore, a sacrifice having been offered according to the custom of the law, and their vow being perfected, **they left the virgin within the enclosures of the temple, there to be educated with the other virgins, and themselves returned home.**

Wisdom 8:19-20

"And I was a witty child and had received a good soul. And whereas I was more good, I came to a body undefiled."

"The Birth and Life of Mary"

The Arabic Gospel of the Infancy of the Saviour

3. Wherefore, after sunset, the old woman, and Joseph with her, came to the cave, and they both went in. And, behold, it was filled with lights more beautiful than the gleaming of lamps and candles, **(4)** and more splendid than the light of the sun. The child, enwrapped in swaddling clothes, was sucking the breast of the Lady Mary His mother, being placed in a stall. And when both were wondering at this light, the old woman asks the **Lady Mary**: Art thou the mother of this Child? And when the Lady Mary gave her assent, she says: **Thou art not at all like the daughters of Eve.** The **Lady Mary said: As my son has no equal among children, so his mother has no equal among women.**

THE BIBLE

"The Birth and Life of Mary"

Matthew

Chapter 1

18. Now the birth of Jesus Christ was on this wise: **When as his mother Mary was espoused to Joseph, before they came together, she was found with child of the Holy Ghost.**
19. Then Joseph her husband, being a just man, and not willing to make her a publick example, was minded to put her away privily.

20. But while he thought on these things, behold, the angel of the Lord appeared unto him in a dream, saying, Joseph, thou son of David, fear not to take unto thee Mary thy wife: for that which is conceived in her is of the Holy Ghost.

21. And she shall bring forth a son, and thou shalt call his name JESUS: for he shall save his people from their sins.

22. Now all this was done, that it might be fulfilled which was spoken of the Lord by the prophet, saying,

23. Behold, a virgin shall be with child, and shall bring forth a son, and they shall call his name Emmanuel, which being interpreted is, God with us.

24. Then Joseph being raised from sleep did as the angel of the Lord had bidden him, and *took unto him his wife:*

25. And knew her not till she had brought forth her firstborn son: and he called his name JESUS.

Luke

Chapter 1

26. And in the sixth month the **angel Gabriel was sent from God unto a city of Galilee, named Nazareth,**

27. To a virgin espoused to a man whose name was Joseph, of the house of David; and the virgin's name was Mary.

28. And the angel came in unto her, and said, Hail, thou that art highly favoured, the Lord is with thee: blessed art thou among women.

29. And when she saw him, she was troubled at his saying, and cast in her mind what manner of salutation this should be.

30. And the angel said unto her, Fear not, Mary: for thou hast found favour with God.

31. And, behold, thou shalt conceive in thy womb, and bring forth a son, and shalt call his name JESUS.

32. He shall be great, and shall be called the Son of the Highest: and the Lord God shall give unto him the throne of his father David:

33. And he shall reign over the house of Jacob for ever; and of his kingdom there shall be no end.

34. Then said Mary unto the angel, How shall this be, seeing I know not a man?

35. And the angel answered and said unto her, The Holy Ghost shall come upon thee, and **the power of the Highest shall overshadow thee: therefore also that holy thing which shall be born of thee shall be called the Son of God.**

36. And, behold, thy cousin Elisabeth, she hath also conceived a son in her old age: and this is the sixth month with her, who was called barren.

37. For with God nothing shall be impossible.

38. And Mary said, Behold the handmaid of the Lord; be it unto me according to thy word. And the angel departed from her.

39. And Mary arose in those days, and went into the hill country with haste, into a city of Juda;

40. And entered into the house of Zacharias, and saluted Elisabeth.

COMMENTARY

In the Qur'an:

1. This is the story of Mary's birth and youth.

   In the non-canonical book entitled the "Infancy Gospel of James" or, "Protevangelium", we can read this story in greater detail. Great emphasis is made of Mary being an unusual girl; she was born and placed into a special room so that nothing "unclean" would come into her presence *(a very strange explanation).*

2. In the Qur'an she lived in the Temple: *"whenever Zakariya entered the sanctuary to (see) her, he found with her food. He said: O Marium! Whence comes this to you? She said: It is from Allah. Surely Allah gives to whom He pleases without measure."*

   In the non-canonical "gospel" we read the same story: *"And Mary was"* in the temple *"of the Lord as a dove that is nurtured: and she received food from the hand of an angel."*

3. We can only find reference to Mary's parents in the Apocrypha, which is a portion of writings not considered to be inspired of God and therefore not included in the Bible. It seems that the Qur'an used some of the tales from the Apocrypha.

   According to the Qur'an, Mary met Zechariah in her childhood: **Sura 3:37** *"... gave her into the charge of Zakariya;"*

4. In the "Infancy Gospel of James" we see that major emphasis was placed upon the statement that Mary was "clean" and recognized by people as "special"; so the high priest had put her in the Temple to live. Also we learn that Mary regained her virginity after the birth of Jesus and remained a perpetual virgin: *"9:3 A virgin hath brought forth, which her nature alloweth not"*. In this text we can see the influence of the Cult of the Virgin Mary which began in the 5th century (The Council of Ephesus in 431AD sanctioned the cult of the Virgin as the Mother of God; thus the dissemination of images of the Virgin and Child, which came to embody church doctrine, soon followed.). This contradicts the Bible: *"... There is none righteous, no, not one..."* **(Romans, Chapter 3:10)**. And *"... since all have sinned and fall short of the glory of God"* **(Romans 3:23)**

5. The Apocrypha tries to deny that Joseph was Mary's husband:
   > *"2 And Joseph refused, saying: **I have sons, and I am an old man, but she is a girl**: lest I became a laughing-stock to the children of Israel.",*
   > *"...And Joseph was afraid, and took her to keep her for himself..."*
   > *"...It is Mary that was nurtured up in the temple of the Lord: and I received her to wife by lot: and she is not my wife, but she hath conception by the Holy Ghost...".*

6. Mary was a daughter of Imran (Amram) and sister of Haroun (Aaron).

In the Bible:

1. We first learn about Mary when the angel Gabriel comes to visit her with a special message.

2. According to the Bible no woman (even as a child) was allowed to enter the Sanctuary (and certainly not to live there), only male priests.

Exodus, Chapter 28:1, 41

"1. And take thou unto thee Aaron thy brother, and his sons with him, from among the children of Israel, that he may minister unto me in the priest's office, even

Aaron, Nadab and Abihu, Eleazar and Ithamar, Aaron's sons…..

41. And thou shalt put them upon Aaron thy brother, and his sons with him; and shalt anoint them, and consecrate them, and sanctify them, that they may minister unto me in the priest's office."

3. Mary came to the house of Zechariah only after she became pregnant.

4. Mary received the Holy Spirit together with the disciples and the apostles:

Acts, Chapter 1:

12. Then returned they unto Jerusalem from the mount called Olivet, which is from Jerusalem a sabbath day's journey.

13. And when they were come in, they went up into an upper room, where abode both Peter, and James, and John, and Andrew, Philip, and Thomas, Bartholomew, and Matthew, James the son of Alphaeus, and Simon Zelotes, and Judas the brother of James. 14. These all continued with one accord in prayer and supplication, with the women, and Mary the mother of Jesus, and with his brethren.

Acts, Chapter 2:

1. And when the day of Pentecost was fully come, they were all with one accord in one place.

2. And suddenly there came a sound from heaven as of a rushing mighty wind, and it filled all the house where they were sitting.

3. And there appeared unto them cloven tongues like as of fire, and it sat upon each of them.

4. And they were all filled with the Holy Ghost, and began to speak with other tongues, as the Spirit gave them utterance.

The Bible declares that Jesus was the firstborn of Mary, indicating that she had more children with her husband Joseph:

Luke, Chapter 2:

1. And it came to pass in those days, that there went out a decree from Caesar Augustus, that all the world should be
taxed.
2. (And this taxing was first made when Cyrenius was governor of Syria.)
3. And all went to be taxed, every one into his own city.
4. And Joseph also went up from Galilee, out of the city of Nazareth, into Judaea, unto the city of David, which is called Bethlehem; (because he was of the house and lineage of David)
*5. To be taxed with **Mary his espoused wife**, being great with child.*
6. And so it was, that, while they were there, the days were accomplished that she should be delivered.
*7. And she brought forth **her firstborn son**, and wrapped him in swaddling clothes, and laid him in a manger; because there was no room for them in the inn.*

Mark, Chapter 3:

*31. There came then **his brethren and his mother,** and, standing without, sent unto him, calling him.*
*32. And the multitude sat about him, and they said unto him, **Behold, thy mother and thy brethren without seek for thee.***
33. And he answered them, saying, Who is my mother, or my brethren?
34. And he looked round about on them which sat about him, and said, Behold my mother and my brethren!
35. For whosoever shall do the will of God, the same is my brother, and my sister, and mother.

5. The Bible speaks of Joseph as Mary's husband:

> **Matthew, Chapter 1:**
> "*...19. Then **Joseph her husband**, being a just man, and not willing to make her a publick example, was minded to put her away privily ...*"

6. There are several Miriams in the Bible, not only one. The first one is Miriam, the sister of Moses and Aaron, and the second one we are concerned with in this reference is Mary, the mother of Jesus. Miriam is their Hebrew name. The names of Mary's parents are not recorded in Scripture, but Miriam, the sister of Moses and Aaron, had a father named Amram.

> **Numbers, Chapter 26:**
> "*...59. And the name of Amram's wife was Jochebed, the daughter of Levi, whom her mother bare to Levi in Egypt: and she bare unto Amram Aaron and Moses, and **Miriam their sister...**"

The Qur'an confuses the two women as one person; Miriam, the sister of Aaron and Moses, with Mary/Miriam, the mother of Jesus.

THE QUR'AN

"The Father of John the Baptist"

Sura 3

The Family of Imran

38. There did Zakariya pray to his Lord; he said: My Lord! Grant me from Thee good offspring; surely Thou art the Hearer of prayer.

39. Then the angels called to him as he stood praying in the sanctuary: That Allah gives you the good news of Yahya (John) verifying a Word from Allah, and **honorable and chaste and a prophet from among the good ones.**

40. He said: My Lord! When shall there be a son (born) to me and old age has already come upon me, and my wife is barren? He said: even thus does Allah what He pleases.

41. He said: My Lord! Appoint a sign for me. Said He: **Your sign is that you should not speak to men for three days except by signs;** and remember your Lord much and glorify Him in the evening and the morning.

Sura 19

Marium

7. O Zakariya! surely We give you good news of a boy whose name shall be Yahya: We have not made before anyone his equal.

8. He said: O my Lord! when shall I have a son, and my wife is barren, and I myself have reached indeed the extreme degree of old age?

9. He said: So shall it be, your Lord says: It is easy to Me, and indeed I created you before, when you were nothing.

10. He said: **My Lord! give me a sign. He said: Your sign is that you will not be able to speak to the people three nights while in sound health.**

11. So he went forth to his people from his place of worship, then he made known to them that they should glorify (Allah) morning and evening.

THE BIBLE

"The Father of John the Baptist"

Luke

Chapter 1

5. There was in the days of Herod, the king of Judaea, a certain priest named Zacharias, of the course of Abia: and his wife was of the daughters of Aaron, and her name was Elisabeth.

6. And they were both righteous before God, walking in all the commandments and ordinances of the Lord blameless.

7. And they had no child, because that Elisabeth was barren, and they both were now well stricken in years.

8. And it came to pass, that while he executed the priest's office before God in the order of his course,

9. According to the custom of the priest's office, his lot was to burn incense when he went into the temple of the Lord.

10. And the whole multitude of the people were praying without at the time of incense.

11. And there appeared unto him an angel of the Lord standing on the right side of the altar of incense.

12. And when Zacharias saw him, he was troubled, and fear fell upon him.

13. But the angel said unto him, Fear not, Zacharias: for thy prayer is heard; and thy wife Elisabeth shall bear thee a son, and thou shalt call his name John.

14. And thou shalt have joy and gladness; and many shall rejoice at his birth.

15. For he shall be great in the sight of the Lord, and shall drink neither wine nor strong drink; and he shall be filled with the Holy Ghost, even from his mother's womb.

16. And many of the children of Israel shall he turn to the Lord their God.

17. And he shall go before him in the spirit and power of Elias, to turn the hearts of the fathers to the children, and the disobedient to the wisdom of the just; to make ready a people prepared for the Lord.

18. And Zacharias said unto the angel, Whereby shall I know this? for I am an old man, and my wife well stricken in years.

19. And the angel answering said unto him, I am Gabriel, that stand in the presence of God; and am sent to speak unto thee, and to shew thee these glad tidings.

20. And, behold, thou shalt be dumb, and not able to speak, until the day that these things shall be performed, because thou believest not my words, which shall be fulfilled in their season.

21. And the people waited for Zacharias, and marvelled that he tarried so long in the temple.

22. And when he came out, he could not speak unto them: and they perceived that he had seen a vision in the temple: for he beckoned unto them, and remained speechless.

23. And it came to pass, that, as soon as the days of his ministration were accomplished, he departed to his own house.

24. And after those days his wife Elisabeth conceived, and hid herself five months, saying,

25. Thus hath the Lord dealt with me in the days wherein he looked on me, to take away my reproach among men.

57. Now Elisabeth's full time came that she should be delivered; and she brought forth a son.

58. And her neighbours and her cousins heard how the Lord had shewed great mercy upon her; and they rejoiced with her.

59. And it came to pass, that on the eighth day they came to circumcise the child; and they called him Zacharias, after the name of his father.

60. And his mother answered and said, Not so; but he shall be called John.

61. And they said unto her, There is none of thy kindred that is called by this name.

62. And they made signs to his father, how he would have him called.

63. And he asked for a writing table, and wrote, saying, His name is John. And they marvelled all.

64. And his mouth was opened immediately, and his tongue loosed, and he spake, and praised God.

COMMENTARY

In the Qur'an:

1. More that one angel talked to Zacharias: "*Then **the angels** called to him...*".
2. Zacharias was silent for just three days.

In the Bible:

1. There was only one angel, Gabriel, who addressed Zacharias.
2. The period of silence was more than nine months:

> *And, behold, thou shalt be dumb, and not able to speak, until the day that these things shall be performed, "[24]. And **after** those days his wife Elisabeth conceived... [59]. And it came to pass, that on the eighth day they came to circumcise the child;... [64]. And **his mouth was opened immediately**, and his tongue loosed, and he spake, and praised God."*

THE QUR'AN

"Young Jesus"

Sura 3

The Family of Imran

42. And when **the angels said: O Marium! surely Allah has chosen you and purified you and chosen you above the women of the world.**

43. O Marium! keep to obedience to your Lord and humble yourself, and bow down with those who bow.

44. This is of the announcements relating to the unseen which We reveal to you; and you were not with them when they cast their pens (to decide) which of them should have Marium in his charge, and you were not with them when they contended one with another.

45. When the angels said: **O Marium, surely Allah gives you good news with a Word from Him (of one) whose name is the '. Messiah, Isa son of Marium, worthy of regard in this world and the hereafter and of those who are made near (to Allah).**

46. And he shall speak to the people when in the cradle and when of old age, and (he shall be) one of the good ones.

47. She said: My Lord! when shall there be a son (born) to me, and man has not touched me? He said: Even so, Allah creates what He pleases; when He has decreed a matter, He only says to it, Be, and it is.

48. And He will teach him the Book and the wisdom and the **Tavrat (Torah)** and the **Injeel (Gospel).**

49. And (make him) an apostle to the children of Israel: That I have come to you with a sign from your Lord, that **I determine for you out of dust like the form of a bird, then I breathe into it and it becomes a bird with Allah's permission** and I heal the blind and the leprous, and bring the dead to life with Allah's permission and I inform you of what you should eat and what you should store in your houses; most surely there is a sign in this for you, if you are believers.

50. And a verifier of that which is before me of the **Tavrat (Torah)** and that I may allow you part of that which has been forbidden to you, and I have come to you with a sign from your Lord therefore be careful of (your duty to) Allah and obey me.

Sura 5

The Dinner Table

46. And We sent after them in their footsteps Isa, son of Marium, **verifying what was before him of the Taurat and We gave him the Injeel in which was guidance and light, and verifying what was before it of Taurat** and a guidance and an admonition for those who guard (against evil).

110. When Allah will say: O Isa son of Marium! **Remember My favor** on you and on your mother, when I strengthened you with the holy Spirit, **you spoke to the people in the cradle and when of old age, and when I taught you the Book and the wisdom and the Taurat(Torah) and the Injeel(Gospel); and when you determined out of clay a thing like the form of a bird by My permission, then you breathed into it and it became a bird by My permission,** and you healed the blind and the leprous by My permission; and when you brought forth the dead by My permission; and when I withheld the children of Israel from you when you came to them with clear arguments, but those who disbelieved among them said: This is nothing but clear enchantment.

Sura 19

Marium

16. And mention Marium in the Book when **she drew aside from her family to an eastern place;**

17. So she took a veil (to screen herself) from them; then We sent to her Our spirit, and there appeared to her a well-made man.

18. She said: Surely I fly for refuge from you to the Beneficent God, if you are one guarding (against evil).

19. He said: I am only a messenger of your Lord: That I will give you a pure boy.

20. She said: When shall I have a boy and no mortal has yet touched me, nor have I been unchaste?

21. He said: Even so; your Lord says: It is easy to Me: and that We may make him a sign to men and a mercy from Us, and it is a matter which has been decreed.

22. So she conceived him; then withdrew herself with him to a remote place.

23. And the throes (of childbirth) compelled her to betake herself to the trunk of a palm tree. She said: Oh, would that I had died before this, and had been a thing quite forgotten!

24. Then (the child) called out to her from beneath her: Grieve not, surely your Lord has made a stream to flow beneath you;

25. And shake towards you the trunk of the palmtree, it will drop on you fresh ripe dates:

26. So eat and drink and refresh the eye. Then if you see any mortal, say: Surely I have vowed a fast to the Beneficent God, so I shall not speak to any man today.

27. And she came to her people with him, carrying him (with her). They said: **O Marium! surely you have done a strange thing.**

28. O sister of Haroun! your father was not a bad man, nor, was your mother an unchaste woman.

29. But she pointed to him. They said: How should we speak to one who was a child in the cradle?

30. He said: Surely I am a servant of Allah; He has given me the Book and made me a prophet;

31. And He has made me blessed wherever I may be, and He has enjoined on me prayer and poor-rate so long as I live;

32. And dutiful to my mother, and He has not made me insolent, unblessed;

33. And peace on me on the day I was born, and on the day I die, and on the day I am raised to life.

34. Such is Isa, son of Marium; (this is) the saying of truth about which they dispute.

THE NON-CANONICAL GOSPELS

"Young Jesus"

Gospel of Thomas

II. 1 This little child Jesus when he was five years old was playing at the ford of a brook: and he gathered together the waters that flowed there into pools, and made them straightway clean, and commanded them by his word alone.

2 And having made soft clay, he fashioned thereof twelve sparrows. And it was the Sabbath when he did these things (or made them). And there were also many other little children playing with him.

3 And a certain Jew when he saw what Jesus did, playing upon the Sabbath day, departed straightway and told his father Joseph: Lo, thy child is at the brook, and he hath taken clay and fashioned twelve little birds, and hath polluted the Sabbath day.

4 And Joseph came to the place and saw: and cried out to him, saying: Wherefore doest thou these things on the Sabbath, which it is not lawful to do? **But Jesus clapped his hands together and cried out to the sparrows and said to them: Go! and the sparrows took their flight and went away chirping**. 5 And when the Jews saw it they were amazed, and departed and told their chief men that which they had seen Jesus do.

"Young Jesus"

The Arabic Gospel of the Infancy of the Saviour

With the help and favour of the Most High we begin to write a book of the miracles of our Lord and Master and Saviour Jesus Christ, which is called the Gospel of the Infancy: in the peace of the Lord. Amen.

1. We find **(1)** what follows in the book of Joseph the high priest, who lived in the time of Christ. Some say that he is Caiaphas. **(2)** **He has said that Jesus spoke, and, indeed, when He was lying in His cradle said to Mary His mother: I am Jesus, the Son of God, the Logos, whom thou hast brought forth, as the Angel Gabriel announced to thee; and my Father has sent me for the salvation of the world.**

THE BIBLE

"Young Jesus"

Luke

Chapter 2

21. And when eight days were accomplished for the circumcising of the child, his name was called JESUS, which was so named of the angel before he was conceived in the womb.

22. And when the days of her purification according to the law of Moses were accomplished, **they brought him to Jerusalem**, to present him to the Lord;

39. And when they had performed all things according to the law of the Lord, they returned into Galilee, to their own city Nazareth.

40. And the child grew, and waxed strong in spirit, filled with wisdom: and the grace of God was upon him.

41. Now his parents went to Jerusalem every year at the feast of the passover.

42. And when he was twelve years old, they went up to Jerusalem after the custom of the feast.

43. And when they had fulfilled the days, as they returned, the child Jesus tarried behind in Jerusalem; and Joseph and his mother knew not of it.

44. But they, supposing him to have been in the company, went a day's journey; and they sought him among their kinsfolk and acquaintance.

45. And when they found him not, they turned back again to Jerusalem, seeking him.

46. And it came to pass, that after three days they found him in the temple, sitting in the midst of the doctors, both hearing them, and asking them questions.

47. And all that heard him were astonished at his understanding and answers.

48. And when they saw him, they were amazed: and his mother said unto him, Son, why hast thou thus dealt with us? behold, thy father and I have sought thee sorrowing.

49. And he said unto them, **How is it that ye sought me? wist ye not that I must be about my Father's business?**

50. And they understood not the saying which he spake unto them.

51. And he went down with them, and came to Nazareth, and was subject unto them: **but his mother kept all these sayings in her heart.**

52. And Jesus increased in wisdom and stature, and in favour with God and man.

Mark

Chapter 6

1. And he went out from thence, **and came into his own country;** and his disciples follow him.

2. And when the sabbath day was come, he began to teach in the synagogue: **and many hearing him were astonished, saying, From whence hath this man these things? and what wisdom is this which is given unto him, that even such mighty works are wrought by his hands?**

3. Is not this the carpenter, the son of Mary, the brother of James, and Joses, and of Juda, and Simon? and are not his sisters here with us? And they were offended at him.

4. But Jesus said unto them, A prophet is not without honour, but in his own country, and among his own kin, and in his own house.

5. And he could there do no mighty work, save that he laid his hands upon a few sick folk, and healed them.

6. And he marvelled because of their unbelief. And he went round about the villages, teaching.

John

Chapter 7

1. After these things Jesus walked in Galilee: for he would not walk in Jewry, because the Jews sought to kill him.

2. Now the Jews' feast of tabernacles was at hand.

3. His brethren therefore said unto him, Depart hence, and go into Judaea, that thy disciples also may see the works that thou doest.

4. For there is no man that doeth any thing in secret, and he himself seeketh to be known openly. **If thou do these things, shew thyself to the world.**

5. *For neither did his brethren believe in him.*

6. Then Jesus said unto them, My time is not yet come: but your time is alway ready.

7. The world cannot hate you; but me it hateth, because I testify of it, that the works thereof are evil.

8. Go ye up unto this feast: I go not up yet unto this feast; for my time is not yet full come.

9. When he had said these words unto them, he abode still in Galilee.

COMMENTARY

In the Qur'an:

1. The Qur'an speaks only of *"45...Messiah, Isa son of Marium, worthy of regard in this world and the hereafter...",* and refer to Him us a teacher: *"48. And He will teach him the Book and the wisdom and the Tavrat (Torah) and the Injeel (Gospel)."*

2. The Qur'an again refers to the Apocrypha: *"46. And he shall speak to the people when in the cradle", "49...that I determine for you out of dust like the form of a bird, then I breathe into it and it becomes a bird with Allah's permission...".*

   It is interesting that the middle part of verse one is presented as a true story but the last sentence contradicts the main doctrine in the Qur'an about the deity of Jesus!

In the Bible:

1. The Bible gives us the title and purpose of the coming of Jesus:

   ### Matthew, Chapter 1:
   *"21.And she shall bring forth a son, and thou shalt call his name JESUS (Saviour): for **he shall save his people from their sins**."*

2. The Bible does not give us the details of Jesus' life before His mission which began at the age of 30, except for one event that occurred when He was 12 years old. According to the Qur'an and the non-canonical texts, He was recognized as an extraordinary child even at five years of age by His neighbors and friends. But the Biblical text gives us an opposite view. Not only did His neighbors not believe Him, but also His brothers! It shows us that the text in the Qur'an (which I believe was taken from non-canonical sources) is in direct contradiction to the canonical (inspired by God) Gospels of the Bible.

THE QUR'AN

"The Crucifixion of Jesus"

Sura 4

The Women

157. And their saying: Surely we have killed the Messiah, Isa son of Marium, the apostle of Allah; **and they did not kill him nor did they crucify him, but it appeared to them so (like Isa)** and most surely those who differ therein are only in a doubt about it; they have no knowledge respecting it, but only follow a conjecture, **and they killed him not for sure.**
158. Nay! **Allah took him up to Himself;** and Allah is Mighty, Wise.

Sura 6

The Cattle

164. Say: What! shall I seek a Lord other than Allah? And He is the Lord of all things; and no soul earns (evil) but against itself, **and no bearer of burden shall bear the burden of another;** then to your Lord is your return, so He will inform you of that in which you differed.

THE BIBLE

"The Crucifixion of Jesus"

Isaiah

Chapter 53

3. He is despised and rejected of men; a man of sorrows, and acquainted with grief: and we hid as it were our faces from him; he was despised, and we esteemed him not.

4. Surely he hath borne our griefs, and carried our sorrows: yet we did esteem him stricken, smitten of God, and afflicted.

5. But he was wounded for our transgressions, he was bruised for our iniquities: the chastisement of our peace was upon him; and with his stripes we are healed.

6. All we like sheep have gone astray; we have turned every one to his own way; and the **LORD hath laid on him the iniquity of us all.**

7. He was oppressed, and he was afflicted, yet he opened not his mouth: he is brought as a lamb to the slaughter, and as a sheep before her shearers is dumb, so he openeth not his mouth.

8. He was taken from prison and from judgment: and who shall declare his generation? for he was cut off out of the land of the living: **for the transgression of my people was he stricken.**

9. And he made his grave with the wicked, and with the rich in his death; because he had done no violence, neither was any deceit in his mouth.

10. Yet it pleased the LORD to bruise him; he hath put him to grief: **when thou shalt make his soul an offering for sin, he shall see his seed, he shall prolong his days, and the pleasure of the LORD shall prosper in his hand.**

11. He shall see of the travail of his soul, and shall be satisfied: **by his knowledge shall my righteous servant justify many; for he shall bear their iniquities.**

12. Therefore will I divide him a portion with the great, and he shall divide the spoil with the strong; because **he hath poured out his soul unto death:** and he was numbered with the transgressors; and **he bare the sin of many, and made intercession for the transgressors.**

Acts

Chapter 8

26. And the angel of the Lord spake unto Philip, saying, Arise, and go toward the south unto the way that goeth down from Jerusalem unto Gaza, which is desert.

27. And he arose and went: and, behold, a man of Ethiopia, an eunuch of great authority under Candace queen of the Ethiopians, who had the charge of all her treasure, and had come to Jerusalem for to worship,

28. Was returning, and sitting in his chariot read Esaias the prophet.

29. Then the Spirit said unto Philip, Go near, and join thyself to this chariot.

30. And Philip ran thither to him, and heard him read the prophet Esaias, and said, Understandest thou what thou readest?

31. And he said, How can I, except some man should guide me? And he desired Philip that he would come up and sit with him.

32. The place of the scripture which he read was this, He was led as a sheep to the slaughter; and like a lamb dumb before his shearer, so opened he not his mouth:

33. In his humiliation his judgment was taken away: and who shall declare his generation? for his life is taken from the earth.

34. And the eunuch answered Philip, and said, **I pray thee, of whom speaketh the prophet this? of himself, or of some other man?**

35. Then Philip opened his mouth, *and began at the same scripture, and preached unto him Jesus.*

36. And as they went on their way, they came unto a certain water: and the eunuch said, See, here is water; what doth hinder me to be baptized?

37. And Philip said, If thou believest with all thine heart, thou mayest. And he answered and said, **I believe that Jesus Christ is the Son of God.**

38. And he commanded the chariot to stand still: and they went down both into the water, both Philip and the eunuch; and **he baptized him.**

First Corinthians

Chapter 15

1. Moreover, brethren, I declare unto you **the gospel which I preached unto you**, which also ye have received, and wherein ye stand;

2. By which also ye are saved, if ye keep in memory what I preached unto you, unless ye have believed in vain.

3. For I delivered unto you first of all that which I also received, how that Christ died for our sins according to the scriptures;

4. And that he was buried, and that he rose again the third day according to the scriptures:

Psalms

Chapter 49

5. Wherefore should I fear in the days of evil, when the iniquity of my heels shall compass me about?

6. They that trust in their wealth, and boast themselves in the multitude of their riches;

7. None of them can by any means redeem his brother, nor give to God a ransom for him:

8. (For the redemption of their soul is precious, and it ceaseth for ever:)

COMMENTARY

In the Qur'an:

1. The Qur'an denies Jesus' death on the cross. *"... and they did not kill him nor did they crucify him, but it appeared to them so (like Isa)..."*

2. This is a clear statement that no man can take away the sin of another man. Nobody is able to redeem the iniquity of another. Each human is responsible for his own sins.

In the Bible:

1. The Bible teaches us that He was born to die for sinners:
    ### Isaiah, Chapter 53:
    *"...**8.**...for the transgression of my people was he stricken... **6.**...and the LORD hath laid on him the iniquity of us all... **12.**...he bare the sin of many, and made intercession for the transgressors..."*

Jesus said:

John, Chapter 12:

27. Now is my soul troubled; and what shall I say? Father, save me from this hour: but for this cause came I unto this hour 32. And I, if I be lifted up from the earth, will draw all men unto me. 33. This he said, signifying what death he should die."

Christianity in it's entirety is based on this fact; otherwise, believing in God is in vain.

First Corinthians, Chapter 15:

13. But if there be no resurrection of the dead, then is Christ not risen:

14. And if Christ be not risen, then is our preaching vain, and your faith is also vain.

15. Yea, and we are found false witnesses of God; because we have testified of God that he raised up Christ: whom he raised not up, if so be that the dead rise not.

16. For if the dead rise not, then is not Christ raised:

17. And if Christ be not raised, your faith is vain; ye are yet in your sins.

18. Then they also which are fallen asleep in Christ are perished.

19. If in this life only we have hope in Christ, we are of all men most miserable.

20. But now is Christ risen from the dead, and become the firstfruits of them that slept.

21. For since by man came death, by man came also the resurrection of the dead.

22. For as in Adam all die, even so in Christ shall all be made alive.

*23. But every man in his own order: **Christ the firstfruits; afterward they that are Christ's at his coming.***

2. Here it is very clear that no sinful human can save other person from their sin. It is only the Sinless Son of God Who can do it as the Perfect Sacrifice:

> "...*because he had done no violence, neither was **any deceit in his mouth**..*", "*... **he bare the sin of many**, and made intercession for the transgressors...*"

THE QUR'AN

"The Deity of Jesus"

Sura 4

The Women

171. O followers of the Book! do not exceed the limits in your religion, and do not speak (lies) against Allah, but (speak) the truth; **the Messiah, Isa son of Marium is only an apostle of Allah** and His Word which He communicated to Marium and a spirit from Him; believe therefore in Allah and His apostles, **and say not, Three. Desist, it is better for you; Allah is only one God; far be It from His glory that He should have a son,** whatever is in the heavens and whatever is in the earth is His, and Allah is sufficient for a Protector.
172. The Messiah does by no means disdain that **he should be a servant of Allah,** nor do the angels who are near to Him, and whoever disdains His service and is proud, He will gather them all together to Himself.

Sura 5

The Dinner Table

17. Certainly they disbelieve who say: Surely, Allah-- He is the Messiah, son of Marium. Say: Who then could control anything as against Allah when He wished to destroy the Messiah son of Marium and his mother and all those on the earth? And Allah's is the kingdom of the heavens and the earth and what is between them; He creates what He pleases; and Allah has power over all things,
72. Certainly they disbelieve who say: Surely Allah, He is the Messiah, son of Marium; and the Messiah said: O Children of Israel!

serve Allah, my Lord and your Lord. Surely whoever associates (others) with Allah, then Allah has forbidden to him the garden, and his abode is the fire; and there shall be no helpers for the unjust.

73. Certainly they disbelieve who say: Surely Allah is the third (person) of the three; and there is no god but the one God, and if they desist not from what they say, a painful chastisement shall befall those among them who disbelieve.

75. The Messiah, son of Marium is but an apostle; apostles before him have indeed passed away; and his mother was a truthful woman; they both used to eat food. See how We make the communications clear to them, then behold, how they are turned away.

116. And when Allah will say: O Isa son of Marium! did you say to men *Take me and my mother for two gods besides Allah* he will say: Glory be to Thee, it did not befit me that I should say what I had no right to (say); if I had said it, Thou wouldst indeed have known it; Thou knowest what is in my mind, and I do not know what is in Thy mind, surely Thou art the great Knower of the unseen things.

THE BIBLE

"The Deity of Jesus"

Witnesses Among People

Matthew

Chapter 14

24. But the ship was now in the midst of the sea, tossed with waves: for the wind was contrary.

25. And in the fourth watch of the night Jesus went unto them, walking on the sea.

26. And when the disciples saw him walking on the sea, they were troubled, saying, It is a spirit; and they cried out for fear.

27. But straightway Jesus spake unto them, saying, Be of good cheer; it is I; be not afraid.

28. And Peter answered him and said, Lord, if it be thou, bid me come unto thee on the water.

29. And he said, Come. And when Peter was come down out of the ship, he walked on the water, to go to Jesus.

30. But when he saw the wind boisterous, he was afraid; and beginning to sink, he cried, saying, Lord, save me.

31. And immediately Jesus stretched forth his hand, and caught him, and said unto him, O thou of little faith, wherefore didst thou doubt?

32. And when they were come into the ship, the wind ceased.

33. Then they that were in the ship came and worshipped him, saying, Of a truth thou art the Son of God.

John

Chapter 1

29. The next day John seeth Jesus coming unto him, and saith, **Behold the Lamb of God, which taketh away the sin of the world.**

34. And I saw, and **bare record that this is the Son of God.**

45. Philip findeth Nathanael, and saith unto him, We have found him, of whom Moses in the law, and the prophets, did write, Jesus of Nazareth, the son of Joseph.

49. Nathanael answered and saith unto him, Rabbi, thou art the *Son of God*; **thou art the King of Israel.**

Romans

Chapter 1

3. Concerning his Son Jesus Christ our Lord, which was made of the seed of David according to the flesh;

4. And declared to be the Son of God with power, according to the spirit of holiness, by the resurrection from the dead.

Belief in God's Son as Necessary for Salvation

John

Chapter 3

14. And as Moses lifted up the serpent in the wilderness, even so must the **Son of man be lifted up:**

15. That whosoever believeth in him should not perish, but have eternal life.

16. For God so loved the world, that he gave his only begotten Son, that whosoever believeth in him should not perish, but have everlasting life.

35. The Father loveth the Son, and hath given all things into his hand.

36. He that believeth on the Son hath everlasting life: and he that believeth not the Son shall not see life; but the wrath of God abideth on him.

John

Chapter 6

40. And this is the will of him that sent me, that every one which seeth the **Son, and believeth on him, may have everlasting life: and I will raise him up at the last day.**

John

Chapter 20

31. But these are written, that **ye might believe that Jesus is the Christ, the Son of God; and that believing ye might have life through his name.**

First John

Chapter 5

5. Who is he that overcometh the world, but he that believeth that Jesus is the Son of God?

12. He that hath the Son hath life; and he that hath not the Son of God hath not life.

13. These things have I written unto you that believe on the name of the Son of God; that ye may know that **ye have eternal life**, and that **ye may believe on the name of the Son of God.**

God's Plan for His Son

First John

Chapter 4

9. In this was manifested the love of God toward us, because that **God sent his only begotten Son into the world, that we might live through him**.
10. Herein is love, not that we loved God, but that he loved us, and **sent his Son to be the propitiation for our sins**.

Romans

Chapter 8

3. For what the law could not do, in that it was weak through the flesh, **God sending his own Son in the likeness of sinful flesh, and for sin, condemned sin in the flesh:**

The Deity of Jesus

John

Chapter 20

24. But Thomas, one of the twelve, called Didymus, was not with them when Jesus came.
25. The other disciples therefore said unto him, We have seen the Lord. But he said unto them, Except I shall see in his hands the print of the nails, and put my finger into the print of the nails, and thrust my hand into his side, I will not believe.
26. And after eight days again his disciples were within, and Thomas with them: then came Jesus, the doors being shut, and stood in the midst, and said, Peace be unto you.
27. Then saith he to Thomas, reach hither thy finger, and behold my hands; and reach hither thy hand, and thrust it into my side: and be not faithless, but believing.
28. And Thomas answered and said unto him, My Lord and my God.

29. Jesus saith unto him, Thomas, because thou hast seen me, thou hast believed: **blessed are they that have not seen, and yet have believed.**

Romans
Chapter 9

4. Who are Israelites; to whom pertaineth the adoption, and the glory, and the covenants, and the giving of the law, and the service of God, and the promises;
5. Whose are the fathers, and of whom as concerning the flesh **Christ** came, **who is over all, God blessed for ever. Amen.**

COMMENTARY

In the Qur'an:

1.   The Qur'an denies the deity of Jesus.

In the Bible:

1.   The Bible speaks of Jesus as the Son of the Living God, unique from other humans. The Qur'an warns Christians not to call Jesus the Son of God, as it is blasphemy against the One and Only True God!

For this same reason Jesus was hated and crucified:

John, Chapter 8:
54. Jesus answered, If I honour myself, my honour is nothing: it is my Father that honoureth me; of whom ye say, that he is your God:
55. Yet ye have not known him; but I know him: and if I should say, I know him not, I shall be a liar like unto you: but I know him, and keep his saying.
56. Your father Abraham rejoiced to see my day: and he saw it, and was glad.
57. Then said the Jews unto him, Thou art not yet fifty years old, and hast thou seen Abraham?

58. *Jesus said unto them,* **Verily, verily, I say unto you, Before Abraham was, I am.**

59. *Then took they up stones to cast at him: but Jesus hid himself, and went out of the temple, going through the midst of them, and so passed by.*

John, Chapter 10:

27. *My sheep hear my voice, and I know them, and they follow me:*

28. *And I give unto them eternal life; and they shall never perish, neither shall any man pluck them out of my hand.*

29. *My Father, which gave them me, is greater than all; and no man is able to pluck them out of my Father's hand.*

30. *I and my Father are one.*

31. *Then the Jews took up stones again to stone him.*

32. *Jesus answered them, Many good works have I shewed you from my Father; for which of those works do ye stone me?*

33. *The Jews answered him, saying, For a good work we stone thee not; but for blasphemy; and because that thou, being a man, makest thyself God.*

34. *Jesus answered them, Is it not written in your law, I said, Ye are gods?*

35. *If he called them gods, unto whom the word of God came, and the scripture cannot be broken;*

36. *Say ye of him, whom the Father hath sanctified, and sent into the world, Thou blasphemest;* **because I said, I am the Son of God?**

37. *If I do not the works of my Father, believe me not.*

38. *But if I do, though ye believe not me, believe the works: that ye may know, and believe, that the Father is in me, and I in him.*

Matthew, Chapter 26:

62. And the high priest arose, and said unto him, Answerest thou nothing? what is it which these witness against thee?

63. But Jesus held his peace. And the high priest answered and said unto him, I adjure thee by the living God, that thou tell us whether thou be the **Christ, the Son of God***.*

64. Jesus saith unto him, **Thou hast said***: nevertheless I say unto you, Hereafter* **shall ye see the Son of man sitting on the right hand of power, and coming in the clouds of heaven***.*

65. Then the high priest rent his clothes, saying, He hath spoken blasphemy; what further need have we of witnesses? behold, now ye have heard his blasphemy.

66. What think ye? They answered and said, He is guilty of death.

According to the Bible, Jesus is the Creator, not a creature.

Colossians, Chapter 1:

14. In whom we have redemption through his blood, even the forgiveness of sins:

15. Who is the image of the invisible God, the firstborn of every creature:

16. For **by him** *were* **all things created***, that are in heaven, and that are in earth, visible and invisible, whether they be thrones, or dominions, or principalities, or powers:* **all things were created by him, and for him***:*

17. And he is before all things, and by him all things consist.

Therefore, the Qur'an calls Jesus' words blasphemy. By doing so, it takes the position of Jesus' enemies, who were the high priest and most of Pharisees in the Sanhedrin. Moreover, it condemns Jesus to the cross for what He had said concerning His nature.

However, according to the Bible, only those who believe in Jesus as the Son of God will be saved:

John, Chapter 3
36 He that believeth on the Son hath everlasting life: and he that believeth not the Son shall not see life; but the wrath of God abideth on him.
John, Chapter 8
24. I said therefore unto you, that ye shall die in your sins: **for if ye believe not that I am he**, ye shall die in your sins.

THE QUR'AN

"The Son of God"

Sura 2

The Cow

116. And they say: **Allah has taken to himself a son**. Glory be to Him; rather, whatever is in the heavens and the earth is His; all are obedient to Him.

Sura 17

The children of Israel

111. And say: (All) praise is due to Allah, **Who has not taken a son and Who has not a partner in the kingdom**, and Who has not a helper to save Him from disgrace; and proclaim His greatness magnifying (Him).

Sura 19

Marium

88. And they say: The Beneficent God has taken (to Himself) a son.
89. Certainly you have made an abominable assertion
90. The heavens may almost be rent thereat, and the earth cleave asunder, and the mountains fall down in pieces,
91. That they ascribe a son to the Beneficent God.

92. And it is not worthy of the Beneficent God that He should take (to Himself) a son.

93. There is no one in the heavens and the earth but will come to the Beneficent God as a servant.

Sura 21

The Prophets

26. And they say: The Beneficent God has taken to Himself a son. Glory be to Him. Nay! they are honored servants

27. They do not precede Him in speech and (only) according to His commandment do they act.

28. He knows what is before them and what is behind them, and they do not intercede except for him whom He approves and for fear of Him they tremble.

29. And whoever of them should say: Surely I am a god besides Him, such a one do We recompense with hell; thus do, We recompense the unjust.

Sura 23

The Believers

91. Never did Allah take to Himself a son, and never was there with him any (other) god-- in that case would each god have certainly taken away what he created, and some of them would certainly have overpowered others; glory be to Allah above what they describe!

Sura 25

The Distinction

1. Blessed is He Who sent down the Furqan upon His servant that he may be a warner to the nations;

2. He, Whose is the kingdom of the heavens and the earth, and **Who did not take to Himself a son**, and Who has no associate in the kingdom, and Who created everything, then ordained for it a measure.

THE BIBLE

"The Son of God"

Exodus

Chapter 4

21. And the LORD said unto Moses, When thou goest to return into Egypt, see that thou do all those wonders before Pharaoh, which I have put in thine hand: but I will harden his heart, that he shall not let the people go.

22. And thou shalt say unto Pharaoh, Thus saith the LORD, **Israel is my son, even my firstborn**:

23. And I say unto thee, Let my son go, that he may serve me: and if thou refuse to let him go, behold, I will slay thy son, even thy firstborn.

Psalms

Chapter 2

1. Why do the heathen rage, and the people imagine a vain thing?

2. The kings of the earth set themselves, and the rulers take counsel together, against the LORD, and against his anointed, saying,

3. Let us break their bands asunder, and cast away their cords from us.

4. He that sitteth in the heavens shall laugh: the Lord shall have them in derision.

5. Then shall he speak unto them in his wrath, and vex them in his sore displeasure.

6. Yet have I set my king upon my holy hill of Zion.

7. I will declare the decree: the LORD hath said unto me, **Thou art my Son; this day have I begotten thee.**

8. Ask of me, and I shall give thee the heathen for thine inheritance, and the uttermost parts of the earth for thy possession.

9. Thou shalt break them with a rod of iron; thou shalt dash them in pieces like a potter's vessel.

Proverbs

Chapter 30

1. The words of Agur the son of Jakeh, even the prophecy: the man spake unto Ithiel, even unto Ithiel and Ucal,

2. Surely I am more brutish than any man, and have not the understanding of a man.

3. I neither learned wisdom, nor have the knowledge of the holy.

4. Who hath ascended up into heaven, or descended? who hath gathered the wind in his fists? who hath bound the waters in a garment? **who hath established all the ends of the earth? what is his name, and what is *his son's name*, if thou canst tell?**

5. Every word of God is pure: he is a shield unto them that put their trust in him.

Jeremiah

Chapter 31

1. At the same time, saith the LORD, will I be the God of all the families of Israel, and they shall be my people.

8. Behold, I will bring them from the north country, and gather them from the coasts of the earth, and with them the blind and the lame, the woman with child and her that travaileth with child together: a great company shall return thither.

9. They shall come with weeping, and with supplications will I lead them: I will cause them to walk by the rivers of waters in a straight way, wherein they shall not stumble: **for I am a father to Israel, and Ephraim is my firstborn.**

Hosea

Chapter 11

1. When Israel was a child, then I loved him, **and called my son out of Egypt.**

Luke

Chapter 3

21. Then said Mary unto the angel, How shall this be, seeing I know not a man?

35. And the angel answered and said unto her, The Holy Ghost shall come upon thee, and the power of the Highest shall overshadow thee: therefore also that holy thing which shall be born of thee shall be called the Son of God.

Luke

Chapter 3

21. Now when all the people were baptized, it came to pass, that Jesus also being baptized, and praying, the heaven was opened,

22. And the Holy Ghost descended in a bodily shape like a dove upon him, and a voice came from heaven, which said, **Thou art my beloved Son; in thee I am well pleased.**

23. And Jesus himself began to be about thirty years of age, being (as was supposed) the son of Joseph, which was the son of Heli,

Second Peter

Chapter 1

1. Simon Peter, a servant and an apostle of Jesus Christ, to them that have obtained like precious faith with us through the righteousness of God and our Saviour Jesus Christ:

16. For we have not followed cunningly devised fables, when we made known unto you the power and coming of our Lord Jesus Christ, but were eyewitnesses of his majesty.

17. For he received from God the Father honour and glory, when there came such a voice to him from the excellent glory, **This is my beloved Son, in whom I am well pleased.**

Acts

Chapter 13

29. And when they had fulfilled all that was written of him, they took him down from the tree, and laid him in a sepulchre.

30. But God raised him from the dead:

31. And he was seen many days of them which came up with him from Galilee to Jerusalem, who are his witnesses unto the people.

32. And we declare unto you glad tidings, how that the promise which was made unto the fathers,

33. God hath fulfilled the same unto us their children, in that he hath raised up Jesus again; as it is also written in the second psalm, **Thou art my Son, this day have I begotten thee**.

Hebrews
Chapter 1

1. God, who at sundry times and in divers manners spake in time past unto the fathers by the prophets,

2. Hath in these last days spoken unto us by his Son, whom he hath appointed heir of all things, by whom also he made the worlds;

3. Who being the brightness of his glory, and the express image of his person, and upholding all things by the word of his power, when he had by himself purged our sins, sat down on the right hand of the Majesty on high;

4. Being made so much better than the angels, as he hath by inheritance obtained a more excellent name than they.

5. For unto which of the angels said he at any time, **Thou art my Son, this day have I begotten thee? And again, I will be to him a Father, and he shall be to me a Son?**

6. And again, when he bringeth in the firstbegotten into the world, he saith, **And let all the angels of God worship him**.

7. And of the angels he saith, Who maketh his angels spirits, and his ministers a flame of fire.

8. But unto the Son he saith, Thy throne, O God, is for ever and ever: a sceptre of righteousness is the sceptre of thy kingdom.

COMMENTARY

In the Qur'an:

1. The Qur'an clearly rejects the possibility of anybody being called the "Son of God".

In the Bible:

1. In both the Old and New Testaments, we find that God calls the nation of Israel "My Son", as well as calling Jesus "My Son":

Exodus 4:22

22. *And thou shalt say unto Pharaoh, Thus saith the LORD, Israel is my son, even my firstborn:*

God called the Messiah, Jesus, "My Son":

Psalm 2:6,7

6. *Yet have I set my king upon my holy hill of Zion.* **7.** *I will declare the decree: the LORD hath said unto me, Thou art my Son; this day have I begotten thee.*

THE QUR'AN
"The Camel and the Eye of a Needle"

Sura 7
The Elevated Places

40. Surely (as for) those who reject Our communications and turn away from them haughtily, the doors of heaven shall not be opened for them, **nor shall they enter the garden until the camel pass through the eye of the needle**; and thus do We reward the guilty.

THE BIBLE
"The Camel and the Eye of a Needle"

Matthew
Chapter 19

21. Jesus said unto him, **If thou wilt be perfect**, go and sell that thou hast, and give to the poor, and thou shalt have treasure in heaven: **and come and follow me.**

231

22. But when the young man heard that saying, he went away sorrowful: for he had great possessions.

23. Then said Jesus unto his disciples, Verily I say unto you, **That a rich man shall hardly enter into the kingdom of heaven.**

24. And again I say unto you, **It is *easier* for a camel to go through the eye of a needle, than for a rich man to enter into the kingdom of God.**

25. When his disciples heard it, they were exceedingly amazed, saying, **Who then can be saved?**

26. But Jesus beheld them, and said unto them, With men this is impossible; **but with God all things are possible.**

COMMENTARY

In the Qur'an:

1. The Qur'an refers to the biblical story of Jesus, but without mentioning its source and true context.

   In the Qur'an it is impossible for unbelievers to enter Paradise before a camel will pass through the eye of the needle : " *...the doors of heaven shall not be opened for them, nor shall they enter the garden until the camel pass through the eye of the needle.*"

In the Bible:

1. Jesus spoke this account only to a rich person, not to every unbeliever. He was trying to emphasise how hard it is to rely upon God when one can rely upon one's wealth instead:

   Matthew 19:24 and Mark 10:25
   *"...**a rich man shall hardly enter** into the kingdom of heaven. **It is easier** for a camel to go through the eye of a needle, than for a rich man to enter into the kingdom of God."*

Still here is hope: *"With men, this is impossible; but with God, all things are possible."* (**Matthew 19:26 and Mark 10:27**)

THE QUR'AN

"Jesus Speaks About the Comforter"

Sura 61

The Ranks

6. And when Isa son of Marium said: O children of Israel! surely I am the apostle of Allah to you, verifying that which is before me of the Taurat **and giving the good news of an Apostle who will come after me, his name being Ahmad,** but when he came to them with clear arguments they said: This is clear magic.

THE BIBLE

"Jesus Speaks About the Comforter"

John

Chapter 14

16. And I(*Jesus*) will pray the Father, and he shall give you **another Comforter, that he may abide with you for ever;**
26. But the Comforter, which is the Holy Ghost, whom the Father will send in my name, he shall teach you all things, and bring all things to your remembrance, whatsoever I have said unto you.

John

Chapter 15

26. But when the Comforter is come, whom I will send unto you from the Father, **even the Spirit of truth, which proceedeth from the Father, he shall testify of me:**

John

Chapter 16

7. Nevertheless I tell you the truth; It is expedient for you that I go away: for if I go not away, the Comforter will not come unto you; but if I depart, **I will send him unto you.**

Acts

Chapter 1

6. When they therefore were come together, they asked of him, saying, Lord, wilt thou at this time restore again the kingdom to Israel?

7. And he said unto them, It is not for you to know the times or the seasons, which the Father hath put in his own power.

8. But ye shall receive power, after that the Holy Ghost is come upon you: and ye shall be witnesses unto me both in Jerusalem, and in all Judaea, and in Samaria, and unto the uttermost part of the earth.

Acts

Chapter 2

1. And when the day of Pentecost was fully come, they were all with one accord in one place.

2. And suddenly there came a sound from heaven as of a rushing mighty wind, and it filled all the house where they were sitting.

3. And there appeared unto them cloven tongues like as of fire, and it sat upon each of them.

4. And they were all filled with the Holy Ghost, and began to speak with other tongues, as the Spirit gave them utterance.

Romans

Chapter 8

9. But ye are not in the flesh, but in the Spirit, if so be that the **Spirit of God dwell in you.** Now if any man have not the **Spirit of Christ, he is none of his.**

10. And if Christ be in you, the body is dead because of sin; but the Spirit is life because of righteousness.

11. But if the Spirit of him that raised up Jesus from the dead dwell in you, he that raised up Christ from the dead shall also quicken your mortal bodies by **his Spirit that dwelleth in you.**

12. Therefore, brethren, we are debtors, not to the flesh, to live after the flesh.

13. For if ye live after the flesh, ye shall die: but if ye through the Spirit do mortify the deeds of the body, ye shall live.

14. For as many as are led by the Spirit of God, they are the sons of God.

15. For ye have not received the spirit of bondage again to fear; but ye have received the Spirit of adoption, whereby we cry, Abba, Father.

16. The Spirit itself beareth witness with our spirit, that we are the children of God:

First Corinthians

Chapter 12

13. For by **one Spirit are we all baptized into one body**, whether we be **Jews or Gentiles**, whether we be bond or free; and have been all made to drink into one Spirit.

Second Corinthians

Chapter 1

21. Now he which stablisheth us with you in Christ, and hath anointed us, is God;

22. Who hath also sealed us, **and given the earnest of the Spirit in our hearts.**

Galatians

Chapter 3

14. That the blessing of Abraham might come on the Gentiles through Jesus Christ; **that we might receive the promise of the Spirit through faith.**

Galatians

Chapter 4

6. And because ye are sons, God hath sent forth the Spirit of his Son into your hearts, crying, Abba, Father.

Second Thessalonians

Chapter 2

13. But we are bound to give thanks alway to God for you, brethren beloved of the Lord, because God hath from the beginning **chosen you to salvation through sanctification of the Spirit** and belief of the truth:

First Peter

Chapter 1

1. Peter, an apostle of Jesus Christ, to the strangers scattered throughout Pontus, Galatia, Cappadocia, Asia, and Bithynia,
2. Elect according to the foreknowledge of God the Father, **through sanctification of the Spirit**, unto obedience and sprinkling of the blood of Jesus Christ: Grace unto you, and peace, be multiplied.

First John

Chapter 3

24. And he that keepeth his commandments dwelleth in him, and he in him. And hereby we know that he abideth in us, **by the Spirit which he hath given us.**

Revelation

Chapter 22

16. I Jesus have sent mine angel to testify unto you these things in the churches. I am the root and the offspring of David, and the bright and morning star.

17. And the Spirit and the bride say, Come. And let him that heareth say, Come. And let him that is athirst come. And whosoever will, let him take the water of life freely.

COMMENTARY

In the Qur'an:

1. Jesus revealed that the purpose of His coming was to confirm the Law of Moses and to give *"...the good news of an Apostle who will come after me, his name being Ahmad...".*

In the Bible:

1. Jesus did promise to send the Comforter after Him, but it was not to be "a man". The Comforter is the Holy Spirit of God, equal to God and Jesus. He came on the day of Pentecost (Acts 2:1-4). Since that time, all Christians are waiting for Jesus to return to Earth, not some other prophet from God.

Revelation, Chapter 22:17:
The Spirit(Holy) and the Bride(Church) say, "Come.",

Revelation, Chapter 22:20:
"...He which testifieth these things saith, Surely I come quickly. Amen. Even so, come, Lord Jesus."

SUMMARY

The mission of Jesus, as descrbed in the Qur'an and in the Bible, differ GREATLY. In the Qur'an, Jesus essentially pointed to the next prophet of God who would be greater than Jesus, as it is sensed from this text. But the Biblical Jesus spoke about Himself as a long-ago promised Messiah Who will bring an end to Satan's reign on Earth and will eliminate the root of sin forever.

Part Two

THE DOCTRINES OF THE QUR'AN

Chapter One

JIHAD

THE QUR'AN

"War, Hebrews and Christians, the Punishment of Unbelievers in Allah"

Sura 2

The Cow

190. And fight in the way of Allah with those who fight with you, and do not exceed the limits, surely Allah does not love those who exceed the limits.

191. And kill them wherever you find them, and drive them out from whence they drove you out, and persecution is severer than slaughter, and do not fight with them at the Sacred Mosque until they fight with you in it, but if they do fight you, then slay them; such is the recompense of the unbelievers.

192. But if they desist, then surely Allah is Forgiving, Merciful.

193. And fight with them until there is no persecution, and *religion should be only for Allah*, but if they desist, then there should be no hostility except against the oppressors.

243. Have you not considered those who went forth from their homes, for fear of death, and they were thousands, then Allah said to them, Die; again He gave them life; most surely Allah is Gracious to people, but most people are not grateful.

244. And fight in the way of Allah, and know that Allah is Hearing, Knowing.

Sura 5

The Dinner Table

33. The punishment of those who wage war against Allah and His apostle and strive to make mischief in the land is only this, that **they should be murdered or crucified or their hands and their feet should be cut off on opposite sides or they should be imprisoned;** this shall be as a disgrace for them in this world, and in the hereafter they shall have a grievous chastisement,

34. Except those who repent before you have them in your power; so know that Allah is Forgiving, Merciful.

35. O you who believe! be careful of (your duty to) Allah and seek means of nearness to Him and strive hard in His way that you may be successful.

51. O you who believe! *do not take the Jews and the Christians for friends; they are friends of each other*; **and whoever amongst you takes them for a friend, then surely he is one of them; surely Allah does not guide the unjust people.**

Sura 8

The Accessions

15. O you who believe! when you meet those who disbelieve marching for war, then turn not your backs to them.

16. And whoever shall turn his back to them on that day-- unless he turn aside for the sake of fighting or withdraws to a company-- then he, indeed, becomes deserving of Allah's wrath, and his abode is hell; and an evil destination shall it be.

17. So you did not slay them, but it was Allah Who slew them, and you did not smite when you smote (the enemy), but it was Allah Who smote, and that He might confer upon the believers a good gift from Himself; surely Allah is Hearing, Knowing.

18. This, and that Allah is the weakener of the struggle of the unbelievers.

38. Say to those who disbelieve, if they desist, that which is past shall be forgiven to them; and if they return, then what happened to the ancients has already passed.

39. And fight with them until there is no more persecution *and religion should be only for Allah*; but if they desist, then surely Allah sees what they do.

40. And if they turn back, then know that Allah is your Patron; most excellent is the Patron and most excellent the Helper.

41. And know that whatever thing you gain, a fifth of it is for Allah and for the Apostle and for the near of kin and the orphans and the needy and the wayfarer, if you believe in Allah and in that which We revealed to Our servant, on the day of distinction, the day on which the two parties met; and Allah has power over all things.

58. And if you fear treachery on the part of a people, then throw back to them on terms of equality; surely Allah does not love the treacherous.

59. And let not those who disbelieve think that they shall come in first; surely they will not escape.

60. And prepare against them what force you can and horses tied at the frontier, to frighten thereby the enemy of Allah and your enemy and others besides them, whom you do not know (but) Allah knows them; and whatever thing you will spend in Allah's way, it will be paid back to you fully and you shall not be dealt with unjustly.

61. And if they incline to peace, then incline to it and trust in Allah; surely He is the Hearing, the Knowing.

62. And if they intend to deceive you-- then surely Allah is sufficient for you; He it is Who strengthened you with His help and with the believers

63. And united their hearts; had you spent all that is in the earth, you could not have united their hearts, but Allah united them; surely He is Mighty, Wise.

64. O Prophet! Allah is sufficient for you and (for) such of the believers as follow you.

65. O Prophet! urge the believers to war; if there are twenty patient ones of you they shall overcome two hundred, and if there are a hundred of you they shall overcome a thousand of those who disbelieve, because they are a people who do not understand.

66. For the present Allah has made light your burden, and He knows that there is weakness in you; so if there are a hundred patient ones of you they shall overcome two hundred, and if there are a thousand they shall overcome two thousand by Allah's permission, and Allah is with the patient.

67. It is not fit for a prophet that he should take captives unless he has fought and triumphed in the land; you desire the frail goods of this world, while Allah desires (for you) the hereafter; and Allah is Mighty, Wise.

Sura 9

The Immunity

1. (This is a declaration of) immunity by Allah and His Apostle towards those of the idolaters with whom you made an agreement.

2. So go about in the land for four months and know that you cannot weaken Allah and that Allah will bring disgrace to the unbelievers.

3. And an announcement from Allah and His Apostle to the people on the day of the greater pilgrimage that Allah and His Apostle are free from liability to the idolaters; therefore if you repent, it will be better for you, and if you turn back, then know that you will not weaken Allah; and announce painful punishment to those who disbelieve.

4. Except those of the idolaters with whom you made an agreement, then they have not failed you in anything and have not backed up any one against you, so fulfill their agreement to the end of their term; surely Allah loves those who are careful (of their duty).

5. So when the sacred months have passed away, then slay the idolaters wherever you find them, and take them captives and besiege them and lie in wait for them in every ambush, then if they repent and keep up prayer and pay the poor-rate, leave their way free to them; surely Allah is Forgiving, Merciful.

6. And if one of the idolaters seek protection from you, grant him protection till he hears the word of Allah, then make him attain his place of safety; this is because they are a people who do not know.

7. How can there be an agreement for the idolaters with Allah and with His Apostle; except those with whom you made an agreement at the Sacred Mosque? So as long as they are true to you, be true to them; surely Allah loves those who are careful (of their duty).

8. How (can it be)! while if they prevail against you, they would not pay regard in your case to ties of relationship, nor those of covenant; they please you with their mouths while their hearts do not consent; and most of them are transgressors.

9. They have taken a small price for the communications of Allah, so they turn away from His way; surely evil is it that they do.

10. They do not pay regard to ties of relationship nor those of covenant in the case of a believer; and these are they who go beyond the limits.

11. But if they repent and keep up prayer and pay the poor-rate, they are your brethren in faith; and We make the communications clear for a people who know.

12. And if they break their oaths after their agreement and (openly) revile your religion, then fight the leaders of unbelief-- surely their oaths are nothing-- so that they may desist.

13. What! will you not fight a people who broke their oaths and aimed at the expulsion of the Apostle, and they attacked you first; do you fear them? But Allah is most deserving that you should fear Him, if you are believers.

14. Fight them, Allah will punish them by your hands and bring them to disgrace, and assist you against them and heal the hearts of a believing people.

29. Fight those who do not believe in Allah, nor in the latter day, nor do they prohibit what Allah and His Apostle have prohibited, nor follow the religion of truth, out of those who have been given the Book, until they pay the tax in acknowledgment of superiority and they are in a state of subjection.

30. And the Jews say: Uzair is the son of Allah; and the Christians say: The Messiah is the son of Allah; these are the words of their mouths; they imitate the saying of those who disbelieved before; **may Allah destroy them;** how they are turned away!

31. They have taken their doctors of law and their monks for lords besides Allah, and (also) the Messiah son of Marium and they were enjoined that they should serve one God only, there is no god but He; far from His glory be what they set up (with Him).

32. They desire to put out the light of Allah with their mouths, and Allah will not consent save to perfect His light, though the unbelievers are averse.

33. He it is Who sent His Apostle with guidance and the religion of truth, that He might cause it to prevail over all religions, though the polytheists may be averse.

34. O you who believe! most surely many of the doctors of law and the monks eat away the property of men falsely, and turn (them) from Allah's way; and (as for) those who hoard up gold and silver and do not spend it in Allah's way, announce to them a painful chastisement,

38. O you who believe! What (excuse) have you that when it is said to you: Go forth in Allah's way, you should incline heavily to earth; are you contented with this world's life instead of the hereafter? But the provision of this world's life compared with the hereafter is but little.

39. If you do not go forth, He will chastise you with a painful chastisement and bring in your place a people other than you, and you will do Him no harm; and Allah has power over all things.

41. Go forth light and heavy, and strive hard in Allah's way with your property and your persons; this is better for you, if you know.

73. O Prophet! strive hard against the unbelievers and the hypocrites and be unyielding to them; and their abode is hell, and evil is the destination.

111. Surely Allah has bought of the believers their persons and their property for this, that they shall have the garden; **they fight in Allah's way, so they slay and are slain; a promise which is binding on Him in the Taurat and the Injeel and the Quran;** and who is more faithful to his covenant than Allah? Rejoice therefore in the pledge which you have made; and that is the mighty achievement.

Sura 47

Muhammad

4. So when you meet in battle those who disbelieve, then smite the necks until when you have overcome them, then make (them) prisoners, and afterwards either set them free as a favor or let them ransom (themselves) until the war terminates. That (shall be so); and if Allah had pleased He would certainly have exacted what is due from them, but that He may try some of you by means of others; and (as for) those who are slain in the way of Allah, He will by no means allow their deeds to perish.

5. He will guide them and improve their condition.

6. And cause them to enter the garden which He has made known to them.

Sura 48

The Victory

13. And whoever does not believe in Allah and His Apostle, then surely We have prepared burning fire for the unbelievers.

14. And Allah's is the kingdom of the heavens and the earth; He forgives whom He pleases and punishes whom He pleases, and Allah is Forgiving, Merciful.

29. Muhammad is the Apostle of Allah, and those with him are firm of heart against the unbelievers, compassionate among themselves;

you will see them bowing down, prostrating themselves, seeking grace from Allah and pleasure; their marks are in their faces because of the effect of prostration; that is their description in the Taurat and their description in the Injeel; like as seed-produce that puts forth its sprout, then strengthens it, so it becomes stout and stands firmly on its stem, delighting the sowers that He may enrage the unbelievers on account of them; Allah has promised those among them who believe and do good, forgiveness and a great reward.

Sura 62

The Congregation

5. The likeness of those who were charged with the Taurat, then they did not observe it, is as the likeness of the ass bearing books, evil is the likeness of the people who reject the communications of Allah; and Allah does not guide the unjust people.
6. Say: **O you who are Jews, if you think that you are the favorites of Allah to the exclusion of other people, then invoke death If you are truthful.**
7. And they will never invoke it because of what their hands have sent before; and Allah is Cognizant of the unjust.
8. Say: (As for) the death from which you flee, that will surely overtake you, then you shall be sent back to the Knower of the unseen and the seen, and He will inform you of that which you did.

Sura 66

The Prohibition

9. O Prophet! strive hard against the unbelievers and the hypocrites, and be hard against them; and their abode is hell; and evil is the resort

THE BIBLE

"War, Hebrews and Christians, the Punishment of Unbelievers in Allah"

Exodus

Chapter 23

4. If thou meet thine enemy's ox or his ass going astray, thou shalt surely bring it back to him again.
5. If thou see the ass of him that hateth thee lying under his burden, and wouldest forbear to help him, **thou shalt surely help with him.**

Deuteronomy

Chapter 22

1. Thou shalt not see the brother's ox or his sheep go astray, and hide thyself from them: thou shalt in any case bring them again unto thy brother.
2. And if thy brother be not nigh unto thee, or if thou know him not, then thou shalt bring it unto thine own house, and it shall be with thee until thy brother seek after it, and thou shalt restore it to him again.
3. In like manner shalt thou do with his ass; and so shalt thou do with his raiment; and with all lost thing of thy brother's, which he hath lost, and thou hast found, shalt thou do likewise: thou mayest not hide thyself.
4. Thou shalt not see thy brother's ass or his ox fall down by the way, and hide thyself from them: thou shalt surely help him to lift them up again.

Second Kings

Chapter 6

18. And when they came down to him, Elisha prayed unto the LORD, and said, **Smite this people, I pray thee, with blindness. And he smote them with blindness according to the word of Elisha.**

19. And Elisha said unto them, This is not the way, neither is this the city: follow me, and I will bring you to the man whom ye seek. **But he led them to Samaria.**

20. And it came to pass, when they were come into Samaria, that Elisha said, LORD, open the eyes of these men, that they may see. **And the LORD opened their eyes, and they saw; and, behold, they were in the midst of Samaria.**

21. And the king of Israel said unto Elisha, when he saw them, My father, shall I smite them? shall I smite them?

22. And he answered, **Thou shalt not smite them: wouldest thou smite those whom thou hast taken captive with thy sword and with thy bow? set bread and water before them, that they may eat and drink, and go to their master.**

23. And he prepared great provision for them: **and when they had eaten and drunk, he sent them away, and they went to their master. So the bands of Syria came no more into the land of Israel.**

Proverbs

Chapter 25

21. If thine enemy be hungry, give him bread to eat; and if he be thirsty, give him water to drink:

22. For thou shalt heap coals of fire upon his head, and the LORD shall reward thee.

Matthew

Chapter 5

1. And seeing the multitudes, he *(Jesus)* went up into a mountain: and when he was set, his disciples came unto him:

9. Blessed are the peacemakers: for they shall be called the children of God.

10. Blessed are they which are persecuted for righteousness' sake: for theirs is the kingdom of heaven.

11. Blessed are ye, when men shall revile you, and persecute you, and shall say all manner of evil against you falsely, for my sake.

12. Rejoice, and be exceeding glad: for great is your reward in heaven: **for so persecuted they the prophets which were before you.**

38. Ye have heard that it hath been said, An eye for an eye, and a tooth for a tooth:

39. But I say unto you, That ye resist not evil: but whosoever shall smite thee on thy right cheek, turn to him the other also.

40. And if any man will sue thee at the law, and take away thy coat, let him have thy cloke also.

41. And whosoever shall compel thee to go a mile, go with him twain.

42. Give to him that asketh thee, and from him that would borrow of thee turn not thou away.

43. Ye have heard that it hath been said, Thou shalt love thy neighbour, and hate thine enemy.

44. But I say unto you, Love your enemies, bless them that curse you, do good to them that hate you, and pray for them which despitefully use you, and persecute you;

45. That ye may be the children of your Father which is in heaven: for he maketh his sun to rise on the evil and on the good, and sendeth rain on the just and on the unjust.

46. For if ye love them which love you, what reward have ye? do not even the publicans the same?

47. And if ye salute your brethren only, what do ye more than others? do not even the publicans so?

48. Be ye therefore perfect, even as your Father which is in heaven is perfect.

Matthew

Chapter 10

11. And into whatsoever city or town ye shall enter, inquire who in it is worthy; and there abide till ye go thence.

12. And when ye come into an house, salute it.

13. And if the house be worthy, let your peace come upon it: but if it be not worthy, let your peace return to you.

14. And whosoever shall not receive you, nor hear your words, when ye depart out of that house or city, shake off the dust of your feet.

Romans

Chapter 12

19. Dearly beloved, **avenge not yourselves**, but rather give place unto wrath: for it is written, Vengeance is mine; I will repay, saith the Lord.
20. Therefore if thine enemy hunger, feed him; if he thirst, give him drink: for in so doing thou shalt heap coals of fire on his head.
21. Be not overcome of evil, but overcome evil with good.

Titus

Chapter 3

1. Put them in mind to be subject to principalities and powers, to obey magistrates, to be ready to every good work,
2. To speak evil of no man, to be no brawlers, but gentle, shewing all meekness unto all men.
3. For we ourselves also were sometimes foolish, disobedient, deceived, serving divers lusts and pleasures, living in malice and envy, hateful, and hating one another.
4. But after that the kindness and love of God our Saviour toward man appeared,
5. Not by works of righteousness which we have done, but according to his mercy he saved us, by the washing of regeneration, and renewing of the Holy Ghost;
6. Which he shed on us abundantly through Jesus Christ our Saviour;
7. That being justified by his grace, we should be made heirs according to the hope of eternal life.
8. This is a faithful saying, and these things I will that thou affirm constantly, that they which have believed in God might be careful to maintain good works. These things are good and profitable unto men.
9. But avoid foolish questions, and genealogies, and contentions, and strivings about the law; for they are unprofitable and vain.
10. A man that is an heretick after the first and second admonition reject;
11. Knowing that he that is such is subverted, and sinneth, being condemned of himself.

COMMENTARY

In the Qur'an:

1. The commandment to make war with unbelievers is not only written in the present tense, but also in the future tense. Mohammed declared it not only to provoke an immediate battle with the people of Mecca, but also for a future "relationship" with other unbelievers.

2. The only possible attitude toward unbelievers is to be *"...strong against Unbelievers..."* and if they resist the message of Allah through Mohammed, Muslims have to make war to fulfill their obligation toward Allah, until *"... there is no more persecution and religion should be only for Allah;"*. If the unbelievers will submit to the authority of the Muslims, they will not be killed, but *"...they pay the tax in acknowledgment of superiority and they are in a state of subjection."*

In the Bible:

1. In the Bible we see the opposite commandment from God: *"...If your enemy is hungry, give him bread to eat; and if he is thirsty, give him water to drink..."*, *"...Love your enemies and pray for those who persecute you..."*

2. According to the Bible, believers should offer the message of salvation to unbelievers, and if they will not listen *"...shake off the dust from your feet as you leave that house or town."*

There is no command anywhere in the Bible to kill those who do not want to believe; rather, there is the commandment to leave them alone: *"...after admonishing him once or twice, have nothing more to do with him..."*. It is clear that it is God's responsibility to judge people, not the responsibility of believers.

CONCLUSION

We can see a great difference between the biblical and the qur'anical approach to the issue of converting unbelievers.

The history of the first 300 years of Christianity reveals a peaceful, victorious sweep throughout the Roman Empire, while Islam waged wars with all of its neighbors. Islam was able to expand because of their usage of the method called "sword and fire".

During the first 100 years of the growth of Islam since the death of Mohammed in 632 AD, Muslim armies conquered Christian countries such as Syria (634 AD), Israel (637 AD), Lebanon, Egypt (638 AD), Libya (689 AD), Spain and Portugal (711 AD), and Zoroaster's Persia (640 AD). By 732 AD, Arabic armies under the command of Abd-er-Rahman, Governor of Spain, were stopped by the Christian army under the command of Charles Martel (near the city of Tours in modern France).

The successors to the Arabs in the 11th century were the Turks, who started a long offence against the Eastern Byzantine Empire and never rested until Constantinople fell into their hands in 1453 AD. It opened the door to further Islamic expansion in Europe. This resulted in an occupation in part or in full of such countries as present-day Bulgaria, Greece, Austria, Yugoslavia, Romania, Hungary, Ukraine and Russia.

Only after the destruction of the Turkish armies near Vienna in 1683 AD by Jan III Sobieski, did they lose their power to threaten Europe and the zone of Islamic influence began diminishing. Meanwhile, Russia commenced her period of wars with the Ottoman Empire and it's vassals in 1676 AD and continued until 1918. During this lengthy period of 241 years, Russia and Turkey had eleven wars between themselves. In 1878, Russian General Skobelev captured the city of San-Stefano near Istanbul. As a result, the Ottoman Empire recognized the independence of Romania, Serbia and Montenegro and the autonomy of Bulgaria.

At this same time, Islam expanded towards Africa and the Far East and has acquired many countries which today are ruled by Islamic governments in accordance with Shariah law.

After a short break of thirty years from 1918-1948, Islam began its offensive against the newly-born state of Israel which continues until now and, according to the Bible, will continue until the Second Coming of Christ.

Many Imams in mosques today remind their fellow Muslims that **now is the time** to restore the former glory of the 8th century Muslim Caliphate, not only in Middle East but also in the Western World. The Islamic factor has been active for 1,372 years and has caught a fresh start in 2001!

It will have no end until Muslims will fulfill the Qur'anical call to fight until *"...religion should be only for Allah..."*

Chapter Two

JINN

THE QUR'AN

"Jinn and Men Destined for Hell"

Sura 7

The Elevated Places

178. Whomsoever Allah guides, he is the one who follows the right way; and whomsoever He causes to err, these are the losers.
179. And certainly, We have created for hell many of the jinn and the men; they have hearts, with which they do not understand, and they have eyes, with which they do not see, and they have ears with which they do not hear; they are as cattle, nay, they are in worse errors; these are the heedless ones.

Sura 10

Jonah

99. And if your Lord had pleased, surely all those who are in the earth would have believed, all of them; will you then force men till they become believers?
100. And it is not for a soul to believe except by Allah's permission; and He casts uncleanness on those who will not understand.

Sura 16

The Bee

95. If Allah so willed, He could make you all one people: But He leaves straying whom He pleases, and He guides whom He pleases: but ye shall certainly be called to account for all your actions.

Sura 32

The Adoration

13. If We had so willed, *We could certainly have brought every soul its true guidance:* **but the Word from Me will come true,** *"I will fill Hell with Jinns and men all together."*

THE BIBLE

"Jinn and Men Destined for Hell"

First Timothy

Chapter 2

1. I exhort therefore, that, first of all, supplications, prayers, intercessions, and giving of thanks, be made for all men;

2. For kings, and for all that are in authority; that we may lead a quiet and peaceable life in all godliness and honesty.

3. For this is good and acceptable in the sight **of God our Saviour;**

4. **Who will have** *all men* **to be saved, and to come unto the knowledge of the truth.**

5. For there is one God, and one mediator between God and men, the man Christ Jesus;

6. Who gave himself a ransom for all, to be testified in due time..

Romans

Chapter 10

12. For there is no difference between the Jew and the Greek: for the **same Lord over all is rich unto all that call upon him.**

13. For **whosoever shall call upon the name of the Lord shall be saved.**

John

Chapter 3

16. For **God so loved the world,** that he gave his only begotten Son, that **whosoever believeth in him should not perish, but have everlasting life.**

Second Peter

Chapter 3

9. The Lord is not slack concerning his promise, as some men count slackness; but is longsuffering to us-ward, **not willing that *any should perish*, but that all should come to repentance**.

COMMENTARY

In the Qur'an:

1. God created people not only for serving Him, but to live in hell: *"...I will fill Hell with Jinns and men all together..."*

In the Bible:

1. God wishes to bring ALL men unto salvation and hell was created for fallen angels only:

Matthew, Chapter 25:

31. When the Son of man shall come in his glory, and all the holy angels with him, then shall he sit upon the throne of his glory:

*41. Then shall he say also unto them on the left hand, Depart from me, ye cursed, into **everlasting fire, prepared for the devil and his angels:***

Chapter Three

MECCA

THE QUR'AN

"Mecca as the Place of Worship"

Sura 2

The Cow

124. And when his Lord tried Ibrahim with certain words, he fulfilled them. He said: Surely I will make you an Imam of men. Ibrahim said: **And of my offspring? My covenant does not include the unjust, said He.**

125. And when We made the House a pilgrimage for men and a (place of) security, and: Appoint for yourselves a place of prayer on the standing-place of Ibrahim. And We enjoined Ibrahim and Ismail saying: Purify My House for those who visit (it) and those who abide (in it) for devotion and those who bow down (and) those who prostrate themselves.

126. And when Ibrahim said: My Lord, make it a secure town and provide its people with fruits, such of them as believe in Allah and the last day. He said: And whoever disbelieves, I will grant him enjoyment for a short while, then I will drive him to the chastisement of the fire; and it is an evil destination.

127. And when Ibrahim and Ismail raised the foundations of the House: Our Lord! accept from us; surely Thou art the Hearing, the Knowing:

128. Our Lord! and make us both submissive to Thee and (raise) from our offspring a nation submitting to Thee, and show us our ways of devotion and turn to us (mercifully), surely Thou art the Oft-returning (to mercy), the Merciful.

129. Our Lord! and raise up in them an Apostle from among them who shall recite to them Thy communications and teach them the Book and the wisdom, and purify them; surely Thou art the Mighty, the Wise.

130. And who forsakes the religion of Ibrahim but he who makes himself a fool, and most certainly We chose him in this world, and in the hereafter he is most surely among the righteous.

131. When his Lord said to him, Be a Muslim, he said: I submit myself to the Lord of the worlds.

132. And the same did Ibrahim enjoin on his sons and (so did) Yaqoub. O my sons! surely Allah has chosen for you (this) faith, therefore die not unless you are Muslims.

133. Nay! were you witnesses when death visited Yaqoub, when he said to his sons: What will you serve after me? They said: We will serve your God and the **God of your fathers, Ibrahim and Ismail and Ishaq,** one God only, and to Him do we submit.

134. This is a people that have passed away; they shall have what they earned and you shall have what you earn, and you shall not be called upon to answer for what they did.

135. And they say: **Be Jews or Christians, you will be on the right course. Say: Nay! (we follow) the religion of Ibrahim, the Hanif, and he was not one of the polytheists.**

139. Say: Do you dispute with us about Allah, and He is our Lord and your Lord, and we shall have our deeds and you shall have your deeds, and we are sincere to Him.

140. Nay! do you say that Ibrahim and Ismail and Yaqoub and the tribes were Jews or Christians? Say: Are you better knowing or Allah? And who is more unjust than he who conceals a testimony that he has from Allah? And Allah is not at all heedless of what you do.

Sura 3

The Family of Imran

96. Most surely the first house appointed for men is the one at Bekka, blessed and a guidance for the nations.

97. In it are clear signs, the standing place of Ibrahim, and whoever enters it shall be secure, **and pilgrimage to the House is incumbent upon men for the sake of Allah,** (upon) every one who is able to undertake the journey to it; and whoever disbelieves, then surely Allah is Self-sufficient, above any need of the worlds.

Sura 14

Abraham

35. And when Ibrahim said: My Lord! make this city secure, and save me and my sons from worshipping idols:

36. My Lord! surely they have led many men astray; then whoever follows me, he is surely of me, and whoever disobeys me, Thou surely are Forgiving, Merciful:

37. O our Lord! surely I have settled a part of my offspring in a valley unproductive of fruit near Thy Sacred House, our Lord! that they may keep up prayer; therefore make the hearts of some people yearn towards them and provide them with fruits; haply they may be grateful:

38. O our Lord! Surely Thou knowest what we hide and what we make public, and nothing in the earth nor any thing in heaven is hidden from Allah:

39. Praise be to Allah, Who has given me in old age Ismail and Ishaq; most surely my Lord is the Hearer of prayer:

40. My Lord! make me keep up prayer and from my offspring (too), O our Lord, and accept my prayer:

Sura 22

The Pilgrimage

25. Surely (as for) those who disbelieve, and hinder (men) from Allah's way and from the Sacred Mosque which We have made equally for all men, (for) the dweller therein and (for) the visitor, and whoever shall incline therein to wrong unjustly, We will make him taste of a painful chastisement.

26. And when We assigned to Ibrahim the place of the House, saying: Do not associate with Me aught, and purify My House for those who make the circuit and stand to pray and bow and prostrate themselves.

27. And proclaim among men the Pilgrimage: they will come to you on foot and on every lean camel, coming from every remote path,

28. That they may witness advantages for them and mention the name of Allah during stated days over what He has given them of the cattle quadrupeds, then eat of them and feed the distressed one, the needy.

29. Then let them accomplish their needful acts of shaving and cleansing, and let them fulfill their vows and let them go round the Ancient House.

THE BIBLE

"Mecca as the Place of Worship"

Genesis

Chapter 15

13. And he said unto Abram, Know of a surety that **thy seed shall be a stranger in a land that is not theirs, and shall serve them; and they shall afflict them four hundred years;**

14. And also that nation, whom they shall serve, will I judge: and afterward shall they come out with great substance.

15. And thou shalt go to thy fathers in peace; thou shalt be buried in a good old age.

16. But in the fourth generation they shall come hither again: for the iniquity of the Amorites is not yet full.

17. And it came to pass, that, when the sun went down, and it was dark, behold a smoking furnace, and a burning lamp that passed between those pieces.

18. In the same day the LORD made a covenant with Abram, saying, Unto thy seed have I given this land, from the river of Egypt unto the great river, the river Euphrates:

Genesis

Chapter 16

1. Now Sarai Abram's wife bare him no children: and she had an handmaid, an Egyptian, whose name was Hagar.

2. And Sarai said unto Abram, Behold now, the LORD hath restrained me from bearing: I pray thee, go in unto my maid; it may be that I may obtain children by her. And Abram hearkened to the voice of Sarai.

3. And Sarai Abram's wife took Hagar her maid the Egyptian, after Abram had dwelt ten years in the land of Canaan, and gave her to her husband Abram to be his wife.

4. And he went in unto Hagar, and she conceived: and when she saw that she had conceived, her mistress was despised in her eyes.

5. And Sarai said unto Abram, My wrong be upon thee: I have given my maid into thy bosom; and when she saw that she had conceived, I was despised in her eyes: the LORD judge between me and thee.

6. But Abram said unto Sarai, Behold, thy maid is in thy hand; do to her as it pleaseth thee. And when Sarai dealt hardly with her, she fled from her face.

7. And the angel of the LORD found her by a fountain of water in the wilderness, by the fountain in the way to Shur.

8. And he said, Hagar, Sarai's maid, whence camest thou? and whither wilt thou go? And she said, I flee from the face of my mistress Sarai.

9. And the angel of the LORD said unto her, Return to thy mistress, and submit thyself under her hands.

10. And the angel of the LORD said unto her, I will multiply thy seed exceedingly, that it shall not be numbered for multitude.

11. And the angel of the LORD said unto her, **Behold, thou art with child, and shalt bear a son, and shalt call his name Ishmael; because the LORD hath heard thy affliction.**

12. *And he will be a wild man; his hand will be against every man, and every man's hand against him; and he shall dwell in the presence of all his brethren.*

13. And she called the name of the LORD that spake unto her, Thou God seest me: for she said, Have I also here looked after him that seeth me?

14. Wherefore the well was called Beer-lahai-roi; behold, it is between Kadesh and Bered.

15. And Hagar bare Abram a son: and **Abram called his son's name, which Hagar bare, Ishmael.**

16. And Abram was fourscore and six years old, when Hagar bare Ishmael to Abram.

Genesis

Chapter 17

1. And when Abram was ninety years old and nine, the LORD appeared to Abram, and said unto him, I am the Almighty God; walk before me, and be thou perfect.

2. And I will make my covenant between me and thee, and will multiply thee exceedingly.

3. And Abram fell on his face: and God talked with him, saying,

4. As for me, behold, my covenant is with thee, and thou shalt be a father of many nations.

5. Neither shall thy name any more be called Abram, but thy name shall be Abraham; for a father of many nations have I made thee.

6. And I will make thee exceeding fruitful, and I will make nations of thee, and kings shall come out of thee.

7. And I will establish my covenant between me and thee and thy seed after thee in their generations for an everlasting covenant, to be a God unto thee, and to thy seed after thee.

8. And I will give unto thee, and to thy seed after thee, the land wherein thou art a stranger, all the land of Canaan, for an everlasting possession; and I will be their God.

9. And God said unto Abraham, Thou shalt keep my covenant therefore, thou, and thy seed after thee in their generations.

10. This is my covenant, which ye shall keep, between me and you and thy seed after thee; Every man child among you shall be circumcised.

11. And ye shall circumcise the flesh of your foreskin; and it shall be a token of the covenant betwixt me and you.

12. And he that is eight days old shall be circumcised among you, every man child in your generations, he that is born in the house, or bought with money of any stranger, which is not of thy seed.

13. He that is born in thy house, and he that is bought with thy money, must needs be circumcised: and my covenant shall be in your flesh for an everlasting covenant.

14. And the uncircumcised man child whose flesh of his foreskin is not circumcised, that soul shall be cut off from his people; he hath broken my covenant.

15. And God said unto Abraham, As for Sarai thy wife, thou shalt not call her name Sarai, but Sarah shall her name be.

16. And I will bless her, and give thee a son also of her: yea, I will bless her, and she shall be a mother of nations; kings of people shall be of her.

17. Then Abraham fell upon his face, and laughed, and said in his heart, Shall a child be born unto him that is an hundred years old? and shall Sarah, that is ninety years old, bear?

18. And Abraham said unto God, O that Ishmael might live before thee!

19. And God said, **Sarah thy wife shall bear thee a son indeed; and thou shalt call his name Isaac: and I will establish my covenant with him for an everlasting covenant, and with his seed after him.**

20. And as for Ishmael, I have heard thee: Behold, I have blessed him, and will make him fruitful, and will multiply him exceedingly; twelve princes shall he beget, and I will make him a great nation. 21. *But my covenant will I establish with Isaac, which Sarah shall bear unto thee* at this set time in the next year.

22. And he left off talking with him, and God went up from Abraham.

Genesis

Chapter 21

1. And the LORD visited Sarah as he had said, and the LORD did unto Sarah as he had spoken.

2. For Sarah conceived, and bare Abraham a son in his old age, at the set time of which God had spoken to him.

3. And Abraham called the name of his son that was born unto him, whom Sarah bare to him, Isaac.

4. And Abraham circumcised his son Isaac being eight days old, as God had commanded him.

5. And Abraham was an hundred years old, when his son Isaac was born unto him.

9. And Sarah saw the son of Hagar the Egyptian, which she had born unto Abraham, mocking.

10. Wherefore she said unto Abraham, **Cast out this bondwoman and her son: for the son of this bondwoman shall not be heir with my son, even with Isaac.**

11. And the thing was very grievous in Abraham's sight because of his son.

12. And God said unto Abraham, Let it not be grievous in thy sight because of the lad, and because of thy bondwoman; in all that Sarah hath said unto thee, hearken unto her voice; **for in Isaac shall thy seed be called.**

13. And also of the son of the bondwoman will I make a nation, because he is thy seed.

14. And Abraham rose up early in the morning, and took bread, and a bottle of water, and gave it unto Hagar, putting it on her shoulder, and the child, **and sent her away: and she departed, and wandered in the wilderness of Beer-sheba.**

Genesis

Chapter 12

1. Now the LORD had said unto Abram, Get thee out of thy country, and from thy kindred, and from thy father's house, unto a land that I will shew thee:

2. And I will make of thee a great nation, and I will bless thee, and make thy name great; and thou shalt be a blessing:

3. And I will bless them that bless thee, and curse him that curseth thee: and in thee shall all families of the earth be blessed.

Genesis

Chapter 13

18. Then Abram removed his tent, and came and dwelt in the plain of Mamre, which is in Hebron, **and built there an altar** unto the LORD.

Genesis

Chapter 26

25. And he builded an altar there, and called upon the name of the LORD and **pitched his tent there:** and there Isaac's servants digged a well.

Genesis

Chapter 33

19. And he bought a parcel of a field, where he had spread his tent, at the hand of the children of Hamor, Shechem's father, for an hundred pieces of money.

20. And he erected there an altar, and called it El-elohe- Israel.

Exodus

Chapter 25

22. And there I will meet with thee, and **I will commune with thee from above the mercy seat, from between the two cherubims which are upon the ark of the testimony, of all things which I will give thee in commandment unto the children of Israel.**

COMMENTARY

In the Qur'an:

1. There is a covenant between Ibrahim and Allah, but not with Ibrahim's offspring (thereby excluding Ishmael): *"Ibrahim said: And of my offspring? My covenant does not include the unjust, said He."*

2. This covenant included building a house to worship Allah (in Mecca) by Ibrahim and Ishmael*: "and when Ibrahim and Ismail raised the foundations of the House."… "And proclaim the Pilgrimage among men…"… "Most surely the first house appointed for men is the one at Bekka, blessed and guidance for the nations."*

In the Bible:

1. God made the covenant with Abraham and **his seed** and promised to give to Abraham's seed the Promised Land with specific borders *"… from the river of Egypt unto the great river, the river Euphrates:"*. God was clearly speaking about the nation of people we now know as the Israelites, the descendants of Isaac: *"And God said, Sarah thy wife shall bear thee a son indeed; and thou shalt call his name Isaac: and I will establish my covenant with him for an everlasting covenant, and with his seed after him.", "But my covenant will I establish with Isaac, which Sarah shall bear unto thee at this set time in the next year", "for in Isaac shall thy seed be called". " And also that nation, whom they shall serve, will I judge: and afterward shall they come out with great substance."*. This covenant was unconditional, and included not only Jews, but also people…**of many nations**… who will worship God, for God's intention is to save ALL, and to bring ALL people into His presence, through His Messiah, Jesus, as He commanded:

Matthew, Chapter 28:18-20

18. And Jesus came and spake unto them, saying, All power is given unto me in heaven and in earth. 19. Go ye therefore, and teach all nations, baptizing them in the name of the Father, and of the Son, and of the Holy Ghost: 20. Teaching them to observe all things whatsoever I have commanded you: and, lo, I am with you alway, even unto the end of the world. Amen.

For almost 1500 years from Abraham to Jesus, this covenant included ONLY Jews. Ishmael and his descendants were not included, nor was Esau, the firstborn of Isaac, although Esau became Ishmael's son in-law when he took *"...Ma'halath the daughter of Ish'mael Abraham's son..."* (**Genesis Chapter 28:9**). He was not included in the seed of Promise! That is why in many places in the Bible God called Himself **"The God of Abraham, the God of Isaac, and the God of Jacob".** Soon after Isaac was born, God told Abraham to cast out Hagar with Ishmael. Ishmael was young at that time, being referred to as **"...the child..."**

2. The Bible gives us the location of Abraham's dwelling from birth to the exile of Ishmael. Chapter 18 mentions that Abraham was living in Mamre, near Hebron. From there he could witness the destruction of Sodom and Gomorrah. Chapter 20 tells us that Abraham was dwelling: *"... between Kadesh and Shur, and sojourned in Gerar..."* After the exile of Ishmael, he and his mother Hagar *"... dwelt in the wilderness of Paran: and his mother took him a wife out of the land of Egypt...".* The wilderness of Paran is located south of **Kadesh,** almost in the heart of the Sinai Peninsula. Mecca (that is, the location of the Kaaba) is hundreds of miles south of the location where Abraham had dwelled. The Bible does not support the Qur'an's claim about building a " House of Allah" by Abraham and Ishmael, for since the birth of Isaac, Abraham never saw Ishmael again; that is, since Ishmael was a young boy: *"...Arise, lift up the lad, and hold him in thine hand; for I will make him a great nation..."* The Bible also tells us that Abraham built altars for the Lord, not houses. If he had really built the Kaaba, he should also have built an altar nearby, yet the Qur'an makes no mention

271

of this. According to Sura 2:135,140 Abraham was not a **Jew**, but according to the Bible, he was the first man on earth to be called a **Hebrew**.

Genesis, Chapter 14:

10. And the vale of Siddim was full of slimepits; and the kings of Sodom and Gomorrah fled, and fell there; and they that remained fled to the mountain.

11. And they took all the goods of Sodom and Gomorrah, and all their victuals, and went their way.

12. And they took Lot, Abram's brother's son, who dwelt in Sodom, and his goods, and departed.

13. And there came one that had escaped, and told **Abram the Hebrew**; *for he dwelt in the plain of Mamre the Amorite, brother of Eschol, and brother of Aner: and these were confederate with Abram.*

The Qur'an claims that the *"...first house appointed for men is the one at Bekka..."* and *"pilgrimage to the House is incumbent upon men for the sake of Allah..."*. If Abraham had actually built this house and had dedicated it to God, and if this house had such significance for God, he should have mentioned it to Isaac as he did about the covenant with the Lord and about the Promised Land. Instead, God commanded Moses to build a Tabernacle (mobile Temple) with altars for sacrifices because the priest was not allowed to approach the presence of God (inside the Holy of Holies) without sacrificial blood.

Exodus, Chapter 25:22

And there I will meet with thee, and I will commune with thee from above the mercy seat, from between the two cherubims which are upon the ark of the testimony, of all things which I will give thee in commandment unto the children of Israel."

We note that God had chosen the city of Jerusalem for the site of His Holy dwelling-place, and not another city such as Mecca:

2 Chronicles, Chapter 33:4

... the LORD had said, In Jerusalem shall my name be for ever.

Psalms, Chapter 135:21

Blessed be the LORD out of Zion, which dwelleth at Jerusalem. Praise ye the LORD.

Isaiah, Chapter 2:3

And many people shall go and say, Come ye, and let Us go up to the mountain of the LORD, to the house of the God of Jacob; and he will teach us of his ways, and we will walk in his paths: for out of Zion shall go forth the law, and the word of the LORD from Jerusalem.

Chapter Four

OATH

THE QUR'AN

"Oath to God"

Sura 16

The Bee

91. And fulfill the covenant of Allah when you have made a covenant, and do not break the oaths after making them fast, and you have indeed made Allah a surety for you; surely Allah knows what you do.

94. And do not make your oaths a means of deceit between you, lest a foot should slip after its stability and you should taste evil because you turned away from Allah's way and grievous punishment be your (lot).

95. And do not take a small price in exchange for Allah's covenant; surely what is with Allah is better for you, did you but know.

THE BIBLE

"Oath to God"

Judges

Chapter 11

1. Now Jephthah the Gileadite was a mighty man of valour, and he was the son of an harlot: and Gilead begat Jephthah.

2. And Gilead's wife bare him sons; and his wife's sons grew up, and they thrust out Jephthah, and said unto him, Thou shalt not inherit in our father's house; for thou art the son of a strange woman.

3. Then Jephthah fled from his brethren, and dwelt in the land of Tob: and there were gathered vain men to Jephthah, and went out with him.

4. And it came to pass in process of time, that the children of Ammon made war against Israel.

5. And it was so, that when the children of Ammon made war against Israel, the elders of Gilead went to fetch Jephthah out of the land of Tob:

6. And they said unto Jephthah, Come, and be our captain, that we may fight with the children of Ammon.

29. Then the Spirit of the LORD came upon Jephthah, and he passed over Gilead, and Manasseh, and passed over Mizpeh of Gilead, and from Mizpeh of Gilead he passed over unto the children of Ammon.

30. And Jephthah vowed a vow unto the LORD, and said, If thou shalt without fail deliver the children of Ammon into mine hands,

31. Then it shall be, **that whatsoever cometh forth of the doors of my house to meet me**, when I return in peace from the children of Ammon, shall surely be the LORD's, and **I will offer it up for a burnt offering**.

32. So Jephthah passed over unto the children of Ammon to fight against them; and the LORD delivered them into his hands.

33. And he smote them from Aroer, even till thou come to Minnith, even twenty cities, and unto the plain of the vineyards, with a very great slaughter. Thus the children of Ammon were subdued before the children of Israel.

34. And Jephthah came to Mizpeh unto his house, and, behold, his daughter came out to meet him with timbrels and with dances: and she was his only child; beside her he had neither son nor daughter.

35. And it came to pass, when he saw her, that he rent his clothes, and said, Alas, my daughter! thou hast brought me very low, and thou art one of them that trouble me: for I have opened my mouth unto the LORD, and I cannot go back.

36. And she said unto him, My father, if thou hast opened thy mouth unto the LORD, do to me according to that which hath proceeded out of thy mouth; forasmuch as the LORD hath taken vengeance for thee of thine enemies, even of the children of Ammon.

37. And she said unto her father, Let this thing be done for me: let me alone two months, that I may go up and down upon the mountains, and bewail my virginity, I and my fellows.

38. And he said, Go. And he sent her away for two months: and she went with her companions, and bewailed her virginity upon the mountains.

39. And it came to pass at the end of two months, that she returned unto her father, who did with her according to his vow which he had vowed: and she knew no man. And it was a custom in Israel,

40. That the daughters of Israel went yearly to lament the daughter of Jephthah the Gileadite four days in a year.

Matthew

Chapter 5

33. Again, ye have heard that it hath been said by them of old time, Thou shalt not forswear thyself, but **shalt perform unto the Lord thine oaths:**
34. But I say unto you, **Swear not at all; neither by heaven; for it is God's throne:**
35. Nor by the earth; for it is his footstool: neither by Jerusalem; for it is the city of the great King.
36. Neither shalt thou swear by thy head, because thou canst not make one hair white or black.
37. But let your communication be, Yea, yea; Nay, nay: for whatsoever is more than these cometh of evil.

COMMENTARY

Jesus simply referred to the state of men; namely, that we may think that we will do what we promise, but we do not control the future and should not presume upon it. Moreover, we have no power to keep our promise when something happens apart from our plans.

Chapter Five

PARADISE

THE QUR'AN

"The Destiny of Believers in Paradise"

Sura 2

The Cow

25. And convey good news to those who believe and do good deeds, that they shall have gardens in which rivers flow; whenever they shall be given a portion of the fruit thereof, they shall say: This is what was given to us before; and they shall be given the like of it, and **they shall have pure mates in them,** and in them, they shall abide.

Sura 9

The Immunity

72. Allah has promised to the believing men and the believing women gardens, beneath which rivers flow, to abide in them, and goodly dwellings in gardens of perpetual abode; and best of all is Allah's goodly pleasure; that is the grand achievement.

Sura 13

The Thunder

22. And those who are constant, seeking the pleasure of their Lord, and keep up prayer and spend (benevolently) out of what We have given them secretly and openly and repel evil with good; as for those, they shall have the (happy) issue of the abode

23. The gardens of perpetual abode which they will enter along with those who do good from among their parents and their spouses and their offspring; and the angels will enter in upon them from every gate:

Sura 16

The Bee

31. The gardens of perpetuity, they shall enter them, rivers flowing beneath them; **they shall have in them what they please.** Thus does Allah reward those who guard (against evil).

Sura 18

The Cave

30. Surely (as for) those who believe and do good, We do not waste the reward of him who does a good work.

31. These it is for whom are gardens of perpetuity beneath which rivers flow, ornaments shall be given to them therein of bracelets of gold, and they shall wear **green robes** of fine silk and thick silk brocade interwoven with gold, **reclining therein on raised couches; excellent the recompense and goodly the resting place.**

Sura 22

The Pilgrimage

23. Surely Allah will make those who believe and do good deeds enter gardens beneath which rivers flow; they shall be adorned therein **with bracelets of gold and (with) pearls, and their garments therein shall be of silk.**

Sura 25

The Distinction

16. They shall have therein **what they desire abiding (in it)**; it is a promise which it is proper to be prayed for from your Lord.

Sura 35

The Originator

33. Gardens of perpetuity, they shall enter therein; they shall be made to wear therein **bracelets of gold and pearls, and their dress therein shall be silk.**

Sura 36

Yasin

55. Surely the dwellers of the garden shall on that day be in an occupation quite happy.

56. They and their wives shall be in shades, reclining on raised couches.

57. They shall have fruits therein, **and they shall have whatever they desire.**

58. Peace: a word from a Merciful Lord.

Sura 37

The Rangers

40. Save the servants of Allah, the purified ones.

41. For them is a known sustenance,

42. Fruits, and they shall be highly honored,

43. In gardens of pleasure,

44. On thrones, facing each other.

45. A bowl shall be made to go round them from water running out of springs,

46. White, delicious to those who drink.

47. There shall be no trouble in it, nor shall they be exhausted therewith.

48. And with them shall be those who restrain the eyes, having beautiful eyes;

Sura 38

Suad

49. This is a reminder; and most surely there is an excellent resort for those who guard (against evil),

50. The gardens of perpetuity, the doors are opened for them.

51. Reclining therein, calling therein for many fruits and drink.

52. And with them shall be those restraining their eyes, equals in age.

53. This is what you are promised for the day of reckoning.

54. Most surely this is Our sustenance; it shall never come to an end;

Sura 43

Ornaments of Gold

69. Those who believed in Our communications and were submissive:
70. Enter the garden, **you and your wives**; you shall be made happy.
71. There shall be sent round to them golden bowls and drinking-cups **and therein shall be what their souls yearn after and (wherein) the eyes shall delight, and you shall abide therein.**
72. And this is the garden which you are given as an inheritance on account of what you did.
73. For you therein are many fruits of which you shall eat.

Sura 44

The Smoke

51. Surely those who guard (against evil) are in a secure place,
52. In gardens and springs;
53. They shall wear of fine and thick silk, **(sitting)** *face to face;*
54. Thus (shall it be), and **We will wed them with Houris pure, beautiful ones.**
55. They shall call therein for every fruit in security;

Sura 47

Muhammad

15. A parable of the garden which those guarding (against evil) are promised: **Therein are rivers of water that does not alter, and rivers of milk the taste whereof does not change, and rivers of drink delicious to those who drink, and rivers of honey clarified and for them therein are all fruits and protection from their Lord.** (Are these) like those who abide in the fire and who are made to drink boiling water so it rends their bowels asunder.

Sura 55

The Beneficent

54. Reclining on beds, the inner coverings of which are of silk brocade; and the fruits of the two gardens shall be within reach.

55. Which then of the bounties of your Lord will you deny?

56. In them shall be those who restrained their eyes; before them neither man nor jinn shall have touched them.

57. Which then of the bounties of your Lord will you deny?

58. As though they were rubies and pearls.

59. Which then of the bounties of your Lord will you deny?

60. Is the reward of goodness aught but goodness?

61. Which then of the bounties of your Lord will you deny?

62. And besides these two are two (other) gardens:

63. Which then of the bounties of your Lord will you deny?

64. Both inclining to blackness.

65. Which then of the bounties of your Lord will you deny?

66. In both of them are two springs gushing forth.

67. Which then of the bounties of your Lord will you deny?

68. In both are fruits and palms and pomegranates.

69. Which then of the bounties of your Lord will you deny?

70. In them are goodly things, beautiful ones.

71. Which then of the bounties of your Lord will you deny?

72. Pure ones confined to the pavilions.

73. Which then of the bounties of your Lord will you deny?

74. Man has not touched them before them nor jinn.

75. Which then of the bounties of your Lord will you deny?

76. Reclining on green cushions and beautiful carpets.

Sura 56

The Event

11. These are they who are drawn nigh (to Allah),

12. In the gardens of bliss.

13. A numerous company from among the first,

14. And a few from among the latter.

15. On thrones decorated,

16. Reclining on them, facing one another.

17. Round about them shall go youths never altering in age,

18. With goblets and ewers and a cup of pure drink;

19. They shall not be affected with headache thereby, nor shall they get exhausted,

20. And fruits such as they choose,

21. And the flesh of fowl such as they desire.

22. And pure, beautiful ones,

23. The like of the hidden pearls:

24. A reward for what they used to do.

25. They shall not hear therein vain or sinful discourse,

26. Except the word peace, peace.

27. And the companions of the right hand; how happy are the companions of the right hand!

28. Amid thornless lote-trees,

29. And banana-trees (with fruits), one above another.

30. And extended shade,

31. And water flowing constantly,

32. And abundant fruit,

33. Neither intercepted nor forbidden,

34. And exalted thrones.

35. Surely We have made them to grow into a (new) growth,

36. Then We have made them virgins,

37. Loving, equals in age,

38. For the sake of the companions of the right hand.

39. A numerous company from among the first…

THE BIBLE

"The Destiny of Believers in Paradise"

Job

Chapter 19

25. For I know that my redeemer liveth, and that he shall stand at the latter day upon the earth:

26. And though **after my skin worms destroy this body, yet in my flesh shall I see God:**

27. Whom I shall see for myself, and mine eyes shall behold, and not another; though my reins be consumed within me.

Matthew

Chapter 22

23. The same day came to him the Sadducees, which say that there is no resurrection, and asked him,

24. Saying, Master, Moses said, If a man die, having no children, his brother shall marry his wife, and raise up seed unto his brother.

25. Now there were with us seven brethren: and the first, when he had married a wife, deceased, and, having no issue, left his wife unto his brother:

26. Likewise the second also, and the third, unto the seventh.

27. And last of all the woman died also.

28. Therefore in the resurrection whose wife shall she be of the seven? for they all had her.

29. Jesus answered and said unto them, Ye do err, not knowing the scriptures, nor the power of God.

30. For in the resurrection they neither marry, nor are given in marriage, but are as the angels of God in heaven.

Revelation

Chapter 6

9. And when he had opened the fifth seal, **I saw under the altar the souls of them that were slain for the word of God, and for the testimony which they held:**

10. And they cried with a loud voice, saying, How long, O Lord, holy and true, dost thou not judge and avenge our blood on them that dwell on the earth?

11. And white robes were given unto every one of them; and it was said unto them, that they should rest yet for a little season, until their fellow servants also and their brethren, that should be killed as they were, should be fulfilled.

Revelation

Chapter 7

9. After this I beheld, and, lo, a great multitude, which no man could number, of all nations, and kindreds, and people, and tongues, **stood before the throne, and before the Lamb, clothed with white robes**, and palms in their hands;

10. And cried with a loud voice, saying, Salvation to our God which sitteth upon the throne, and unto the Lamb.

11. And all the angels stood round about the throne, and about the elders and the four beasts, and fell before the throne on their faces, and **worshipped God,**

12. Saying, Amen: Blessing, and glory, and wisdom, and thanksgiving, and honour, and power, and might, be unto our God for ever and ever. Amen.

13. And one of the elders answered, saying unto me, What are these which are arrayed in **white robes**? and whence came they?

14. And I said unto him, Sir, thou knowest. And he said to me, **These are they which came out of great tribulation, and have washed their robes, and made them white in the blood of the Lamb.**

15. Therefore are they before the throne of God, and serve him day and night in his temple: and he that sitteth on the throne shall dwell among them.

16. They shall hunger no more, neither thirst any more; neither shall the sun light on them, nor any heat.

17. For the Lamb which is in the midst of the throne shall feed them, and shall lead them unto living fountains of waters: and God shall wipe away all tears from their eyes.

COMMENTARY

In the Qur'an:

Paradise involves:

1. Relaxation on cushions, facing each other.
2. Satisfaction of EVERY WISH (such as food and drink).
3. Satisfaction of sexual needs, using mostly virgins whom they did not touch before.
4. Wearing green garments and golden jewellery.

In the Bible:

1. Believers stand and worship God, actually beholding at His face, as only Adam did before the fall.
2. God promises satisfaction of EVERY NEED.
3. There are no sexual activities in the presence of God.
4. Believers wear white garments which have been washed in the Blood of Jesus. There are no other jewelled accessories except for golden crowns which will be thrown at the feet of Jesus.

CONCLUSION:

According to the Qur'an, the rewards for Muslims are the enjoyment of pleasures and lusts of earthly life (eating, rest, sex).

According to the Bible, the reward of believers is to see God and to be in His presence!

Chapter Six

PARABLES

The Qur'an

"Parables"

Sura 2

The Cow

15. Allah shall pay them back their mockery, and He leaves them alone in their inordinacy, blindly wandering on.

16. These are they who buy error for the right direction, so their bargain shall bring no gain, nor are they the followers of the right direction.

17. Their parable is like the parable of one who kindled a fire but when it had illumined all around him, Allah took away their light, and left them in utter darkness-- they do not see.

18. Deaf, dumb (and) blind, so they will not turn back.

26. Surely Allah is not ashamed to set forth any parable-- (that of) a gnat or any thing above that; then as for those who believe, they know that it is the truth from their Lord, and as for those who disbelieve, they say: **What is it that Allah means by this parable: He causes many to err by it and many He leads aright by it!** but He does not cause to err by it (any) except the transgressors,

171. And the parable of those who disbelieve is as the parable of one who calls out to that which hears no more than a call and a cry; deaf, dumb (and) blind, so they do not understand.

172. O you who believe! eat of the good things that We have provided you with, and give thanks to Allah if Him it is that you serve.

173. He has only forbidden you what dies of itself, and blood, and flesh of swine, and that over which any other (name) than (that of) Allah has been invoked; but whoever is driven to necessity, not desiring, nor exceeding the limit, no sin shall be upon him; surely Allah is Forgiving, Merciful.

174. Surely those who conceal any part of the Book that Allah has revealed and take for it a small price, they eat nothing but fire into their bellies, and Allah will not speak to them on the day of resurrection, nor will He purify.

261. The parable of those who spend their property in the way of Allah is as the parable of a grain growing seven ears (with) a

hundred grains in every ear; and Allah multiplies for whom He pleases; and Allah is Ample-giving, Knowing

262. (As for) those who spend their property in the way of Allah, then do not follow up what they have spent with reproach or injury, they shall have their reward from their Lord, and they shall have no fear nor shall they grieve.

264. O you who believe! do not make your charity worthless by reproach and injury, like him who spends his property to be seen of men and does not believe in Allah and the last day; **so his parable is as the parable of a smooth rock with earth upon it, then a heavy rain falls upon it, so it leaves it bare; they shall not be able to gain anything of what they have earned;** and Allah does not guide the unbelieving people.

265. And the parable of those who spend their property to seek the pleasure of Allah and for the certainty 'of their souls is as **the parable of a garden on an elevated ground, upon which heavy rain falls so it brings forth its fruit twofold but if heavy rain does not fall upon it, then light rain (is sufficient);** and Allah sees what you do.

Sura 7

The Elevated Places

175. And recite to them the narrative of him to whom We give Our communications, but he withdraws himself from them, so the Shaitan overtakes him, so he is of those who go astray.

176. And if We had pleased, We would certainly have exalted him thereby; but he clung to the earth and followed his low desire, so **his parable is as the parable of the dog; if you attack him he lolls out his tongue; and if you leave him alone he lolls out his tongue; this is the parable of the people who reject Our communications;** therefore relate the narrative that they may reflect.

177. Evil is the likeness of the people who reject Our communications and are unjust to their own souls.

Sura 13

The Thunder

17. He sends down water from the cloud, then watercourses flow (with water) according to their measure, and the torrent bears along the swelling foam, and from what they melt in the fire for the sake of making ornaments or apparatus arises a scum like it; thus does Allah compare truth and falsehood; then as for the scum, it passes away as a worthless thing; and as for that which profits the people, it tarries in the earth; **thus does Allah set forth parables.**

18. For those who respond to their Lord is good; and (as for) those who do not respond to Him, had they all that is in the earth and the like thereof with it they would certainly offer it for a ransom. (As for) those, an evil reckoning shall be theirs and their abode is hell, and evil is the resting-place.

Sura 14

Abraham

18. The parable of those who disbelieve in their Lord: their actions are like ashes on which the wind blows hard on a stormy day; they shall not have power over any thing out of what they have earned; this is the great error.

19. Do you not see that Allah created the heavens and the earth with truth? If He please He will take you off and bring a new creation,

20. And this is not difficult for Allah.

24. Have you not considered how Allah sets forth a parable of a good word (being) like a good tree, whose root is firm and whose branches are in heaven,

25. Yielding its fruit in every season by the permission of its Lord? And Allah sets forth parables for men that they may be mindful.

26. And the **parable of an evil word** is as an evil tree pulled up from the earth's surface; **it has no stability**.

27. Allah confirms those who believe with the sure word in this world's life and in the hereafter, and Allah causes the unjust to go astray, and Allah does what He pleases.

Sura 16

The Bee

75. Allah sets forth a parable: (consider) a slave, the property of another, (who) has no power over anything, and one whom We have granted from Ourselves a goodly sustenance so he spends from it secretly and openly; are the two alike? (All) praise is due to Allah! Nay, most of them do not know.

76. And Allah sets forth a parable of two men; one of them is dumb, not able to do anything, and he is a burden to his master; wherever he sends him, he brings no good; can he be held equal with him who enjoins what is just, and he (himself) is on the right path?

77. And Allah's is the unseen of the heavens and the earth; and the matter of the hour is but as the twinkling of an eye or it is higher still; surely Allah has power over all things.

112. And Allah sets forth a parable: (Consider) a town safe and secure to which its means of subsistence come in abundance from every quarter; but it became ungrateful to Allah's favors, therefore Allah made it to taste the utmost degree of hunger and fear because of what they wrought.

113. And certainly there came to them an Apostle from among them, but they rejected him, so the punishment overtook them while they were unjust.

114. Therefore eat of what Allah has given you, lawful and good (things), and give thanks for Allah's favor if Him do you serve.

Sura 18

The Cave

32. And set forth to them a parable of two men; for one of them We made two gardens of grape vines, and We surrounded them both with palms, and in the midst of them We made cornfields.

33. . Both these gardens yielded their fruits, and failed not aught thereof, and We caused a river to gush forth in their midst,

34. And he possessed much wealth; so he said to his companion, while he disputed with him: I have greater wealth than you, and am mightier in followers.

35. And he entered his garden while he was unjust to himself. He said: I do not think that this will ever perish

36. And I do not think the hour will come, and even if I am returned to my Lord I will most certainly find a returning place better than this,

37. His companion said to him while disputing with him: Do you disbelieve in Him Who created you from dust, then from a small seed, then He made you a perfect man?

38. But as for me, He, Allah, is my Lord, and I do not associate anyone with my Lord.

39. And wherefore did you not say when you entered your garden: It is as Allah has pleased, there is no power save in Allah? If you consider me to be inferior to you in wealth and children,

40. Then maybe my Lord will give me what is better than your garden, and send on it a thunderbolt from heaven so that it shall become even ground without plant,

41. Or its waters should sink down into the ground so that you are unable to find it.

42. And his wealth was destroyed; so he began to wring his hands for what he had spent on it, while it lay, having fallen down upon its roofs, and he said: Ah me! would that I had not associated anyone with my Lord.

43. And he had no host to help him besides Allah nor could he defend himself.

44. Here is protection only Allah's, the True One; He is best in (the giving of) reward and best in requiting.

45. And set forth to them parable of the life of this world: like water which We send down from the cloud so the herbage of the earth becomes tangled on account of it, then it becomes dry broken into pieces which the winds scatter; and Allah is the holder of power over all things.

46. Wealth and children are an adornment of the life of this world; and the ever-abiding, the good works, are better with your Lord in reward and better in expectation.

Sura 22

The Pilgrimage

73. O people! a parable is set forth, therefore listen to it: surely those whom you call upon besides Allah cannot create fly, though they should all gather for it, and should the fly snatch away anything from them, they could not take it back. So weak are the invoker and the invoked.

74. They have not estimated Allah with the estimation that is due to Him; most surely Allah is Strong, Mighty.

75. Allah chooses messengers from among the angels and from among the men; surely Allah is Hearing, Seeing.

76. He knows what is before them and what is behind them and to Allah are all affairs turned back.

77. O you who believe! bow down and prostrate yourselves and serve your Lord, and do good that you may succeed.

Sura 24

The Light

35. Allah is the light of the heavens and the earth; a likeness of His light is as a niche in which is a lamp, the lamp is in a glass, (and) the glass is as it were a brightly shining star, lit from a blessed olive-tree, neither eastern nor western, the oil whereof almost gives light though fire touch it not-- light upon light-- Allah guides to His light whom He pleases, **and Allah sets forth parables for men, and Allah is Cognizant of all things.**

36. In houses which Allah has permitted to be exalted and that His name may be remembered in them; there glorify Him therein in the mornings and the evenings,

37. Men whom neither merchandise nor selling diverts from the remembrance of Allah and the keeping up of prayer and the giving of poor-rate; they fear a day in which the hearts and eyes shall turn about;

38. That Allah may give them the best reward of what they have done, and give them more out of His grace; and Allah gives sustenance to whom He pleases without measure.

39. And (as for) those who disbelieve, their deeds are like the mirage in a desert, which the thirsty man deems to be water; until when he comes to it he finds it to be naught, and there he finds Allah, so He pays back to him his reckoning in full; and Allah is quick in reckoning;

40. Or like utter darkness in the deep sea: there covers it a wave above which is another wave, above which is a cloud, (layers of) utter darkness one above another; when he holds out his hand, he is almost unable to see it; and to whomsoever Allah does not give light, he has no light.

Sura 29

The Spider

41. The parable of those who take guardians besides Allah is as the parable of the spider that makes for itself a house; and most surely the frailest of the houses is the spider's house did they but know.

42. Surely Allah knows whatever thing they call upon besides Him; and He is the Mighty, the Wise.

43. And (as for) these examples, We set them forth for men, and none understand them but the learned.

Sura 30

The Romans

28. He sets forth to you a parable relating to yourselves: Have you among those whom your right hands possess partners in what We have given you for sustenance, so that with respect to it you are alike; you fear them as you fear each other? Thus do We make the communications distinct for a people who understand.

29. Nay! those who are unjust follow their low desires without any knowledge; so who can guide him whom Allah makes to err? And they shall have no helpers.

Sura 47

Muhammad

14. What! is he who has a clear argument from his Lord like him to whom the evil of his work is made fairseeming: and they follow their low desires.

15. A parable of the garden which those guarding (against evil) are promised: Therein are rivers of water that does not alter, and

rivers of milk the taste whereof does not change, and rivers of drink delicious to those who drink, and rivers of honey clarified and for them therein are all fruits and protection from their Lord. (Are these) like those who abide in the fire and who are made to drink boiling water so it rends their bowels asunder.

16. And there are those of them who seek to listen to you, until when they go forth from you, they say to those who have been given the knowledge: What was it that he said just now? These are they upon whose hearts Allah has set a seal and they follow their low desires.

17. And (as for) those who follow the right direction, He increases them in guidance and gives them their guarding (against evil).

Sura 59

The Banishment

21. Had We sent down this Quran on a mountain, you would certainly have seen it falling down, splitting asunder because of the fear of Allah, and We set forth these parables to men that they may reflect.

22. He is Allah besides Whom there is no god; the Knower of the unseen and the seen; He is the Beneficent, the Merciful.

Sura 74

The Covered One

31. And We have not made the wardens of the fire others than angels, and We have not made their number but as a trial for those who disbelieve, that those who have been given the book may be certain and those who believe may increase in faith, and those who have been given the book and the believers may not doubt, and that those in whose hearts is a disease and the unbelievers may say: **What does Allah mean by this parable? Thus does Allah make err whom He pleases, and He guides whom He pleases, and none knows the hosts of your Lord but He Himself; and this is naught but a reminder to the mortals.**

THE BIBLE

"Parables"

Proverbs

Chapter 26

7. The legs of the lame are not equal: so is a parable in the mouth of fools.

8. As he that bindeth a stone in a sling, so is he that giveth honour to a fool.

9. As a thorn goeth up into the hand of a drunkard, so is a parable in the mouth of fools.

10. The great God that formed all things both rewardeth the fool, and rewardeth transgressors.

11. As a dog returneth to his vomit, so a fool returneth to his folly.

Ezekiel

Chapter 17

1. And the word of the LORD came unto me, saying,

2. Son of man, put forth a riddle, and **speak a parable** unto the house of Israel;

3. And say, Thus saith the Lord GOD; A great eagle with great wings, longwinged, full of feathers, which had divers colours, came unto Lebanon, and took the highest branch of the cedar:

4. He cropped off the top of his young twigs, and carried it into a land of traffick; he set it in a city of merchants.

5. He took also of the seed of the land, and planted it in a fruitful field; he placed it by great waters, and set it as a willow tree.

6. And it grew, and became a spreading vine of low stature, whose branches turned toward him, and the roots thereof were under him: so it became a vine, and brought forth branches, and shot forth sprigs.

7. There was also another great eagle with great wings and many feathers: and, behold, this vine did bend her roots toward him, and shot forth her branches toward him, that he might water it by the furrows of her plantation.

8. It was planted in a good soil by great waters, that it might bring forth branches, and that it might bear fruit, that it might be a goodly vine.

9. Say thou, Thus saith the Lord GOD; Shall it prosper? shall he not pull up the roots thereof, and cut off the fruit thereof, that it wither? it shall wither in all the leaves of her spring, even without great power or many people to pluck it up by the roots thereof.

10. Yea, behold, being planted, shall it prosper? shall it not utterly wither, when the east wind toucheth it? it shall wither in the furrows where it grew.

Psalms

Chapter 1

1. Blessed is the man that walketh not in the counsel of the ungodly, nor standeth in the way of sinners, nor sitteth in the seat of the scornful.

2. But his delight is in the law of the LORD; and in his law doth he meditate day and night.

3. And he shall be like a tree planted by the rivers of water, that bringeth forth his fruit in his season; his leaf also shall not wither; and whatsoever he doeth shall prosper.

4. The ungodly are not so: but are like the chaff which the wind driveth away.

5. Therefore the ungodly shall not stand in the judgment, nor sinners in the congregation of the righteous.

6. For the LORD knoweth the way of the righteous: but the way of the ungodly shall perish.

Matthew

Chapter 13

1. The same day went Jesus out of the house, and sat by the sea side.

2. And great multitudes were gathered together unto him, so that he went into a ship, and sat; and the whole multitude stood on the shore.

3. And he spake many things unto them in parables, saying, Behold, a sower went forth to sow;

4. And when he sowed, some seeds fell by the way side, and the fowls came and devoured them up:

5. Some fell upon stony places, where they had not much earth: and forthwith they sprung up, because they had no deepness of earth:

6. And when the sun was up, they were scorched; and because they had no root, they withered away.

7. And some fell among thorns; and the thorns sprung up, and choked them:

8. But other fell into good ground, and brought forth fruit, some an hundredfold, some sixtyfold, some thirtyfold.

9. Who hath ears to hear, let him hear.

18. Hear ye therefore the parable of the sower.

19. When any one heareth the word of the kingdom, and understandeth it not, then cometh the wicked one, and catcheth away that which was sown in his heart. This is he which received seed by the way side.

20. But he that received the seed into stony places, the same is he that heareth the word, and anon with joy receiveth it;

21. Yet hath he not root in himself, but dureth for a while: for when tribulation or persecution ariseth because of the word, by and by he is offended.

22. He also that received seed among the thorns is he that heareth the word; and the care of this world, and the deceitfulness of riches, choke the word, and he becometh unfruitful.

23. But he that received seed into the good ground is he that heareth the word, and understandeth it; which also beareth fruit, and bringeth forth, some an hundredfold, some sixty, some thirty.

24. Another parable put he forth unto them, saying, The kingdom of heaven is likened unto a man which sowed good seed in his field:

25. But while men slept, his enemy came and sowed tares among the wheat, and went his way.

26. But when the blade was sprung up, and brought forth fruit, then appeared the tares also.

27. So the servants of the householder came and said unto him, Sir, didst not thou sow good seed in thy field? from whence then hath it tares?

28. He said unto them, An enemy hath done this. The servants said unto him, Wilt thou then that we go and gather them up?

29. But he said, Nay; lest while ye gather up the tares, ye root up also the wheat with them.

30. Let both grow together until the harvest: and in the time of harvest I will say to the reapers, Gather ye together first the tares, and bind them in bundles to burn them: but gather the wheat into my barn.

31. Another parable put he forth unto them, saying, The kingdom of heaven is like to a grain of mustard seed, which a man took, and sowed in his field:

32. Which indeed is the least of all seeds: but when it is grown, it is the greatest among herbs, and becometh a tree, so that the birds of the air come and lodge in the branches thereof.

33. Another parable spake he unto them; The kingdom of heaven is like unto leaven, which a woman took, and hid in three measures of meal, till the whole was leavened.

34. All these things spake Jesus unto the multitude in parables; and without a parable spake he not unto them:

35. That it might be fulfilled which was spoken by the prophet, saying, I will open my mouth in parables; I will utter things which have been kept secret from the foundation of the world.

36. Then Jesus sent the multitude away, and went into the house: and his disciples came unto him, saying, Declare unto us the parable of the tares of the field.

37. He answered and said unto them, He that soweth the good seed is the Son of man;

38. The field is the world; the good seed are the children of the kingdom; but the tares are the children of the wicked one;

39. The enemy that sowed them is the devil; the harvest is the end of the world; and the reapers are the angels.

40. As therefore the tares are gathered and burned in the fire; so shall it be in the end of this world.

41. The Son of man shall send forth his angels, and they shall gather out of his kingdom all things that offend, and them which do iniquity;

42. And shall cast them into a furnace of fire: there shall be wailing and gnashing of teeth.

43. Then shall the righteous shine forth as the sun in the kingdom of their Father. Who hath ears to hear, let him hear.

44. Again, the kingdom of heaven is like unto treasure hid in a field; the which when a man hath found, he hideth, and for joy thereof goeth and selleth all that he hath, and buyeth that field.

45. Again, the kingdom of heaven is like unto a merchant man, seeking goodly pearls:

46. Who, when he had found one pearl of great price, went and sold all that he had, and bought it.

47. Again, the kingdom of heaven is like unto a net, that was cast into the sea, and gathered of every kind:

48. Which, when it was full, they drew to shore, and sat down, and gathered the good into vessels, but cast the bad away.

49. So shall it be at the end of the world: the angels shall come forth, and sever the wicked from among the just,

50. And shall cast them into the furnace of fire: there shall be wailing and gnashing of teeth.

51. Jesus saith unto them, Have ye understood all these things? They say unto him, Yea, Lord.

52. Then said he unto them, Therefore every scribe which is instructed unto the kingdom of heaven is like unto a man that is an householder, which bringeth forth out of his treasure things new and old.

53. And it came to pass, that when Jesus had finished these parables, he departed thence.

Luke

Chapter 12

16. And he*(Jesus)* spake a parable unto them, saying, The ground of a certain rich man brought forth plentifully:

17. And he thought within himself, saying, What shall I do, because I have no room where to bestow my fruits?

18. And he said, This will I do: I will pull down my barns, and build greater; and there will I bestow all my fruits and my goods.

19. And I will say to my soul, Soul, thou hast much goods laid up for many years; take thine ease, eat, drink, and be merry.

20. But God said unto him, Thou fool, this night thy soul shall be required of thee: then whose shall those things be, which thou hast provided?

21. So is he that layeth up treasure for himself, and is not rich toward God.

CONCLUSION

According to Islamic scholars, one of the many conclusive proofs of the divine origin of the Qur'an and its clear superiority above the Bible, which they claim to have been corrupted, has to be the "Parables from God" as recorded in the Qur'an.

I am confident that the reader will use an objective viewpoint in examining the parables in the Qur'an and the Bible by comparing them to each other in style and content.

Chapter Seven

SEVEN HEAVENS

THE QUR'AN

"Seven Heavens"

Sura 2

The Cow

29. He it is Who created for you all that is in the earth, and He directed Himself to the heaven, so **He made them complete seven heavens**, and He knows all things.

Sura 17

The Children of Israel

44. **The seven heavens** declare His glory and the earth (too), and those who are in them; and there is not a single thing but glorifies Him with His praise, but you do not understand their glorification; surely He is Forbearing, Forgiving.

Sura 41

Ha Mim

12. So **He ordained them seven heavens in two periods**, and revealed in every heaven its affair; and **We adorned the lower heaven with brilliant stars and (made it) to guard;** that is the decree of the Mighty, the Knowing.

Sura 65

The Divorce

12. **Allah is He Who created seven heavens**, and of the earth the like of them; the decree continues to descend among them, that you may know that Allah has power over all things and that Allah indeed encompasses all things in (His) knowledge.

Sura 67

The Kingdom

3. Who created the seven heavens one above another; you see no incongruity in the creation of the Beneficent God; then look again, **can you see any disorder?**
4. Then turn back the eye again and again; your look shall come back to you confused while it is fatigued.
5. And certainly We have adorned this lower heaven with lamps and We have made these missiles for the Shaitans, and We have prepared for them the chastisement of burning.
6. And for those who disbelieve in their Lord is the punishment of hell, and evil is the resort.

Sura 71

Nuh

14. And indeed He has created you through various grades:
15. Do you not see how Allah has created the seven heavens, one above another,
16. And made the moon therein a light, and made the sun a lamp?

Sura 7

The Elevated Places

54. Surely your Lord is Allah, Who created the **heavens and the earth in six periods of time**, and He is firm in power; He throws the veil of night over the day, which it pursues incessantly; and (He created) the sun and the moon and the stars, made subservient by His command; surely His is the creation and the command; blessed is Allah, the Lord of the worlds.

Sura 41

Ha Mim

9. Say: What! do you indeed disbelieve in Him Who created the **earth in two periods**, and do you set up equals with Him? That is the Lord of the Worlds.

10. And He made in it mountains above its surface, and He blessed therein and made therein its foods, **in four periods**: alike for the seekers.

11. Then He directed Himself to the heaven and it is a vapor, so He said to it and to the earth: Come both, willingly or unwillingly. They both said: We come willingly.

12. So He ordained them **seven heavens in two periods**, and revealed in every heaven its affair; and We adorned the lower heaven with brilliant stars and (made it) to guard; that is the decree of the Mighty, the Knowing.

THE BIBLE

"Seven Heavens"

Second Corinthians

Chapter 12

1. It is not expedient for me doubtless to glory. I will come to visions and revelations of the Lord.

2. I knew a man in Christ above fourteen years ago, (whether in the body, I cannot tell; or whether out of the body, I cannot tell: God knoweth;) such an one caught up to the **third heaven.**

3. And I knew such a man, (whether in the body, or out of the body, I cannot tell: God knoweth;)

4. How that he was caught up **into paradise**, and heard unspeakable words, which it is not lawful for a man to utter.

5. Of such an one will I glory: yet of myself I will not glory, but in mine infirmities.

Genesis

Chapter 1

1. In the beginning God created the heaven and the earth.

5. And God called the light Day, and the darkness he called Night. And the evening and the morning were the first day.

8. And God called the firmament Heaven. And the evening and the morning were the second day.

12. And the earth brought forth grass, and herb yielding seed after his kind, and the tree yielding fruit, whose seed was in itself, after his kind: and God saw that it was good.

13. And the evening and the morning were the third day.

17. And God set them *(the sun, lights, stars, moon - editor)* in the firmament of the heaven to give light upon the earth,

18. And to rule over the day and over the night, and to divide the light from the darkness: and God saw that it was good.

19. And the evening and the morning were the fourth day.

21. And God created great whales, and every living creature that moveth, which the waters brought forth abundantly, after their kind, and every winged fowl after his kind: and God saw that it was good.

23 And the evening and the morning were the fifth day.

24. And God said, Let the earth bring forth the living creature after his kind, cattle, and creeping thing, and beast of the earth after his kind: and it was so.

26. And God said, Let us make man in our image, after our likeness: and let them have dominion over the fish of the sea, and over the fowl of the air, and over the cattle, and over all the earth, and over every creeping thing that creepeth upon the earth.

31 And God saw every thing that he had made, and, behold, it was very good. And the evening and the morning were the **sixth day**.

Genesis

Chapter 2

1. Thus the heavens and the earth were finished, and all the host of them.

2. And **on the seventh day God ended his work** which he had made; and he rested on the seventh day from all his work which he had made.

3. And God blessed the seventh day, and sanctified it: because that in it he had rested from all his work which God created and made.

COMMENTARY

The Qur'an speaks about seven heavens in total. According to Muslim scholars, the first heaven, which contains the sun, moon and stars, is only one known today out of the seven. The reference to verse 15 which asks **"Do you not see how Allah has created the seven heavens, ~ one above another"**, sounds strange, because no one (even with a modern telescope) can actually see more than one heaven.

The Bible speaks about only three heavens:
- **the first heaven**: our planetary atmosphere.
- **the second heaven**: the universe with its stars and galaxies.
- **the third heaven**: invisible, where God dwells.

The Qur'an makes two contradictory statements about the time period of the creation of heaven and earth:
1. -in 6 periods (or, *days*).
2. -in 2 plus 4, plus 2 periods, equaling 8 periods (or, *days*).

The Bible claims that God created the earth in six literal days, and He rested on the seventh day.

Chapter Eight

MOHAMMED

The Qur'an

"The Statement of Mohammed"

Sura 46

The Sandhills

9. Say: I am not the first of the apostles, and **I do not know what will be done with me or with you:** I do not follow anything but that which is revealed to me, and I am nothing but a plain warner.
10. Say: Have you considered if it is from Allah, and you disbelieve in it, and a witness from among the children of Israel has borne witness of one like it, so he believed, while you are big with pride; surely Allah does not guide the unjust people.

Sura 2

The Cow

136. Say: **We believe** in Allah and (in) that which had been revealed to us, and (in) **that which was revealed to Ibrahim and Ismail and Ishaq and Yaqoub and the tribes, and (in) that which was given to Musa and Isa, and (in) that which was given to the prophets from their Lord, we do not make any distinction between any of them**, and to Him do we submit.

Sura 5

The Dinner Table

48. And We have revealed to you the Book with the truth, **verifying what is before it of the Book and a guardian over it**, therefore judge between them by what Allah has revealed, and do not follow their low desires (to turn away) from the truth that has come to you; for every one of you did We appoint a law and a way, and if Allah had pleased He would have made you (all) a single people, but that He might try you in what He gave you, therefore strive with one another to hasten to virtuous deeds; to Allah is your return, of all (of you), so He will let you know that in which you differed;

Sura 23

The Believers

116. So exalted be Allah, the True King; no god is there but He, the Lord of the honorable dominion.
117. And whoever invokes with Allah another god-- he has no proof of this-- his reckoning is only with his Lord; surely the unbelievers shall not be successful.

Sura 29

The Spider

45. Recite that which has been revealed to you of the Book and keep up prayer; surely prayer keeps (one) away from indecency and evil, and certainly the remembrance of Allah is the greatest, and Allah knows what you do.
46. And do not dispute with the followers of the Book except by what is best, except those of them who act unjustly, and say: **We believe in that which has been revealed to us and revealed to you, and our God and your God is One**, and to Him do we submit.

THE BIBLE

"The Statement of Jesus"

John

Chapter 14

1. Let not your heart be troubled: **ye believe in God, believe also in me.**
2. In my Father's house are many mansions: if it were not so, I would have told you. I go to prepare a place for you.
3. And if I go and prepare a place for you, I will come again, and receive you unto myself; that where I am, there ye may be also.
4. And whither I go ye know, and the way ye know.
5. Thomas saith unto him, Lord, we know not whither thou goest; and how can we know the way?
6. Jesus saith unto him, *I am the way, the truth, and the life: no man cometh unto the Father, but by me.*

7. If ye had known me, ye should have known my Father also: and from henceforth ye know him, and have seen him.

COMMENTARY

In the Qur'an:

1. Here we have a very bold statement for every Muslim believer: to believe in that *"which was revealed"* to Abraham, Isaac, Jacob, Moses, and even Jesus! It summarizes the Old and the New Testaments, but never in the Qur'an do we find a command to search these Scriptures. It is actually the opposite: the Qur'an admonishes the reader to not believe the Bible, for it has been corrupted. Therefore Muslims have only one way to know about that which *"was revealed"* **and that way can only be** through the Qur'an. Although the Qur'an contains small portions of Biblical stories, in most cases it contradicts the Bible in small details, as well as in major topics.

2. A significant statement of Mohammed's clarifies his position: *"I do not know what will be done with me or with you."*

3. Mohammed said that he is the first to submit himself (to Allah). The word "submit" is also interpreted as the word "Muslim".

In several places, the Qur'an states that before Mohammed's time, all prophets and many believers were submitted to God, or in other words, were "Muslims". For example:

Sura 5

*44. Surely **We revealed the Taurat in which was guidance and light; with it the prophets who submitted** themselves (to Allah) judged (matters) for those who were Jews, and the masters of Divine knowledge and the doctors, **because they were required to guard (part) of the Book of Allah,** and they were witnesses thereof; therefore fear not the people and fear Me, and do not take a small price for My communications; and whoever did not judge by what Allah revealed, those are they that are the unbelievers.*

110. When Allah will say: O Isa son of Marium! Remember My favor on you and on your mother, when I strengthened you with the holy Spirit, you spoke to the people in the cradle and when of old age, and when I taught you the Book and the wisdom and the Taurat and the Injeel; and when you determined out of clay a thing like the form of a bird by My permission, then you breathed into it and it became a bird by My permission, and you healed the blind and the leprous by My permission; and when you brought forth the dead by My permission; and when I withheld the children of Israel from you when you came to them with clear arguments, but those who disbelieved among them said: This is nothing but clear enchantment.

*111. And when I revealed to the disciples, saying, Believe in Me and My apostle, they said: We believe and bear witness that we **submit** (ourselves).*

Sura 10

*84. And Musa said: O my people! if you believe in Allah, then rely on Him (alone) if you **submit** (to Allah).*

*90. And We made the children of Israel to pass through the sea, then Firon and his hosts followed them for oppression and tyranny; until when drowning overtook him, he said: I believe that there is no god but He in Whom the children of Israel believe and I am of those who **submit**.*

In the Bible:

1. The Bible is the final revelation to mankind from God. We do not need to be guided by new laws such as Shariah, etc. God already gave us His plan of redemption through the atoning death of His Son, as written clearly in the Bible.

2. A) Compare that with the statement of Jesus:

John, Chapter 14:6

And whither I go ye know, and the way ye know... I am the way, the truth, and the life: no man cometh unto the Father, but by me...

As Jesus said about the false prophet:

Luke, Chapter 6:29

... And he spake a parable unto them, Can the blind lead the blind? shall they not both fall into the ditch?

B) Also all believers in Jesus have the assurance of eternal life:

First John, Chapter 5:13

... These things have I written unto you that believe on the name of the Son of God; that ye may know that ye have eternal life, and that ye may believe on the name of the Son of God.

3. The name "Allah" was unknown to the Hebrews and Christians until Mohammed introduced Him to the Arabs as the one and only God, and Mohammed had to be the first Muslim on this planet.

There is a theory that the root of the name "Allah" is the equivalent of the Hebrew word *El*, which means "god". But according to the Hebrew Scriptures, one can call God *'El 'Olam* (the Eternal God), *'El 'Elyon* (the Most High God), *'Elohe Sabaoth* (God of Hosts), for example, and at the same time refer to one of the pagan gods as *El Murdock*. Therefore, the word *'El* is not exclusively the title or name for only one "god".

In the Arabic language, the word *Allah* consists of two words:

"Al"- means "The" and "Ilah"- meaning "Divinity" or "God". This leads us to accept another possibility: this name "Allah" could be unique and have no connection with Hebrew or any other language.

In spite of the name's origin, Allah was worshipped alongside with other pagan gods or idols in Kaaba. There is no evidence that either Christians or Jews ever made pilgrimages to Mecca. Based on this fact, they simply never regarded Allah or other idols as gods.

Chapter Nine

MERCY VERSUS LOVE

The Qur'an

"The Mercy of Allah"

Sura 2

The Cow

163. And your God is one God! there is no god but He; **He is the Beneficent, the Merciful.**

243. Have you not considered those who went forth from their homes, for fear of death, and they were thousands, then Allah said to them, Die; again He gave them life; **most surely Allah is Gracious to people,** but most people are not grateful.

Sura 4

The Women

29. O you who believe! do not devour your property among yourselves falsely, except that it be trading by your mutual consent; and do not kill your people; **surely Allah is Merciful to you.**

Sura 7

The Elevated Places

23. They said: Our Lord! We have been unjust to ourselves, **and if Thou forgive us not, and have (not) mercy on us,** we shall certainly be of the losers.

Sura 9

The Immunity

71. And (as for) the believing men and the believing women, they are guardians of each other; they enjoin good and forbid evil and keep up prayer and pay the poor-rate, and obey Allah and His Apostle; (as for) these, **Allah will show mercy to them; surely Allah is Mighty, Wise.**

Sura 10

Jonah

60. And what will be the thought of those who forge lies against Allah on the day of resurrection? **Most surely Allah is the Lord of grace towards men**, but most of them do not give thanks.

Sura 11

The Holy Prophet

3. And you that ask forgiveness of your Lord, then turn to Him; He will provide you with a goodly provision to an appointed term **and bestow His grace on every one endowed with grace, and if you turn back, then surely I fear for you the chastisement of a great day.**

Sura 17

The Children of Israel

54. Your Lord knows you best; **He will have mercy on you if He pleases, or He will chastise you if He pleases;** and We have not sent you as being in charge of them.

Sura 19

Marium

96. Surely (as for) those who believe and do good deeds for them **will Allah bring about love**.

Sura 20

Ta Ha

36. He said: You are indeed granted your petition, O Musa. And certainly We bestowed on you a favor at another time;
38. When We revealed to your mother what was revealed;
39. Saying: Put him into a chest, then cast it down into the river, then the river shall throw him on the shore; there shall take him up one who is an enemy to Me and enemy to him, **and I cast down upon you love from Me**, and that you might be brought up before My eyes;

Sura 25

The Distinction

25. And on the day when the heaven shall burst asunder with the clouds, and the angels shall be sent down descending (in ranks).
26. The kingdom on that day shall rightly belong to the **Beneficent God**, and a hard day shall it be for the unbelievers.

Sura 36

Yasin

23. What! shall I take other gods besides Him, if **the Beneficent God** should desire to afflict me with a harm, shall not avail me aught, nor shall they be able to deliver me?
24. In that case I shall most surely be in clear error:

THE BIBLE

"The Love of God"

Deuteronomy

Chapter 23

5. Nevertheless the LORD thy God would not hearken unto Balaam; but the LORD thy God turned the curse into a blessing unto thee, **because the LORD thy God loved thee**.

First Kings

Chapter 10

9. Blessed be the LORD thy God, which delighted in thee, to set thee on the throne of Israel: **because the LORD loved Israel for ever**, therefore made he thee king, to do judgment and justice.

Second Chronicles

Chapter 9

8. Blessed be the LORD thy God, which delighted in thee to set thee on his throne, to be king for the LORD thy God: **because thy God loved Israel**, to establish them for ever, therefore made he thee king over them, to do judgment and justice.

Jeremiah

Chapter 2

2. Go and cry in the ears of Jerusalem, saying, Thus saith the LORD; **I remember thee, the kindness of thy youth, the love of thine espousal**s, when thou wentest after me in the wilderness, in a land that was not sown.

Jeremiah

Chapter 31

3. The LORD hath appeared of old unto me, saying, Yea, **I have loved thee with an everlasting love**: therefore with lovingkindness have I drawn thee.

20. Is Ephraim my dear son? is he a pleasant child? for since I spake against him, I do earnestly remember him still: therefore my bowels are troubled for him; I will surely have mercy upon him, saith the LORD.

Zephaniah

Chapter 3

17. The LORD thy God in the midst of thee is mighty; he will save, he will rejoice over thee with joy; **he will rest in his love**, he will joy over thee with singing

John

Chapter 3

14. And as Moses lifted up the serpent in the wilderness, even so must the **Son of man be lifted up**:

15. That whosoever **believeth in him should not perish**, but have eternal life.

16. For God so loved the world, that **he gave his only begotten Son,** that whosoever believeth in him should not perish, but have everlasting life.

17. For **God sent not his Son into the world to condemn** the world; **but that the world through him might be saved.**

18. He that believeth on him is not condemned: but he that believeth not is condemned already, because he hath not believed in the name of the only begotten Son of God.

Romans

Chapter 5

5. And hope maketh not ashamed; because **the love of God is shed abroad in our hearts by the Holy Ghost which is given unto us.**

6. For when we were yet without strength, in due time Christ died for the ungodly.

8. But God commendeth his love toward us, in that, while we were yet sinners, Christ died for us.

Romans

Chapter 8

35. Who shall separate us **from the love of Christ?** shall tribulation, or distress, or persecution, or famine, or nakedness, or peril, or sword?

39. Nor height, nor depth, nor any other creature, shall be able to separate us from **the love of God**, which is in Christ Jesus our Lord.

First Corinthians

Chapter 13

1. Though I speak with the tongues of men and of angels, and have not charity (love), I am become as sounding brass, or a tinkling cymbal.

2. And though I have the gift of prophecy, and understand all mysteries, and all knowledge; and **though I have all faith, so that I could remove mountains, and have not charity (love), I am nothing.**

3. And though I bestow all my goods to feed the poor, and though I give my body to be burned, **and have not charity (love), it profiteth me nothing.**

4. Charity (love) suffereth long, and is kind; charity (love) envieth not; charity vaunteth not itself, is not puffed up,

5. Doth not behave itself unseemly, seeketh not her own, is not easily provoked, thinketh no evil;

6. Rejoiceth not in iniquity, but rejoiceth in the truth;

7. Beareth all things, believeth all things, hopeth all things, endureth all things.

8. Charity (love) never faileth: but whether there be prophecies, they shall fail; whether there be tongues, they shall cease; **whether there be knowledge, it shall vanish away.**

9. For we know in part, and we prophesy in part.

10. But when that which is perfect is come, then that which is in part shall be done away.

11. When I was a child, I spake as a child, I understood as a child, I thought as a child: but when I became a man, I put away childish things.

12. For now we see through a glass, darkly; but then face to face: now I know in part; but then shall I know even as also I am known.

13. And now abideth **faith, hope, charity (love)**, these three; but **the greatest of these is charity (love).**

Second Corinthians

Chapter 13

11. Finally, brethren, farewell. Be perfect, be of good comfort, be of one mind, live in peace; **and the God of love and peace shall be with you.**

Ephesians

Chapter 2

4. But God, who is **rich in mercy, for his great love wherewith he loved us,**
5. Even when we were dead in sins, hath quickened us together with Christ, (by grace ye are saved ;)
6. And hath raised us up together, and made us sit together in heavenly places in Christ Jesus:

First John

Chapter 3

1. Behold, **what manner of love the Father hath bestowed upon us**, that we should be called the sons of God: therefore the world knoweth us not, because it knew him not.
16. Hereby perceive **we the love of God, because he laid down his life for us**: and we ought to lay down our lives for the brethren.
17. But whoso hath this world's good, and seeth his brother have need, and shutteth up his bowels of compassion from him, how dwelleth the love of God in him?

First John

Chapter 4

7. Beloved, let us love one another: **for love is of God**; and every one that loveth is born of God, and knoweth God.
8. He that loveth not knoweth not God; **for God is love.**
9. In this was manifested the love of God toward us, because that God sent his only begotten Son into the world, that we might live through him.

10. Herein is love, not that we loved God, but that **he loved us, and sent his Son to be the propitiation for our sins**.

11. Beloved, **if God so loved us**, we ought also to love one another.

12. No man hath seen God at any time. If we love one another, God dwelleth in us, and his love is perfected in us.

15. Whosoever shall confess that Jesus is the Son of God, God dwelleth in him, and he in God.

16. And we have known and believed the love that God hath to us. **God is love**; and he that dwelleth in love dwelleth in God, and God in him.

17. Herein is our love made perfect, that we may have boldness in the day of judgment: because as he is, so are we in this world.

First John

Chapter 5

1. Whosoever believeth that Jesus is the Christ is born of God: and every one that loveth him that begat loveth him also that is begotten of him.

2. By this we know that we love the children of God, when we love God, and keep his commandments.

3. For this is the love of God, that we keep his commandments: and his commandments are not grievous.

COMMENTARY

In the Qur'an:

1. Allah's character is most frequently referred to as being merciful, and He will decide to save us or to punish and condemn us. As the Creator, He is too far above His creatures to have personal contact with them. He demands obedience and offers a reward to those who submit themselves to Him. It resembles a relationship between a master and his slave.

In the Bible:

1. God is the supreme Creator Who made the human race for the purpose of having a close relationship with Him. Because God

gave us free choice, we can choose to either obey and believe in Him, thereby securing a place for us in His presence in heaven, or disobey Him and face the consequences of a life separated from God for all eternity. We lost this bond after Adam and Eve sinned in the Garden of Eden. God, in His great love for us, reached out to us not to condemn us, but to save us from our sin and to restore our broken relationship with Him. Since we cannot reach Him, He came down to meet His creation and to pay the ransom, the sacrifice for our sins, with His own blood on the cross. From that time on, His righteousness and holiness has been satisfied. The people who accept His ultimate sacrifice will enjoy His presence in eternity, not because **we** are good, but because **His righteousness** became our very own.

Chapter Ten

ISLAM AND ISRAEL

THE QUR'AN

"The Last Religion Until the End of the World"

Sura 2

The Cow

111. And they say: None shall enter the garden (or paradise) except he who is a Jew or a Christian. **These are their vain desires. Say: Bring your proof if you are truthful.**

112. Yes! whoever submits himself entirely to Allah and he is the doer of good (to others) he has his reward from his Lord, and there is no fear for him nor shall he grieve.

113. And **the Jews say: The Christians do not follow anything (good) and the Christians say: The Jews do not follow anything (good) while they recite the (same) Book.** Even thus say those who have no knowledge, like to what they say; so Allah shall judge between them on the day of resurrection in what they differ.

120. And the Jews will not be pleased with you, nor the Christians until you follow their religion. Say: Surely Allah's guidance, that is the (true) guidance. **And if you follow their desires after the knowledge that has come to you, you shall have no guardian from Allah,** nor any helper.

135. And they say: Be Jews or Christians, you will be on the right course. **Say: Nay! (we follow) the religion of Ibrahim, the Hanif, and he was not one of the polytheists.**

137. If then they believe as you believe in Him, they are indeed on the right course, and if they turn back, then they are only in great opposition, so Allah will suffice you against them, and He is the Hearing, the Knowing.

138. (Receive) the baptism of Allah, and who is better than Allah in baptising? and Him do we serve.

Sura 3

The Family of Imran

19. Surely the (true) religion with Allah is Islam, and those to whom the Book had been given did not show opposition but after knowledge had come to them, out of envy among themselves; and whoever disbelieves in the communications of Allah then surely Allah is quick in reckoning.

20. But if they dispute with you, say: I have submitted myself entirely to Allah and (so) every one who follows me; and say to those who have been given the Book and the unlearned people: Do you submit yourselves? **So if they submit then indeed they follow the right way**; and if they turn back, then upon you is only the delivery of the message and Allah sees the servants.

64. Say: **O followers of the Book! come to an equitable proposition between us and you that we shall not serve any but Allah** and (that) we shall not associate aught with Him, and (that) some of us shall not take others for lords besides Allah; but if they turn back, then say: Bear witness that we are Muslims.

65. O followers of the Book! why do you dispute about Ibrahim, when the Taurat and the Injeel were not revealed till after him; do you not then understand?

66. Behold! you are they who disputed about that of which you had knowledge; why then do you dispute about that of which you have no knowledge? And Allah knows while you do not know.

67. Ibrahim was not a Jew nor a Christian but he was (an) upright (man), a Muslim, and he was not one of the polytheists.

69. A party of the followers of the Book desire that they should lead you astray, and they lead not astray but themselves, and they do not perceive.

85. And whoever desires a religion other than Islam, it shall not be accepted from him, and in the hereafter he shall be one of the losers.

99. Say: **O followers of the Book! why do you hinder him who believes from the way of Allah?** You seek (to make) it crooked, while you are witness, and Allah is not heedless of what you do.

Sura 4

The Women

46. Of those who are Jews (there are those who) alter words from their places and say: We have heard and we disobey and: Hear, may you not be made to hear! and: Raina, distorting (the word) with their tongues and taunting about religion; and if they had said (instead): We have heard and we obey, and hearken, it would have been better for them and more upright; **but Allah has cursed them on account of their unbelief, so they do not believe but a little.**

47. O you who have been given the Book! believe that which We have revealed, verifying what you have, before **We alter faces then turn them on their backs, or curse them as We cursed the violaters of the Sabbath,** and the command of Allah shall be executed.

48. Surely Allah does not forgive that anything should be associated with Him, and forgives what is besides that to whomsoever He pleases; and whoever associates anything with Allah, he devises indeed a great sin.

51. Have you not seen those **to whom a portion of the Book has been given? They believe in idols and false deities** and say of those who disbelieve: These are better guided in the path than those who believe.

52. Those are they whom Allah has cursed, and whomever Allah curses you shall not find any helper for him.

Sura 5

The Dinner Table

57. O you who believe! do not take for guardians those who take your religion for a mockery and a joke, from **among those who were given the Book before you** and the unbelievers; and be careful of (your duty to) Allah if you are believers.

58. And when you call to prayer they make it a mockery and a joke; this is because they are a people who do not understand.

59. Say: **O followers of the Book! do you find fault with us (for aught) except that we believe in Allah and in what has been revealed to us** and what was revealed before, and that **most of you are transgressors?**

60. Say: Shall I inform you of (him who is) worse than this in retribution from Allah? **(Worse is he) whom Allah has cursed and brought His wrath upon**, and **of whom He made apes and swine, and he who served the Shaitan**; these are worse in place and more erring from the straight path.

64. And the Jews say: The hand of Allah is tied up! Their hands shall be shackled and they shall be cursed for what they say. Nay, both His hands are spread out, He expends as He pleases; and what has been revealed to you from your Lord will certainly make many of them increase in inordinacy and unbelief; and **We have put enmity and hatred among them till the day of resurrection;** whenever they kindle a fire for war Allah puts it out, and they strive to make mischief in the land; and Allah does not love the mischief-makers.

65. And if the followers of the Book had believed and guarded (against evil) **We would certainly have covered their evil deeds and We would certainly have made them enter gardens of bliss**

66. And if they had kept up the Taurat and the Injeel and that which was revealed to them from their Lord, they would certainly have eaten from above them and from beneath their feet there is a party of them keeping to the moderate course, and (as for) most of them, evil is that which they do

67. O Apostle! deliver what has been revealed to you from your Lord; and if you do it not, then you have not delivered His message, and Allah will protect you from the people; surely Allah will not guide the unbelieving people.

68. Say: **O followers of the Book! you follow no good till you keep up the Taurat and the Injeel and that which is revealed to you from your Lord; and surely that which has been revealed to you from your Lord shall make many of them increase in inordinacy and unbelief;** grieve not therefore for the unbelieving people.

69. Surely those who believe and those who are Jews and the Sabians and the Christians whoever believes in Allah and the last day and does good-- they shall have no fear nor shall they grieve.

80. You will see many of them befriending those who disbelieve; certainly evil is that which their souls have sent before for them, that Allah became displeased with them and in chastisement shall they abide.

81. And had they believed in Allah and the prophet and what was revealed to him, they would not have taken them for friends but! most of them are transgressors.

82. Certainly you will find the most violent of people in enmity for those who believe (to be) the Jews and those who are polytheists, and you will certainly find the nearest in friendship to those who believe (to be) those who say: We are Christians; this is because there are priests and monks among them and because they do not behave proudly.

83. And when they hear what has been revealed to the apostle you will see their eyes overflowing with tears on account of the truth that they recognize; they say: Our Lord! we believe, so write us down with the witnesses (of truth).

84. And what (reason) have we that we should not believe in Allah and in the truth that has come to us, while we earnestly desire that our Lord should cause us to enter with the good people?

85. Therefore Allah rewarded them on account of what they said, with gardens in which rivers flow to abide in them; and this is the reward of those who do good (to others).

86. And (as for) those who disbelieve and reject Our communications, these are the companions of the flame.

Sura 9

The Immunity

33. He it is Who sent His Apostle with guidance and the religion of truth, that He might cause it **to prevail over all religions,** though the polytheists may be averse.

Sura 29

The Spider

46. And do **not dispute with the followers of the Book** except by what is best, except those of them who act unjustly, and say: We believe in that which has been revealed to us and revealed to you, and **our God and your God is One**, and to Him do we submit.

Sura 98
The Clear Evidence

1. Those who disbelieved from among the followers of the Book and the polytheists could not have separated (from the faithful) until there had come to them the clear evidence:

2. An apostle from Allah, reciting pure pages,

3. Wherein are all the right ordinances.

4. And those who were given the Book **did not become divided except after clear evidence had come to them**.

THE BIBLE

"One Faith Until the End Times"

Isaiah

Chapter 1

24. Therefore saith the **Lord, the LORD of hosts, the mighty One of Israel,** Ah, I will ease me of mine adversaries, and avenge me of mine enemies:

25. And I will turn my hand upon thee, and purely purge away thy dross, and take away all thy tin:

26. And I will restore thy judges as at the first, and thy counsellers as at the beginning: **afterward thou shalt be called, The city of righteousness, the faithful city.**

27. Zion shall be redeemed with judgment, and her converts with righteousness.

28. And the destruction of the transgressors and of the sinners shall be together, and they that forsake the LORD shall be consumed.

Isaiah

Chapter 2

1. the word that Isaiah the son of Amoz saw **concerning Judah and Jerusalem.**

2. And it shall come to pass in the last days, **that the mountain of the LORD's house shall be established in the top of the mountains,** and shall be exalted above the hills; **and all nations shall flow unto it.**

3. And many people shall go and say, Come ye, and let us go up to the mountain of the LORD, to the house of the God of Jacob; and he will teach us of his ways, and we will walk in his paths: for out of Zion shall go forth the law, and the word of the LORD from Jerusalem.

4. And he shall judge among the nations, and shall rebuke many people: and they shall beat their swords into plowshares, and their spears into pruninghooks: nation shall not lift up sword against nation, neither shall they learn war any more.

Isaiah

Chapter 33

20. Look upon Zion, the city of our solemnities: thine eyes shall see Jerusalem a quiet habitation, a tabernacle that shall not be taken down; not one of the stakes thereof shall ever be removed, neither shall any of the cords thereof be broken.

21. But there the glorious LORD will be unto us a place of broad rivers and streams; wherein shall go no galley with oars, neither shall gallant ship pass thereby.

22. For the LORD is our judge, the LORD is our lawgiver, **the LORD is our king; he will save us.**

24. And the inhabitant shall not say, I am sick: **the people that dwell therein shall be forgiven their iniquity.**

Isaiah

Chapter 34

1. Come near, **ye nations**, to hear; and hearken, ye people: let the earth hear, and all that is therein; the world, and all things that come forth of it.

2. For the indignation of the LORD is upon all nations, and his fury upon all their armies: he hath utterly destroyed them, he hath delivered them to the slaughter.

3. Their slain also shall be cast out, and their stink shall come up out of their carcases, and the mountains shall be melted with their blood.

8. For it is the day of the LORD's vengeance, and the year of recompences **for the controversy of Zion.**

Isaiah

Chapter 60

1. Arise, shine; for thy light is come, **and the glory of the LORD is risen upon thee.**

3. And the Gentiles shall come to thy light, and kings to the brightness of thy rising.

11. Therefore thy gates shall be open continually; they shall not be shut day nor night; **that men may bring unto thee the forces of the Gentiles, and that their kings may be brought.**

12. For the nation and kingdom that will not serve thee shall perish; yea, those nations shall be utterly wasted.

14. The sons also of them that afflicted thee shall come bending unto thee; and all they that despised thee shall bow themselves down at the soles of thy feet; **and they shall call thee, The city of the LORD, The Zion of the Holy One of Israel.**

18. Violence shall no more be heard in thy land, wasting nor destruction within thy borders; but thou shalt call thy walls Salvation, and thy gates Praise.

19. The sun shall be no more thy light by day; neither for brightness shall the moon give light unto thee: but the LORD shall be unto thee an everlasting light, and thy God thy glory.

20. Thy sun shall no more go down; neither shall thy moon withdraw itself: for the LORD shall be thine everlasting light, and the days of thy mourning shall be ended.

21. Thy people also shall be all righteous: they shall inherit the land for ever, the branch of my planting, the work of my hands, that I may be glorified.

Isaiah

Chapter 62

1. For Zion's sake will I not hold my peace, and for Jerusalem's sake I will not rest, until the righteousness thereof go forth as brightness, and the salvation thereof as a lamp that burneth.

2. And the Gentiles shall see thy righteousness, and all kings thy glory: and thou shalt be called by a new name, which the mouth of the LORD shall name.

3. Thou shalt also be a crown of glory in the hand of the LORD, and a royal diadem in the hand of thy God.

4. Thou shalt no more be termed Forsaken; **neither shall thy land any more be termed Desolate:** but thou shalt be called Hephzi-bah, and thy land Beulah: for the LORD delighteth in thee, and thy land shall be married.

5. For as a young man marrieth a virgin, so shall thy sons marry thee: and as the bridegroom rejoiceth over the bride, so shall thy God rejoice over thee.

6. I have set watchmen upon thy walls, O Jerusalem, which shall never hold their peace day nor night: ye that make mention of the LORD, keep not silence,

7. And give him no rest, till he establish, and till he make Jerusalem a praise in the earth.

Isaiah

Chapter 63

1. Who is this that cometh from Edom, **with dyed garments** from Bozrah? this that is glorious in his apparel, travelling in the greatness of his strength? I that speak in righteousness, mighty to save.

2. Wherefore **art thou red in thine apparel, and thy garments like him that treadeth in the winefat?**

3. I have trodden the winepress alone; and of the people there was none with me: for I will tread them in mine anger, and trample them in my fury; and **their blood shall be sprinkled upon my garments, and I will stain all my raiment.**

4. For the day of vengeance is in mine heart, and the year of my redeemed is come.

5. And I looked, and there was none to help; and I wondered that there was none to uphold: therefore mine own arm brought salvation unto me; and my fury, it upheld me.

6. And **I will tread down the people in mine anger, and make them drunk in my fury, and I will bring down their strength to the earth.**

Isaiah

Chapter 65

17. For, behold, **I create new heavens and a new earth**: and the former shall not be remembered, nor come into mind.

18. But be ye glad and rejoice for ever in that which I create: for, behold, **I create Jerusalem a rejoicing, and her people a joy.**

19. And I will rejoice in Jerusalem, and joy in my people: and the voice of weeping shall be no more heard in her, nor the voice of crying.

20. There shall be no more thence an **infant of days, nor an old man that hath not filled his days: for the child shall die an hundred years old; but the sinner being an hundred years old shall be accursed.**

21. And **they shall build houses, and inhabit them; and they shall plant vineyards, and eat the fruit of them.**

22. They shall not build, and another inhabit; they shall not plant, and another eat: for as the days of a tree are the days of my people, **and mine elect shall long enjoy the work of their hands.**

23. They shall not labour in vain, nor bring forth for trouble; for they are the seed of the blessed of the LORD, **and their offspring with them.**

24. And it shall come to pass, that before they call, I will answer; and while they are yet speaking, I will hear.

25. The wolf and the lamb shall feed together, and the lion shall eat straw like the bullock: and dust shall be the serpent's meat. They shall not hurt nor destroy in all my holy mountain, saith the LORD.

Daniel

Chapter 9

2. In the first year of his reign **I Daniel understood by books the number of the years,** wherefore the word of the LORD came to Jeremiah the prophet, that **he would accomplish seventy years in the desolations of Jerusalem**.

3. And I set my face unto the Lord God, to seek by prayer and supplication, with fasting, and sackcloth, and ashes:

4. And I prayed unto the LORD my God,

20. And whiles I was speaking, and praying, and **confessing my sin and the sin of my people Israel,** and presenting my supplication before the LORD my God for the holy mountain of my God;

21. Yea, whiles I was speaking in prayer, even **the man Gabriel,** whom I had seen in the vision at the beginning, being caused to fly swiftly, **touched me about the time of the evening oblation.**

22. And he informed me, and talked with me, and said, O Daniel, I am now come forth to give thee skill and understanding.

23. At the beginning of thy supplications the commandment came forth, and I am come to shew thee; for thou art greatly beloved: therefore understand the matter, and consider the vision.

24. Seventy weeks are determined upon thy people and upon thy holy city, to finish the transgression, and to make an end of sins, and to make reconciliation for iniquity, and to bring in everlasting righteousness, and to seal up the vision and prophecy, and to anoint the most Holy.

25. Know therefore and understand, that **from the going forth of the commandment to restore and to build Jerusalem unto the Messiah the Prince shall be seven weeks**, and **threescore and two weeks**: the street shall be built again, and the wall, **even in troublous times.**

26. And **after threescore and two weeks shall Messiah be cut off,** but not for himself: **and the people of the prince that shall come shall destroy the city and the sanctuary**; and the end thereof shall be with a flood, and unto the end of the war desolations are determined.

27. And he shall confirm the covenant with many for one week: and in the midst of the week he shall cause the sacrifice and the oblation to cease, and for the overspreading of abominations he shall make it desolate, even until the consummation, and that determined shall be poured upon the desolate.

Daniel

Chapter 11

21. And in his estate shall stand up a **vile person**, to whom they shall not give the honour of the kingdom: but **he shall come in peaceably, and obtain the kingdom by flatteries.**

22. And with the arms of a flood shall they be overflown from before him, and shall be broken; yea, **also the prince of the covenant.**

25. And he shall stir up his power and his courage against the king of the south with a great army; and the king of the south shall be stirred up to battle with a very great and mighty army; but he shall not stand: for they shall forecast devices against him.

31. And arms shall stand on his part, and they shall pollute the sanctuary of strength, and shall take away the daily sacrifice, and they shall place the abomination that maketh desolate.

32. And such as do wickedly against the covenant shall he corrupt by flatteries: but the people that do know their God shall be strong, and do exploits.

33. And they that understand among the people shall instruct many: **yet they shall fall by the sword, and by flame, by captivity, and by spoil, many days.**

36. And the king shall do according to his will; and he shall exalt himself, and magnify himself above every god, and shall **speak marvellous** things **against the God of gods**, and shall prosper till the indignation be accomplished: for that that is determined shall be done.

37. Neither shall he regard the God of his fathers, nor the desire of women, nor regard any god: for he shall magnify himself above all.

38. But in his estate shall he honour the God of forces: and a god whom his fathers knew not shall he honour with gold, and silver, and with precious stones, and pleasant things.

40. And at the time of the end shall the king of the south push at him: and the king of the north shall come against him like a whirlwind, with chariots, and with horsemen, and with many ships; and he shall enter into the countries, and shall overflow and pass over.

41. He shall enter also into the glorious land, and many countries shall be overthrown: but these shall escape out of his hand, even Edom, and Moab, and the chief of the children of Ammon.

42. He shall stretch forth his hand also upon the countries: and the land of Egypt shall not escape.

43. But he shall have power over the treasures of gold and of silver, and over all the precious things of Egypt: and the Libyans and the Ethiopians shall be at his steps.

44. But tidings out of the east and out of the north shall trouble him: therefore he shall go forth with great fury to destroy, and utterly to make away many.

45. And he shall plant the tabernacles of his palace between the seas in the glorious holy mountain; yet he shall come to his end, and none shall help him.

Daniel

Chapter 12

1. And at that time shall Michael stand up, the great prince which standeth **for the children of thy people: and there shall be a time of trouble, such as never was since there was a nation even to that same time: and at that time thy people shall be delivered, every one that shall be found written in the book.**

2. And many of them that sleep in the dust of the earth shall awake, some to everlasting life, and some to shame and everlasting contempt.

3. And they that be wise shall shine as the brightness of the firmament; and they that turn many to righteousness as the stars for ever and ever.

Zechariah

Chapter 10

6. And **I will strengthen the house of Judah**, and I will save the **house of Joseph**, and **I will bring them again to place them; for I have mercy upon them**: and they shall be as though I had not cast them off: for **I am the LORD their God**, and will hear them.

10. I will bring them again also out of the land of Egypt, and gather them out of Assyria; and I will bring them into the land of Gilead and Labanon; **and place shall not be found for them**.

11. And he shall pass through the sea with affliction, and shall smite the waves in the sea, and all the deeps of the river shall dry up: **and the pride of Assyria shall be brought down, and the sceptre of Egypt shall depart away.**

12. And I will strengthen them in the LORD; and they shall walk up and down in his name, saith the LORD.

Zechariah

Chapter 11

1. Open thy doors, **O Lebanon, that the fire may devour thy cedars.**

2. Howl, fir tree; for the cedar is fallen; because the mighty are spoiled: howl, O ye oaks of Bashan; for the forest of the vintage is come down.

3. There is a voice of the howling of the shepherds; for their glory is spoiled: a voice of the roaring of young lions; for the **pride of Jordan is spoiled.**

Zechariah

Chapter 12

1.The burden of the word of the LORD for Israel, saith the LORD, which stretcheth forth the heavens, and layeth the foundation of the earth, and formeth the spirit of man within him.

2.Behold, I will make Jerusalem a cup of trembling unto all the people round about, when they shall be in the siege both against Judah and against Jerusalem.

3.And in that day will I make Jerusalem a burdensome stone for all people: all that burden themselves with it shall be cut in pieces, though all the people of the earth be gathered together against it.

4.In that day, saith the LORD, I will smite every horse with astonishment, and his rider with madness: and I will open mine eyes upon the house of Judah, and will smite every horse of the people with blindness.

5.And the governors of Judah shall say in their heart, The inhabitants of Jerusalem shall be my strength in the LORD of hosts their God.

6.In that day will I make the governors of Judah like an hearth of fire among the wood, and like a torch of fire in a sheaf; and they shall devour all the people round about, on the right hand and on the left: and Jerusalem shall be inhabited again in her own place, even in Jerusalem.

9.And it shall come to pass in that day, **that I will seek to destroy all the nations that come against Jerusalem.**

10.And I will pour upon the house of David, and upon the inhabitants of Jerusalem, the spirit of grace and of supplications:

and they shall look upon me whom they have pierced, and they shall mourn for him, as one mourneth for his only son, and shall be in bitterness for him, as one that is in bitterness for his firstborn.

11.In that day shall there be a great mourning in Jerusalem, as the mourning of Hadadrimmon in the valley of Megiddon.

12. And the land shall mourn, **every family apart;** the family of the house of David apart, and their wives apart; the family of the house of Nathan apart, and their wives apart;

13. The family of the house of Levi apart, and their wives apart; the family of Shimei apart, and their wives apart;

14.All the families that remain, every family apart, and their wives apart.

Zechariah

Chapter 13

8.And it shall come to pass, **that in all the land,** saith the LORD, **two parts therein shall be cut off and die; but the third shall be left therein.**

9. And **I will bring the third part through the fire**, and will refine them as silver is refined, and will try them as gold is tried: they shall call on my name, and I will hear them: I will say, It is my people: and **they shall say, The LORD is my God.**

Zechariah

Chapter 14

1. Behold, the day of the LORD cometh, and **thy spoil shall be divided in the midst of thee.**

2. For **I will gather all nations against Jerusalem to battle; and the city shall be taken, and the houses rifled, and the women ravished; and half of the city shall go forth into captivity, and the residue of the people shall not be cut off from the city.**

3. Then shall the LORD go forth, and fight against those nations, as when he fought in the day of battle.

4. And his feet shall stand in that day upon the mount of Olives, which is before Jerusalem on the east, and the mount of Olives shall cleave in the midst thereof toward the east and toward the west, and there shall be a very great valley; and half of the mountain shall remove toward the north, and half of it toward the south.

5. And ye shall flee to the valley of the mountains; for the valley of the mountains shall reach unto Azal: yea, ye shall flee, like as ye fled from before the earthquake in the days of Uzziah king of Judah: **and the LORD my God shall come, and all the saints with thee.**

6. And it shall come to pass in that day, that the light shall not be clear, nor dark:

7. But it shall be one day which shall be known to the LORD, not day, nor night: but it shall come to pass, that at evening time it shall be light.

8. And it shall be in that day, that living waters shall go out from Jerusalem; half of them toward the former sea, and half of them toward the hinder sea: in summer and in winter shall it be.

9. And the LORD shall be king over all the earth: in that day shall there be one LORD, and his name one.

12. And this shall be the plague wherewith **the LORD will smite all the people that have fought against Jerusalem**; Their flesh shall consume away while they stand upon their feet, and their eyes shall consume away in their holes, and their tongue shall consume away in their mouth.

13. And it shall come to pass in that day, that a great tumult from the LORD shall be among them; and they shall lay hold every one on the hand of his neighbour, and his hand shall rise up against the hand of his neighbour.

16. And it shall come to pass, that **every one that is left of all the nations which came against Jerusalem shall even go up from year to year to worship the King, the LORD of hosts,** and to keep the feast of tabernacles.

Matthew

Chapter 24

1. And Jesus went out, and departed from the temple: and his disciples came to him for to shew him **the buildings of the temple.**

2 And Jesus said unto them, See ye not all these things? verily I say unto you, **There shall not be left here one stone upon another, that shall not be thrown down.**

3. And as **he sat upon the mount of Olives**, the disciples came unto him privately, saying, **Tell us, when shall these things be? and what shall be the sign of thy coming, and of the end of the world?**

4. And Jesus answered and said unto them, Take heed that no man deceive you.

5. For many shall come in my name, saying, I am Christ; and shall deceive many.

6. And ye shall hear of wars and rumours of wars: see that ye be not troubled: for all these things must come to pass, but the end is not yet.

7. For nation shall rise against nation, and kingdom against kingdom: and there shall be famines, and pestilences, and earthquakes, in divers places.

8. All these are the beginning of sorrows.

9. Then shall they deliver you up to be afflicted, and shall kill you: and ye shall be hated of all nations for my name's sake.

10. And then shall many be offended, and shall betray one another, and shall hate one another.

11. And many false prophets shall rise, and shall deceive many.

12. And because iniquity shall abound, the love of many shall wax cold.

13. But he that shall endure unto the end, the same shall be saved.

14. And this gospel of the kingdom shall be preached in all the world for a witness unto all nations; and then shall the end come.

15. When ye therefore shall see the abomination of desolation, spoken of by Daniel the prophet, stand in the holy place, (whoso readeth, let him understand:)

16. Then let them which be in Judaea flee into the mountains:

17. Let him which is on the housetop not come down to take any thing out of his house:

18. Neither let him which is in the field return back to take his clothes.

19. And woe unto them that are with child, and to them that give suck in those days!

20. But pray ye that your flight be not in the winter, neither on the sabbath day:

21. For then shall be great tribulation, such as was not since the beginning of the world to this time, no, nor ever shall be.

22. And except those days should be shortened, there should no flesh be saved: **but for the elect's sake those days shall be shortened.**

23. Then if any man shall say unto you, Lo, here is Christ, or there; believe it not.

27. **For as the lightning cometh out of the east, and shineth even unto the west; so shall also the coming of the Son of man be.**

29. Immediately after the tribulation of those days shall the sun be darkened, and the moon shall not give her light, and the stars shall fall from heaven, and the powers of the heavens shall be shaken:

30. And then shall appear the sign of the Son of man in heaven: and then shall all the tribes of the earth mourn, and they shall see the Son of man coming in the clouds of heaven with power and great glory.

31. And he shall send his angels with a great sound of a trumpet, and they shall gather together his elect from the four winds, from one end of heaven to the other.

Matthew

Chapter 25

31. When the Son of man shall come in his glory, and all the holy angels with him, then shall he sit upon the throne of his glory:

32. And before him shall be gathered all nations: and he shall separate them one from another, as a shepherd divideth his sheep from the goats:

33. And he shall set the sheep on his right hand, but the goats on the left.

34. Then shall the King say unto them on his right hand, Come, ye blessed of my Father, inherit the kingdom prepared for you from the foundation of the world:

35. For I was an hungred, and ye gave me meat: I was thirsty, and ye gave me drink: I was a stranger, and ye took me in:

36. Naked, and ye clothed me: I was sick, and ye visited me: I was in prison, and ye came unto me.

37. Then shall the righteous answer him, saying, Lord, when saw we thee an hungred, and fed thee? or thirsty, and gave thee drink?

38. When saw we thee a stranger, and took thee in? or naked, and clothed thee?

39. Or when saw we thee sick, or in prison, and came unto thee?

40. And the King shall answer and say unto them, Verily I say unto you, Inasmuch as ye have done it unto one of the least of these **my brethren**, ye **have done it unto me.**

41. Then shall he say also unto them on the left hand, Depart from me, ye cursed, into everlasting fire, prepared for the devil and his angels:

42. For I was an hungred, and ye gave me no meat: I was thirsty, and ye gave me no drink:

43. I was a stranger, and ye took me not in: naked, and ye clothed me not: sick, and in prison, and ye visited me not.

44. Then shall they also answer him, saying, Lord, when saw we thee an hungred, or athirst, or a stranger, or naked, or sick, or in prison, and did not minister unto thee?

45. Then shall he answer them, saying, Verily I say unto you, Inasmuch as ye **did it not to one of the least of these, ye did it not to me.**

46. And these shall go away into everlasting punishment: but the righteous into life eternal.

Romans

Chapter 9

1. I say the truth in Christ, I lie not, my conscience also bearing me witness in the Holy Ghost,

2. That I have great heaviness and continual sorrow in my heart.

3. For I could wish that myself were accursed from **Christ for my brethren, my kinsmen according to the flesh:**

4. Who are Israelites; to whom pertaineth the adoption, and the glory, and the covenants, and the giving of the law, and the service of God, and the promises;

5. Whose are the fathers, and of whom as concerning the flesh Christ came, who is over all, God blessed for ever. Amen.

Romans

Chapter 10

1. Brethren, my heart's desire and prayer to God for Israel is, that they might be saved.

2. For I bear them record that they have a zeal of God, but not according to knowledge.

3. For **they being ignorant of God's righteousness,** and going about to **establish their own righteousness, have not submitted themselves unto the righteousness of God.**

4. For **Christ is the end of the law for righteousness to every one that believeth.**

12. For **there is no difference between the Jew and the Greek: for the same Lord over all is rich unto all that call upon him.**

13. For **whosoever shall call upon the name of the Lord shall be saved.**

Romans

Chapter 11

1. I say then, **Hath God cast away his people? God forbid.** For **I also am an Israelite, of the seed of Abraham, of the tribe of Benjamin.**

2. **God hath not cast away his people which he foreknew.** Wot ye not what the scripture saith of Elias? how he maketh intercession to God against Israel, saying,

3. Lord, they have killed thy prophets, and digged down thine altars; and I am left alone, and they seek my life.

4. But what saith the answer of God unto him? I have reserved to myself seven thousand men, who have not bowed the knee to the image of Baal.

5. **Even so then at this present time also there is a remnant according to the election of grace.**

7. What then? Israel hath not obtained that which he seeketh for; **but the election hath obtained it, and the rest were blinded**

25. For I would not, brethren, that ye should be ignorant of this mystery, lest ye should be wise in your own conceits; **that blindness in part is happened to Israel, until the fulness of the Gentiles be come in.**

26. **And so all Israel shall be saved:** as it is written, There shall come out of Sion the Deliverer, and shall turn away ungodliness from Jacob:

27. For **this is my covenant unto them, when I shall take away their sins.**

28. As concerning the gospel, they are enemies for your sakes: but as touching the election, they are beloved for the fathers' sakes.
29. *For the gifts and calling of God are without repentance.*
30. For as ye in times past have not believed God, yet have now obtained mercy through their unbelief:
31. Even so have these also now not believed, that through your mercy they also may obtain mercy.
32. For God hath concluded them all in unbelief, that he might have mercy upon all.

COMMENTARY

In the Qur'an:

1. Allah warned Mohammed to avoid friendly contact with Jews and Christians, for they *"...will not be pleased with you... until you follow their religion"*. He clearly rejects their assertion of having a good relationship with God by claiming that the faith of Abraham (who was a Muslim) was distinct from Judaism and Christianity: *"...Ibrahim was not a Jew nor a Christian..."* Mohammed was clearly instructed by Allah that the Jews and Christians of that time period and of the future cannot be saved from hellfire unless they accept Allah and His messenger, Mohammed. Only those who lived before the time of Mohammed will be saved based on the Torah and the Gospel, if they obey what was written in these books. Jews in particular sinned greatly against God and *"...Allah has cursed them on account of their unbelief, so they do not believe but a little..."* Because the Qur'an is the final religion and final revelation from God to the whole world and by virtue of the fact of its existence, all other religions on the planet are void.

2. Being a follower of the last religion simply means that Muslims will enter Paradise and will be rewarded by Allah at the End of the Days, as we can read in the chapter entitled "Paradise", and all unbelievers in Allah will be headed towards the fires of hell.

In the Bible:

1. In many places in the Scriptures, God refers to the Jews as His own people. He said that He will never curse them (meaning complete damnation without hope). Christians are instructed not

to be ignorant of the fact that Israel will be saved by God in the future, and they should not act proudly nor neglect Jews:

Romans, Chapter 11

28. *As concerning the gospel, they are enemies for your sakes: but as touching the election, they are beloved for the fathers' sakes.*

29. *For the gifts and calling of God are without repentance.*

2. Many prophecies speak about the future conflict which will take place in Israel and in particular, Jerusalem, just before the King (Jesus) returns. God spoke through the prophets Daniel, Isaiah and Zechariah, warning that all the nations surrounding Israel, including other nations in the world, will hate her and will eventually use their military power to attack the Jewish people who will be living in Israel at that time. Nevertheless before that, the military might of Israel will prevail over armies of **surrounding nations**: *"…and they shall devour all the people round about…"*, and in the result of this *"…the pride of **Assyria** shall be brought down, and the sceptre of **Egypt** shall depart away…"*, *"…Open thy doors, O **Lebanon**, that the fire may devour thy cedars… pride of **Jordan** is spoiled."*

However, in the last days Israel will be in even greater trouble and will stand at the edge of extermination: *"…the city shall be taken, and the houses rifled, and the women ravished; and half of the city shall go forth into captivity…"*

Exactly what kind of event that will cause such a conflict is not revealed in the Bible, but it says that Jews will return to the land and *"…place shall not be found for them…"*

Based on the fact that we know that present day Israel has been at war for over sixty years just because of it's existence, any attack on Israel will eventually trigger a worldwide conflict. Today, it is much easier to count the friends of Israel using the fingers on one hand than to count her enemies using a calculator! Jesus predicted that Jerusalem will be attacked and the Jews will find their salvation in His return only:

Matthew, Chapter 24

21. For then shall be great tribulation, such as was not since the beginning of the world to this time, no, nor ever shall be.

22. And except those days should be shortened, there should no flesh be saved: **but for the elect's sake those days shall be shortened.**

30. And then shall appear the sign of the Son of man in heaven: and then shall all the tribes of the earth mourn, and they shall see the **Son of man coming in the clouds of heaven with power and great glory.**

Daniel had a revelation from God that the tribulation period will last for only seven years and it will get much worse after the first three and a half years, but it will be followed by the miraculous salvation of all the remaining people of Israel.

In the return of Jesus there is a hope not only for Christians but for Jews as well. Based on the fact that most of the enemies of Israel are Muslims, we can come to the conclusion that they will be among these nations who will attack Jerusalem and *"…Then shall the LORD go forth, and fight against those nations, as when he fought in the day of battle… the LORD will smite* **all the people** *that have fought against Jerusalem;"*

SUMMARY

Jesus said that when He returns, all nations will be gathered unto Him and He will judge them on the basis of simple acts of help toward **Jesus' brethren**: *"…Inasmuch as ye have done it unto one of the least of these my brethren, ye have done it unto me… Inasmuch as ye did it not to one of the least of these, ye did it not to me…"*

The Bible is very clear that Israel is distinct from the Church, and when it uses the word "nations", it means also "non-Jews", since Jesus is The Jew, and His brethren are also Jews. During the tribulation period, people will enter the Millennial Kingdom of Christ on the basis of their belief in Him, which was proven by helping Jewish people in the great time of trouble for them. Others, who will be enemies of the Jews during the seven-year period, will suffer loss: *"...And these shall go away into everlasting punishment."* Unfortunately without a single doubt, Muslims do fit into this category, together with all other anti-Semites. This claim of Jesus clearly denounces the qur'anical claim that Muslims will be in Paradise, but Jews and Christians will not.

Chapter Eleven

THE BOOK

THE QUR'AN

"The True Book"

Sura 10

Jonah

37. And this Quran is not such as could be forged by those besides Allah, but it is a verification of that which is before it and a clear explanation of the book, there is no doubt in it, from the Lord of the worlds.

38. Or do they say: He has forged it? Say: **Then bring a chapter like this and invite whom you can besides Allah, if you are truthful.**

39. Nay, they reject that of which they have no comprehensive knowledge, and the final sequel of it has not yet come to them; even thus did those before them reject (the truth); see then what was the end of the unjust.

Sura 11

The Holy Prophet

12. Then, it may be that you will give up part of what is revealed to you and your breast will become straitened by it because they say: Why has not a treasure been sent down upon him or an angel come with him? You are only a warner; and Allah is custodian over all things.

13. Or, do they say: He has forged it. Say: **Then bring ten forged chapters like it and call upon whom you can besides Allah, if you are truthful.**

Sura 13

The Thunder

1. Alif Lam Mim Ra. These are the verses of the Book; and that which is **revealed to you from your Lord is the truth**, but most people do not believe..

Sura 15

The Rock

1. Alif Lam Ra. These are the verses of the Book and (of) a Quran that makes (things) clear.

2. Often will those who disbelieve wish that they had been Muslims.

Sura 16

The Bee

64. And We have not revealed to you the Book except that you may make clear to them that about which they differ, ind (as) **a guidance and a mercy for a people who believe**.

89. And on the day when We will raise up in every people a witness against them from among themselves, and bring you as a witness against these. And **We have revealed the Book to you explaining clearly everything, and a guidance and mercy and good news for those who submit.**

Sura 17

The Children of Israel

45. And when you recite the Quran, We place between you and those who do not believe in the hereafter a hidden barrier;

46. And **We have placed coverings on their hearts and a heaviness in their ears lest they understand it, and when you mention your Lord alone in the Quran they turn their backs in aversion.**

47. We know best what they listen to when they listen to you, and when they take counsel secretly, when the unjust say: You follow only a man deprived of reason.

48. See what they liken you to! So they have gone astray and cannot find the way.

49. And they say: What! when we shall have become bones and decayed particles, shall we then certainly be raised up, being a new creation?

88. Say: If men and jinn should combine together to bring the like of this Quran, they could not bring the like of it, though some of them were aiders of others.

106. And it is a Quran which We have revcaled in portions so that you may read it to the people by slow degrees, and We have revealed it, revealing in portions.
107. Say: **Believe in it or believe not; surely those who are given the knowledge before it fall down on their faces, making obeisance when it is recited to them**.
108. And they say: Glory be to our Lord! most surely the promise of our Lord was to be fulfilled.
109. And they fall down on their faces weeping, and it adds to their humility.

Sura 18

The Cave

1. (All) praise is due to **Allah, Who revealed the Book to His servant and did not make in it any crookedness.**
2. Rightly directing, that he might give warning of severe punishment from **Him and give good news to the believers who do good that they shall have a goodly reward,**
3. Staying in it for ever;

Sura 24

The Light

1. (This is) **a chapter which We have revealed and made obligatory and in which We have revealed clear communications that you may be mindful.**

Sura 27

The Ant

1. Ta Sin! **These are the verses of the Quran and the Book that makes (things) clear**
2. A guidance and good news for the believers,

3. Who keep up prayer and pay the poor-rate, and of the hereafter, they are sure.

4. As to those who do not believe in the hereafter, We have surely made their deeds fair-seeming to them, but they blindly wander on.

5. These are they who shall have an evil punishment, and in the hereafter they shall be the greatest losers.

6. And most surely you are made to receive the Quran from the Wise, the Knowing God.

Sura 28

The Narratives

2. These are the verses of the Book that **makes (things) clear**.

Sura 29

The Spider

47. And thus have **We revealed the Book to you. So those whom We have given the Book believe in it, and of these there are those who believe in it, and none deny Our communications except the unbelievers.**

48. And you did not recite before it any book, nor did you transcribe one with your right hand, for then could those who say untrue things have doubted.

49. Nay! these are clear communications in the breasts of those who are granted knowledge; and none deny Our communications except the unjust.

Sura 32

The Adoration

2. The revelation of the **Book, there is no doubt in it, is from the Lord of the worlds.**

Sura 39

The Companions

1. The revelation of the Book is from Allah, the Mighty, the Wise.
2. Surely We have revealed to you the **Book with the truth, therefore serve Allah,** being sincere to Him in obedience.

23. Allah has revealed the best announcement, a book conformable in its various parts, repeating, whereat do shudder the skins of those who fear their Lord, then their skins and their hearts become pliant to the remembrance of Allah; this is Allah's guidance, He guides with it whom He pleases; and (as for) him whom Allah makes err, there is no guide for him.

Sura 40

The Believer

2. The revelation of the Book is from Allah, the Mighty, the Knowing,

Sura 54

The Moon

17, 22, 32, 40. And certainly **We have made the Quran easy for remembrance**, but is there anyone who will mind?

THE BIBLE

"The True Book"

Exodus

Chapter 24

7. And he took the **book of the covenant**, and read in the audience of the people: and they said, All that the **LORD hath said** will we do, and be obedient.

Deuteronomy

Chapter 28

58. If thou wilt not observe to do all the words of this law that are written in this **book**, that thou mayest fear this glorious and fearful name, THE LORD THY GOD;

Deuteronomy

Chapter 31

24. And it came to pass, when Moses had made **an end of writing the words of this law in a book, until they were finished,**
25. That Moses commanded the Levites, which bare the ark of the covenant of the LORD, saying,
26. Take this book of the law, and put it in the side of the ark of the covenant of the LORD your God, that it may be there for a witness against thee.

Joshua

Chapter 1

8. This book of the law shall not depart out of thy mouth; but thou shalt meditate therein day and night, that thou mayest observe to do according to all that is written therein: for then thou shalt make thy way prosperous, and then thou shalt have good success.

Second Chronicles

Chapter 34

14. And when they brought out the money that was brought into the house of the LORD, Hilkiah the priest found **a book of the law of the LORD given by Moses.**

Isaiah

Chapter 34

16. Seek ye out of **the book of the LORD**, and read: no one of these shall fail, none shall want her mate: for my mouth it hath commanded, and his spirit it hath gathered them.

Acts

Chapter 1

16. Men and brethren, **this scripture must needs have been fulfilled,** which the Holy Ghost by the mouth of David spake before concerning Judas, which was guide to them that took Jesus.

Second Peter

Chapter 1

20. Knowing this first, that **no prophecy of the scripture is of any private interpretation.**
21. For the prophecy came not in old time by the will of man: but holy men of God **spake as they were moved by the Holy Ghost.**

Second Timothy

Chapter 3

16. All scripture is given by inspiration of God, and is profitable for doctrine, for reproof, for correction, for instruction in righteousness:
17. That the man of God may be perfect, thoroughly furnished unto all good works.

COMMENTARY

The Qur'an calls itself God's word and claims that it came directly from God. The Bible also claims to be the word of God. Both books contradict each other on almost every subject.

The major theme of this book is to show this gaping contradiction between these two Books. This leads us to the question: **Are they given by the same One Supreme Author?**

Only one Book can be God's Word. It is our duty to make the right choice between the two.

Part Three

COMPARISON OF THE NON-CANONICAL GOSPELS WITH THE BIBLE

Chapter One

MARY'S PARENTS

THE NON-CANONICAL GOSPELS

"Ioacim (Joachim) and Anna are Mocked"

Infancy Gospel of James, or Protevangelium

I. 1. In the histories of the twelve tribes of Israel it is written that there was one Ioacim, exceeding rich: and he offered his gifts twofold, saying: That which is of my superfluity shall be for the whole people, **and that which is for my forgiveness shall be for the Lord, for a propitiation unto me.**

2. Now the great day of the Lord drew nigh and the children of Israel offered their gifts. And **Reuben** stood over against him saying: **It is not lawful for thee to offer thy gifts first,-forasmuch as thou hast gotten no seed in Israel.** And Ioacim was sore grieved, and went **unto the record of the twelve tribes of the people, saying: I will look upon the record of the twelve tribes of Israel, whether I only have not gotten seed in Israel. And he searched, and found concerning all the righteous that they had raised up seed in Israel.**

3 And Anna was sore grieved and mourned with a great mourning because she was *reproached by all the tribes of Israel....*

III. 1 And looking up to the heaven she espied a nest of sparrows in the laurel-tree, and made a lamentation within herself, saying: Woe unto me, who begat me ? And what womb brought me forth for I am become a curse *before the children of Israel, and I am reproached, and they have mocked me forth out of the temple of the Lord?*

The Gospel of the Nativity of Mary

CHAP. 2- **And it came to pass that the festival of the dedication was at hand;** wherefore also Joachim went up to Jerusalem with some men of his own tribe. Now at that time **Issachar** was high priest there. And when he saw Joachim with his offering among his other fellow-citizens, he despised him, and spurned his gifts, asking why he, who had no offspring, presumed to stand among those who had; saying that his gifts could not by any means be acceptable to God, since He had deemed him unworthy of off-spring: for the Scripture said, Cursed is every one who has not begot a male or a female in Israel.

THE BIBLE AND COMMENTARY

The Bible never states anywhere that some of the great prophets of God had descendants. Daniel, Isaiah, Ezekiel, Jonah, etc., nor Hosea, whose wife was a prostitute, ever had children. It is not necessary to have children to be qualified as "righteous" before God.

It is difficult to believe that **all Hebrews** (*"because she was reproached by all the tribes of Israel…"*) had concern over Anna's inability to bear a child.

THE NON-CANONICAL GOSPELS
"Anna Gives Birth"
Infancy Gospel of James, or Protevangelium

VI. 1 And day by day the child waxed strong, and when she **was six months old her mother stood her upon the ground to try if she would stand; and she walked seven steps and returned unto her bosom.** And she caught her up, saying: As the Lord my God liveth, thou shalt walk no more upon this ground, until I bring thee into the temple of the Lord. **And she made a sanctuary in her bed chamber and suffered nothing common or unclean to pass through it. And she called for the daughters of the Hebrews that were undefiled, and they carried her hither and thither.**

2 And the first year of the child was fulfilled, and Ioacim made a great feast and bade the priests and the scribes and the assembly of the elders and the **whole people of Israel**. And Ioacim brought the child to the priests, and they blessed her, saying: O God of our fathers, **bless this child and give her a name renowned for ever among all generations. And all the people said: So be it, so be it.** Amen. And he brought

her to the high priests, and they blessed her, saying: O God of the high places, look upon this child, **and bless her with the last blessing which hath no successor.**

3. And the priest received her and kissed her and blessed her and said: **The Lord hath magnified thy name among all generations: in thee in the latter days shall the Lord make manifest his redemption unto the children of Israel.** And he made her to **sit upon the third step of the altar.** And the Lord put grace upon her and she danced with her feet **and all the house of Israel loved her.**

VIII. 1 And her parents gat them down marveling, and praising the Lord God because tile child was not turned away backward.
And Mary was in the temple of the Lord as a dove that is nurtured: and she received food from the hand of an angel.

The Gospel of the Nativity of Mary

CHAP. 4- Thereafter he appeared to Anna his wife, saying: Fear not, Anna, nor think that it is a phantom which thou seest. For I am that angel who has presented your prayers and alms before God; and now have I been sent to you to announce to you that thou shalt bring forth a daughter, who shall be called Mary, and who shall be blessed above all women. She, full of the favour of the Lord even from her birth, shall remain three years in her father's house until she be weaned. Thereafter, being delivered to the service of the Lord, she shall not depart from the temple until she reach the years of discretion. There, serving God day and night in fastings and prayers, she shall abstain from every unclean thing; **she shall never know man, but alone, without example, immaculate, uncorrupted, without intercourse with man, she, a virgin, shall bring forth a son**; she, His hand-maiden, shall bring forth the Lord--both in grace, and in name, and in work, the Saviour of the world.

CHAP. 6- And when the circle of three years had rolled round, and the time of her weaning was fulfilled, they brought the virgin to the temple of the Lord with offerings. Now there were round the temple, according to the fifteen Psalms of Degrees, fifteen steps going up; for, on account of the temple having been built on a mountain, **the altar of burnt-offering, which stood outside, could not be reached except by steps.**

...the virgin of the Lord went up all the steps, one after the other, without the help of any one leading her or lifting her, in such a manner that, in this respect at least, you would think that she had already attained full age. For already the Lord in the infancy of His virgin wrought a great thing, and by the indication of this miracle foreshowed how great she was to be. Therefore, a sacrifice having been offered according to the custom of the law, and their vow being perfected, they left the virgin within the enclosures of the temple, there to be educated with the other virgins,

CHAP. 7- But the virgin of the Lord advanced in age and in virtues; and though, in the words of the Psalmist, her father and mother had forsaken her, the Lord took her up.[2] For daily was she visited by angels, daily did she enjoy a divine vision, which preserved her from all evil, and made her to abound in all good. And so she reached her fourteenth year; and not only were the wicked unable to charge her with anything worthy of reproach, but all the good, who knew her life and conversation, judged her to be worthy of admiration.

The Bible

"Anna Gives Birth"

Luke

Chapter 2

22. And when the days of her purification according to the law of Moses were accomplished, they brought him to Jerusalem, to present him to the Lord;

25. And, behold, there was a man in Jerusalem, whose name was Simeon; and the same man was just and devout, waiting for the consolation of Israel: and the Holy Ghost was upon him.

26. And it was revealed unto him by the Holy Ghost, that he should not see death, before he had seen the Lord's Christ.

28. Then took he him up in his arms, and blessed God, and said,

29. Lord, now lettest thou thy servant depart in peace, according to thy word:

30. For mine eyes have seen thy salvation,

31. Which thou hast prepared before the face of all people;

32. A light to lighten the Gentiles, and the glory of thy people Israel.

33. And Joseph and his mother marvelled at those things which were spoken of him.

34. And Simeon blessed them, and said unto Mary his mother, **Behold, this child is set for the fall and rising again of many in Israel; and for a sign which shall be spoken against;**

35. (Yea, a sword shall pierce through thy own soul also,) that the thoughts of many hearts may be revealed.

36. And there was one Anna, a prophetess, the daughter of Phanuel, of the tribe of Aser: she was of a great age, and had lived with an husband seven years from her virginity;

37. And she was a widow of about fourscore and four years, which departed not from the temple, but served God with fastings and prayers night and day.

38. And she coming in that instant gave thanks likewise unto the Lord, and **spake of him to all them that looked for redemption in Jerusalem.**

39. And when they had performed all things according to the law of the Lord, they returned into Galilee, to their own city Nazareth.

Exodus

Chapter 20

24. An altar of earth thou shalt make unto me, and shalt sacrifice thereon thy burnt offerings, and thy peace offerings, thy sheep, and thine oxen: in all places where I record my name I will come unto thee, and I will bless thee.

25. And if thou wilt make me an altar of stone, thou shalt not build it of hewn stone: for if thou lift up thy tool upon it, thou hast polluted it.

26. Neither shalt thou go up by steps unto mine altar, that thy nakedness be not discovered thereon.

Exodus

Chapter 28

40. And for Aaron's sons thou shalt make coats, and thou shalt make for them girdles, and bonnets shalt thou make for them, for glory and for beauty.

41. And thou shalt put them upon Aaron thy brother, and his sons with him; and shalt anoint them, and consecrate them, and sanctify them, that they may minister unto me in the priest's office.

42. And thou shalt make them linen breeches to cover their nakedness; from the loins even unto the thighs they shall reach:

43. And they shall be upon Aaron, and upon his sons, **when they come in unto the tabernacle of the congregation, or when they come near unto the altar to minister in the holy place; that they bear not iniquity, and die: it shall be a statute for ever unto him and his seed after him.**

COMMENTARY

In the Non-Canonical Text:

1. The High Priest praised Mary while she was yet a toddler, recognising her uniqueness among **all generations**, and that redemption would be manifested through her later in life.

   The text shows that she was loved by everyone, just as she is praised and adored by certain denominations these days.

2. It looks like the writer of this text tried to prove that Mary was sinless right from birth and perpetual virgin, and that she had taken a rightful position in heaven near her son, Jesus.

3. The writer gives a picture of the "altar of burnt offering" as having steps: Mary sat "… upon the third step of the altar…"

4. Mary was living inside the Temple and an angel from the Lord fed her on daily basis.

In the Bible:

1. Jesus (not Mary) was recognized as the unique child who was to be the Redemption of Israel. This acknowledgement came not from the priesthood of the Temple, but by Simeon and Anna. Nothing is mentioned about the uniqueness of Mary or Joseph, for they are not (and cannot be) portrayed as co-redeemers of humanity with Jesus. Neither can they be placed on the same level of praise or worship and must not be prayed to.

Exodus 20:4-6

⁴Thou shalt not make unto thee any graven image, or any likeness of any thing that is in heaven above, or that is in the earth beneath, or that is in the water under the earth.

⁵Thou shalt not bow down thyself to them, nor serve them: for I the LORD thy God am a jealous God, visiting the iniquity of the fathers upon the children unto the third and fourth generation of them that hate me;

⁶And shewing mercy unto thousands of them that love me, and keep my commandments.

Exodus 34:14

*For thou shalt **worship no other god**: for the LORD, whose name is Jealous, is **a jealous God**.*

(See also Deuteronomy 5:9)

John 10:30

(Jesus says...)*I and my Father are one.*

Acts 4:12 *(referring to Jesus)*

Neither is there salvation in any other: for there is none other name under heaven given among men, whereby we must be saved.

Here we read that redemption was found in Jesus, not Mary.

2. Mary was "highly favoured" by God in being chosen as the person through whom the redemption of mankind would come, but not taking the position of Jesus who is the **only** sinless representative of the human race.

John 1:29
The next day John seeth Jesus coming unto him, and saith, Behold the Lamb of God, which taketh away the sin of the world.

3. The altar did not have any steps. In Solomon's Temple,   the altar was about 5 meters high, and it had a ramp from the eastern side.
4. It was only the privilege of the tribe of Levi to serve near the altar inside the Tabernacle and later in the Temple itself. Nobody from another tribe was allowed to come near the altar, and especially not girls or women.

Chapter Two

MARY

THE NON-CANONICAL GOSPELS

"Mary and Joseph"

Infancy Gospel of James, or Protevangelium

VIII 2 And when she was twelve years old, there was a council of the priests, saying: Behold **Mary is become twelve years old in the temple of the Lord**. What then shall we do with her? **lest she pollute the sanctuary of the Lord.** And they said unto the high priest: Thou standest over the altar of the Lord. Enter in and pray concerning her: And whatsoever the Lord shall reveal to thee, that let us do.

3 And the high priest took the vestment with the twelve bells and **went in unto the Holy of Holies and prayed concerning her**.

And lo, an angel of the Lord appeared saying unto him: **Zacharias, Zacharias, go forth and assemble them that are widowers of the people, and let them bring every man a rod, and to whomsoever the Lord show a sign, his wife shall shall she be.** And the heralds went forth over all the country round about Judaea, and the trumpet of the Lord sounded, and all men ran thereto.

IX **2 And Joseph refused, saying: I have sons, and I am an old man, but she is a girl: lest I become a laughing-stock to the children of Israel.**

XL 8 And she abode three months with Elizabeth, and day by day her womb grew: and Mary was afraid and departed unto her house **and hid herself from the children of Israel**. Now she was sixteen years old when these mysteries came to pass

XV. I Now Annas the scribe came unto him and said to him: Wherefore didst thou not appear in our assembly? and Joseph said unto him: I was weary with the journey, and I rested the first day. And Annas turned him about and saw Mary great with child. 2 And he went hastily to the priest and said unto him: Joseph, to whom thou bearest witness [that he is righteous] **hath sinned grievously**. And the priest said: Wherein? And he said: **The virgin whom he received out of the temple of the Lord, he hath defiled her**, and married her by stealth (lit. stolen her marriage), and hath not declared it to the children of Israel. And the priest said: Bear no false witness but speak the truth: thou hast married her by stealth and hast not declared it unto the children of Israel

XVII. 1 Now there went out a decree from Augustus the king **that all that were in Bethlehem of Judaea should be recorded.** And Joseph said: I will record my sons: but this child, what shall I do with her? **how shall I record her ? as my wife ? nay, I am ashamed. Or as my daughter? but all the children of Israel know that she is not my daughter.**

XVIII. 1 And he found a cave there and brought her into it, and set his sons by her: and he went forth and sought for a midwife of the Hebrews in the country of Bethlehem.

2 Now I Joseph was walking, and I walked not. And I looked up to the air and saw the air in amazement. And I looked up unto the pole of the heaven and saw it standing still, and the fowls of the heaven without motion. And I looked upon the earth and saw a dish set, and workmen lying by it, and their hands were in the dish: and they that were chewing chewed not, and they that were lifting the food lifted it not, and they that put it to their mouth put it not thereto, but the faces of all of them were looking upward. And behold there were sheep being driven, and they went not forward but stood still; and the shepherd lifted his hand to smite them with his staff, and his hand remained up. And I looked upon the stream of the river and saw the mouths of the kids upon the water and they drank not. And of a sudden all things moved onward in their course.

XIX 2 And the midwife cried aloud and said: Great unto me to-day is this day, in that ! have seen this new sight.

3 And the midwife went forth of the cave and Salome met her. And she said to her: Salome, Salome, a new sight have I to tell thee. A virgin hath brought forth, which her nature alloweth not. And Salome said: As the Lord my God liveth, if I make not trial and prove her nature I will not believe that a virgin hath brought forth.
And Salome made trial and cried out and said: Woe unto mine iniquity and mine unbelief, because I have tempted the living God, and lo, my hand falleth away from me in fire.

The Gospel of the Nativity of Mary

CHAP. 7- But the virgin of the Lord advanced in age and in virtues; and though, in the words of the Psalmist, her father and mother had forsaken her, the Lord took her up.[2] **For daily was she visited by angels,** daily did she enjoy a divine vision, **which preserved her from all evil, and made her to abound in all good**. And so she reached her fourteenth year; and **not only were the wicked unable to charge her with anything worthy of reproach, but all the good, who knew her life and conversation, judged her to be worthy of admiration**.

Then the high priest publicly announced that the virgins who were publicly settled in the temple, and had reached this time of life, should return home and get married, according to the custom of the nation and the ripeness of their years. The others readily obeyed this command; but Mary alone, the virgin of the Lord, answered that she could not do this, saying both that her parents had devoted her to the service of the Lord, and that, moreover, she herself had made to the Lord a vow of virginity, which she would never violate by any intercourse with man.

...the high priest went to consult God in the usual way. Nor had they long to wait: in the hearing of all a voice issued from the oracle and from the **mercy-seat, that, according to the prophecy of Isaiah, a man should be sought out to whom the virgin ought to be entrusted and espoused**. For it is clear that Isaiah says: **A rod shall come forth from the root of Jesse, and a flower shall ascend from his root; and the Spirit of the Lord shall rest upon him, the spirit of wisdom and understanding, the spirit of counsel and strength, the spirit of wisdom and piety; and he shall be filled with the spirit of the fear of the Lord.[2] According to this prophecy, therefore, he predicted that all of the house and family of David** that *were unmarried and fit for marriage* **should bring there rods to the altar; and that he whose rod after it was brought should produce a flower, and upon the end of whose rod the Spirit of the Lord should settle in the form of a dove, was the man to whom the virgin ought to be entrusted and espoused.**

CHAP. 9- And in those days, that is, at the time of her first coming into Galilee, the angel Gabriel was sent to her by God,

he said: Hail, Mary! O virgin highly favoured by the Lord, virgin full of grace, the Lord is with thee;

For in choosing chastity, thou hast found favour with the Lord; and therefore thou, a virgin, **shalt conceive without sin, and shalt bring forth a son.**

Think not, Mary, that thou shalt conceive in the manner of mankind: for without any intercourse with man, thou, a virgin, wilt conceive; thou, a virgin, wilt bring forth; thou, a virgin, wilt nurse...

THE BIBLE

"Mary and Joseph"

Leviticus

Chapter 16

2. And the LORD said unto Moses, Speak unto Aaron thy brother, that **he come not at all times into the holy place** within the vail before the mercy seat, which is upon the ark; that he die not: for I will appear in the cloud upon the mercy seat.
34. And this shall be an everlasting statute unto you, to make atonement for the children of Israel for all their sins **once a year**. And he did as the LORD commanded Moses.

Luke

Chapter 1

26. And in the sixth month the angel Gabriel was sent from God unto a city of Galilee, named Nazareth,
27. To a virgin espoused to a man whose name was Joseph, of the house of David; and the virgin's name was Mary.

Luke

Chapter 2

1. And it came to pass in those days, that there went out a decree from Caesar Augustus, that all the world should be taxed.

2. **(And this taxing was first made when Cyrenius was governor of Syria.)**

3. And all went to be taxed, every one into his own city.

4. **And Joseph also went up from Galilee, out of the city of Nazareth, into Judaea, unto the city of David, which is called Bethlehem; (because he was of the house and lineage of David:)**

5. To be taxed with Mary his espoused wife, being great with child.

6. **And so it was, that**, while they were there, **the days were accomplished that she should be delivered.**

7. **And she brought forth her firstborn son, and wrapped him in swaddling clothes, and laid him in a manger; because there was no room for them in the inn.**

Isaiah

Chapter 11

1.And there shall come forth a **rod out of the stem of Jesse, and a Branch shall grow out of his roots:**

2.**And the spirit of the LORD shall rest upon him**, the spirit of wisdom and understanding, the spirit of counsel and might, the spirit of knowledge and of the fear of the LORD;

3. **And shall make him of quick understanding in the fear of the LORD: and he shall not judge after the sight of his eyes, neither reprove after the hearing of his ears:**

4. But with righteousness **shall he judge the poor, and reprove with equity for the meek of the earth: and he shall smite the earth with the rod of his mouth, and with the breath of his lips shall he slay the wicked.**

5. And righteousness shall be the girdle of his loins, and faithfulness the girdle of his reins.

10. And in that day there shall be **a root of Jesse, which shall stand for an ensign of the people; to it shall the Gentiles seek: and his rest shall be glorious.**

COMPARISON AND COMMENTARY

In the Non-Canonical Text:

1. The High Priest went into the Holy of Holies in order to ask God about Mary's future.

2. The High Priest received from God an explanation from the book of Isaiah, Chapter 11 as the way to find *"a man should be sought out to whom the virgin ought to be entrusted and espoused."*

3. An old man named Joseph was chosen by God to be Mary's husband, who was fearful to consider her as his wife or as his daughter.

4. Only those who came from Bethlehem were to be recorded in a census.

5. Mary gave birth in cave, guarded by Joseph's sons from his previous marriage, before they reached the city.

6. Joseph recognised the uniqueness of the moment when Jesus came out of Mary's womb.

7. The attending midwife recognized that Mary was a virgin and that she remained a virgin after the delivery. Salome almost lost her hand trying to disprove it.

8. The passage introduces the belief that the natural way to conceive is sinful.

In the Bible:

1. It is clear that only once a year the High Priest was able to enter into the Holy of Holies. That day is called the Day of Atonement (*Yom Kippur*), when **all the congregation of Israel** was gathered there and waited for the atonement of their sins. It was impossible for the High Priest to go there on any other day of the year, especially for a "local needs" prayer.

2. It is very clear that Isaiah, chapter 11 speaks about the promised Messiah as being a descendant from the lineage of David. Jesus came from this line. The "person" who was to be descendant of the "rod of Jesse" was not designated for the sole purpose of marrying a particular virgin (Mary).

3. The Bible does not give us Joseph's age, but according to the text, he might be as young as Mary and could have really been her betrothed husband, for he did not "know" her (in an intimate way) during her pregnancy, but later we learn that Jesus had brothers and sisters:

Matthew, Chapter 1

25. *...she had brought forth **her firstborn son**: and he called his name JESUS.*

"Firstborn" implies that there were more children after this one.

Matthew, Chapter 12

46. *While he yet talked to the people, behold, **his mother and his brethren** stood without, desiring to speak with him.*

47. *Then one said unto him, Behold, thy mother and thy brethren stand without, desiring to speak with thee.*

48. *But he answered and said unto him that told him, Who is my mother? and who are my brethren?*

49. *And he stretched forth his hand toward his disciples, and said, Behold my mother and my brethren!*

50. *For whosoever shall do the will of my Father which is in heaven, the same is my brother, and sister, and mother.*

Presented in the non-canonical texts is the dogma about the "perpetual virginity" of Mary. The way to ensure this condition was to ensure her husband would be too old to consummate the relationship. No one could doubt Mary's holiness (because to remain a virgin was a sign of true virtue from God). The Bible never supports the idea of such a type of purity.

According to the Bible, neither Mary or her husband Joseph were hiding because of her pregnancy. However, Joseph had decided to let her go after her pregnancy became obvious, but after a visitation from the angel, he "took unto him his wife" (**Matthew 1:24b**). It simply means that her pregnancy would not seem to be unusual or unique if she was considered to be Joseph's wife.

4. Not only were the inhabitants of Bethlehem supposed to be recorded in the census, but **everyone** in the land of Israel. The passage mentions that Joseph and Mary came down from Nazareth, with no mention of anybody else accompanying them. It is doubtful that "all the children of Israel" knew about the marriage details of Joseph and Mary.

5. Joseph and Mary were not in a cave before they reached Bethlehem, but had to stay in a stable for animals within the city because all the inns were full of other travelers. They evidently spent some time in Bethlehem trying to find accommodations.

6. There is no description of the actual moment of the birth of Jesus.

7. The idea of "regaining or retaining virginity" by Mary was needed to support the claim of her holiness. The author of the non-canonical text used the testimony of two women to support this claim.

8. There is no indication that the act of conception is sinful, for God Himself designed it to be this way. Only sexual relations outside of the bond of marriage is sinful.

Numbers 5:29

"This is the law of jealousies, when a wife goeth aside to another instead of her husband, and is defiled."

Matthew 5:32

*"But I say unto you, That whosoever shall put away his wife, saving for the cause of **fornication**, causeth her to commit adultery: and whosoever shall marry her that is divorced committeth adultery."* (see also Matthew 19:9)

First Corinthians 6:9-10

*"Know ye not that the unrighteous shall not inherit the kingdom of God? Be not deceived: neither **fornicators**, nor idolaters, nor **adulterers**... shall inherit the kingdom of God".*

Chapter Three

JESUS

THE NON-CANONICAL GOSPELS

"Young Jesus"

Infancy Gospel of James, or Protevangelium

XXI 1 **And behold, Joseph made him ready to go forth into Judaea. And there came a great tumult in Bethlehem of Judaea;**

2 And when Herod heard it he was troubled and sent officers unto the wise men. And he sent for the high priests and examined them, saying: How is it written concerning the Christ, where he is born ? They say unto him: In Bethlehem of Judaea: for so it is written

XXII 2 **And when Mary heard that the children were being slain, she was afraid, and took the young child and wrapped him in swaddling clothes and laid him in an ox-manger.**

3 But Elizabeth when she heard that they sought for John, took him and went up into the hill-country and looked about her where she should hide him: and there was no hiding-place. And Elizabeth groaned and said with a loud voice: O mountain of God, receive thou a mother with a child. For Elizabeth was not able to go up. And immediately the mountain clave asunder and took her in. And there was a light shining always for them: for an angel of the Lord was with them, keeping watch over them.

XXIII. 1 **Now Herod sought for John,** and sent officers to Zacharias, saying: Where hast thou hidden thy son? And he answered and said unto them: I am a minister of God and attend continually upon the temple of the Lord: I know not where my son is. 2 And the officers departed and told Herod all these things. And Herod was wroth and said: **His son is to be king over Israel.**

And he sent unto him again, saying: Say the truth: where is thy son? for thou knowest that thy blood is under my hand. And the officers departed and told him all these things. 3 And Zacharias said: I am a martyr of God if thou sheddest my blood: for my spirit the Lord shall receive, because thou sheddest innocent blood in the fore-court of the temple of the Lord.

And about the dawning of the day Zacharias was slain.

XXIV. And after the three days the priests took counsel whom they should set in his stead: and the lot came up upon **Symeon. Now he it was which was warned by the Holy Ghost that he should not see death until he should see the Christ in the flesh.**

The Arabic Gospel of the Infancy of the Saviour

With the help and favour of the Most High we begin to write a book of the miracles of our Lord and Master and Saviour Jesus Christ, which is called the Gospel of the Infancy: in the peace of the Lord. Amen.

1. We find (1) what follows in the book of Joseph the high priest, who lived in the time of Christ. Some say that he is Caiaphas. (2) **He has said that Jesus spoke, and, indeed, when He was lying in His cradle said to Mary His mother: I am Jesus, the Son of God, the Logos, whom thou hast brought forth, as the Angel Gabriel announced to thee; and my Father has sent me for the salvation of the world.**

3. Wherefore, after sunset, the old woman, and Joseph with her, came to the cave, and they both went in. And, behold, it was filled with lights more beautiful than the gleaming of lamps and candles, (4) and more splendid than the light of the sun. The child, enwrapped in swaddling clothes, was sucking the breast of the Lady Mary His mother, being placed in a stall. And when both were wondering at this light, the old woman asks the Lady Mary: Art thou the mother of this Child? **And when the Lady Mary gave her assent, she says: Thou art not at all like the daughters of Eve. The Lady Mary said: As my son has no equal among children, so his mother has no equal among women.**

5. And the time of circumcision, that is, the eighth day, being at hand, the child was to be circumcised according to the law. Wherefore they circumcised Him in the cave. **And the old Hebrew woman took the piece of skin; but some say that she took the navel-string, and laid it past in a jar of old oil of nard.**

And this is that jar which Mary the sinner bought and poured upon the head and feet of our Lord Jesus Christ, which thereafter she wiped with the hair of her head.

6. **Then old Simeon saw Him shining like a pillar of light,** when the Lady Mary, His virgin mother, rejoicing over Him, was carrying Him in her arms. **And angels, praising Him, stood round Him in a circle, like life guards standing by a king.** Simeon therefore went up in haste to the Lady Mary, and, with hands stretched out before her, said to the Lord Christ: Now, O my Lord, let Thy servant depart in

peace, according to Thy word; for mine eyes have seen Thy compassion, which Thou hast prepared for the salvation of all peoples, a light to all nations, and glory to Thy people Israel. Hanna also, a prophetess, was present, and came up, giving thanks to God, and calling the Lady Mary blessed.

7.... magi came from the east to Jerusalem, as Zeraduscht (5) had predicted; and there were with them gifts, gold, and frankincense, and myrrh. And they adored Him, and presented to Him their gifts. **Then the Lady Mary took one of the swaddling-bands, and, on account of the smallness of her means, gave it to them; and they received it from her with the greatest marks of honour.**

8. And their kings and chief men came together to them, asking what they had seen or done, how they had gone and come back, what they had brought with them. And they showed them that swathing-cloth which the Lady Mary had given them. Wherefore they celebrated a feast, and, according to their custom, **lighted a fire and worshipped it, and threw that swathing-cloth into it**; and the fire laid hold of it, and enveloped it. And when the fire had gone out, they took out the swathing-cloth exactly as it had been before, just as if the fire had not touched it. **Wherefore they began to kiss it, and to put it on their heads and their eyes, saying: This verily is the truth without doubt. Assuredly it is a great thing that the fire was not able to burn or destroy it.** Then they took it, and with the greatest honour laid it up among their treasures.

23. And turning away from this place, they came to a desert; and hearing that it was infested by robbers, Joseph and the Lady Mary resolved to cross this region by night. But as they go along, behold, they see **two robbers lying in the way**, and along with them a great number of robbers, who were their associates, sleeping. Now those two robbers, into whose hands they had fallen, were Titus and Dumachus. Titus therefore said to Dumachus: I beseech thee to let these persons go freely, and so that our comrades may not see them. And as Dumachus refused, Titus said to him again: Take to thyself forty drachmas from me, and hold this as a pledge. At the same time he held out to him the belt which he had about his waist, to keep him from opening his mouth or speaking. And the Lady Mary, seeing that the robber had done them a kindness, said to him: **The Lord God will sustain thee by His right**

hand, and will grant thee remission of thy sins. And the Lord Jesus answered, and said to His mother: **Thirty years hence, O my mother, the Jews will crucify me at Jerusalem, and these two robbers will be raised upon the cross along with me, Titus on my right hand and Dumachus on my left; and after that day Titus shall go before me into Paradise**. And she said: God keep this from thee, my son. And they went thence towards a city of idols, which, as they came near it, was changed into sand-hills.

24. Hence they turned aside to that sycamore which is now called Matarea, and the Lord Jesus brought forth in Matarea a fountain in which the Lady Mary washed His shirt. **And from the sweat of the Lord Jesus which she sprinkled there, balsam was produced in that region.**

35. Another woman was living in the same place, whose son was tormented by Satan. **He, Judas by name**, as often as Satan seized him, used to bite all who came near him; and if he found no one near him, he used to bite his own hands and other limbs. The mother of this wretched creature, then, hearing the fame of the Lady Mary and her son Jesus, rose up and brought her son Judas with her to the Lady Mary. In the meantime, James and Joses had taken the child the Lord Jesus with them to play with the other children; and they had gone out of the house and sat down, and the Lord Jesus with them. And the demoniac Judas came up, and sat down at Jesus' right hand: then, being attacked by Satan in the same manner as usual, he wished to bite the Lord Jesus, but was not able; **nevertheless he struck Jesus on the right side, whereupon He began to weep**. And immediately Satan went forth out of that boy, fleeing like a mad dog. **And this boy** who struck Jesus, and out of whom Satan went forth in the shape of a dog, **was Judas Iscariot, who betrayed Him to the Jews; and that same side on which Judas struck Him, the Jews transfixed with a lance.**

41. Now in the month Adar, **Jesus, after the manner of a king, assembled the boys together.** They spread their clothes on the ground, and He sat down upon them. Then they put on His head a crown made of flowers, and, like chamber-servants, stood in His presence, on the right and on the left, as if He were a king. **And whoever passed by that way was forcibly dragged by the boys, saying: Come hither, and adore the king; then go thy way.**

43. On another day, Joseph sent his son James to gather wood, and the Lord Jesus went with him as his companion. And when they had come to the place where the wood was, and James had begun to gather it, behold, a venomous viper bit his band, so that he began to cry out and weep. The Lord Jesus then, seeing him in this condition, went up to him, and blew upon the place where the viper had bitten him; and this being done, he was healed immediately.

45. Once upon a time the Lady Mary bad ordered the Lord Jesus to go and bring her water from the well. And when He had gone to get the water, the pitcher already full was knocked against something, and broken. **And the Lord Jesus stretched out His handkerchief, and collected the water, and carried it to His mother; and she was astonished at it**. And she hid and preserved in her heart all that she saw.

47. At another time, when the Lord Jesus was returning home with Joseph in the evening. He met a boy, who ran up against Him with so much force that He fell. And the Lord Jesus said to him: **As thou hast thrown me down, so thou shall fall and not rise again. And the same hour the boy fell down, and expired.**

49. Thereafter they took Him to another and a more learned master, who, when be saw Him, said: Say Aleph. And when **He had said Aleph, the master ordered him to pronounce Beth.** And the Lord Jesus answered him, and said: First tell me the meaning of the letter Aleph, and then I shall pronounce Beth. And when the master hereupon raised his hand and flogged Him, **immediately his hand dried up, and he died.** Then said Joseph, to the Lady Mary: From this time we shall not let him go out of the house, **since every one who opposes him is struck dead.**

51. And a **philosopher** who was there present, a skilful **astronomer, asked the Lord Jesus whether He had studied astronomy.** And the Lord Jesus answered him, and explained the number of the spheres, and of the heavenly bodies, their natures and operations; their opposition; their aspect, triangular, square, and sextile; their course, direct and retrograde; the twenty-fourths, and sixtieths of twenty-fourths; **and other things beyond the reach of reason.**

Gospel of Thomas

I. I, Thomas the Israelite, tell unto you, even all the brethren that are of the Gentiles, to make known unto you **the works of the childhood of our Lord Jesus Christ and his mighty deeds, even all that he did when he was born in our land:** whereof the beginning is thus:

IV. 1 After that again he went through the village, and a child ran and dashed against his shoulder. And Jesus was provoked and said unto him: Thou shalt not finish thy course (lit. go all thy way). **And immediately he fell down and died.**

VI. 1 Now a certain teacher, Zacchaeus by name, stood there and he heard in part when Jesus said these things to his father and he marvelled greatly that being a young child he spake such matters. 2 And after a few days he came near unto Joseph and said unto him: Thou hast a wise child, and he hath understanding. Come, deliver him to me that he may learn letters. And I will teach him with the letters all knowledge and that he salute all the elders and honour them as grandfathers and fathers, and love them of his own years. 3 **And he told him all the letters from Alpha even to Omega clearly, with much questioning.** But Jesus looked upon Zacchaeus the teacher and saith unto him: Thou that knowest not the Alpha according to its nature, how canst thou teach others the Beta? **thou hypocrite, first, if thou knowest it, teach the Alpha, and then will we believe thee concerning the Beta.** Then began he to confound the mouth of the teacher concerning the first letter, **and he could not prevail to answer him.**

Hear, O teacher, the ordinance of the first letter and pay heed to this, how that it hath [what follows is really unintelligible in this and in all the parallel texts: a literal version would run something like this: **how that it hath lines, and a middle mark, which thou seest, common to both, going apart; coming together, raised up on high, dancing (a corrupt word), of three signs, like in kind (a corrupt word), balanced, equal in measure]: thou hast the rules of the Alpha.**

VII. 1 Now when Zacchaeus the teacher heard such and so many allegories of the first letter spoken by the young child, he was perplexed at his answer and his instruction being so great, and said to them that were there: Woe is me, wretch that I am, I am confounded: I have brought shame to myself by drawing to me this young child. 2 Take him away, therefore I beseech thee, my brother Joseph: I cannot endure the severity of his look, I cannot once make clear my (or his) word. **This young child is not earthly born: this is one that can tame even fire: be like this is one begotten before the making of the world. What belly bare this, what womb nurtured it? I know not.**

XI. 1 Now when he was six years old, his mother sendeth him to draw water and bear it into the house, and gave him a pitcher: but in the press he struck it against another and the pitcher was broken. 2 **But Jesus spread out the garment which was upon him and filled it with water and brought it to his mother.** And when his mother saw what was done she kissed him; and she kept within herself the mysteries which she saw him do.

XVIII. 1 And after some time there was work of building. And there came a great tumult, and Jesus arose and went thither: and he saw a man lying dead, and took hold of his hand and said: Man, I say unto thee, arise and do thy work. **And immediately he arose and worshipped him. 2 And when the multitude saw it, they were astonished, and said: This young child is from heaven: for he hath saved many souls from death, and hath power to save them all his life long.**

THE BIBLE

"Young Jesus"

Luke

Chapter 2

22. And when the days of her purification according to the law of Moses were accomplished, they brought him to Jerusalem, to present him to the Lord;

25. And, behold, **there was a man in Jerusalem, whose name was Simeon; and the same man was just and devout,** waiting for the consolation of Israel: and the Holy Ghost was upon him.

Matthew

Chapter 13

54. And when he was come into his own country, he taught them in their synagogue, insomuch that they were astonished, and said, Whence hath this man this wisdom, and these mighty works?

55. Is not this the carpenter's son? is not his mother called Mary? and his brethren, James, and Joses, and Simon, and Judas?

56. And his sisters, are they not all with us? Whence then hath this man all these things?

57. And they were offended in him. But Jesus said unto them, A prophet is not without honour, save in his own country, and in his own house.

COMMENTARY

In the Non-Canonic Text:

1. Magi arrived in Bethlehem and then inquired about the location of Jesus' birth.

2. When Mary learned about children being slain, she hid Jesus in a cradle.

3. Herod was sure that John, the son of Zachariah, was the promised Messiah and in the process of searching for the child, Herod killed Zachariah.

4. Simeon replaced the slain Zachariah in his duties in the Temple and recognized Jesus as the Saviour.

5. Jesus spoke as if He was an adult even though He was just an infant.

6. The midwife spoke about Mary as a super-woman, higher that any human being, and Mary agreed with her.

7. A piece of Jesus' foreskin was preserved in a jar of perfumed oil and later that oil was poured out on Jesus by Mary Magdalene. As in a good Greek drama, the "circle" was complete.

8. Simeon saw a vision of Jesus shining like a beacon of light while in His mother's arms, with angels guarding the holy family.

9. Mary gave away a swaddling-cloth of Jesus to the magi. While the magi celebrated the event, they worshipped the fire they had made and witnessed the miracle that the cloth was not consumed by the fire. They kept the cloth and gave it great honour.

10. The holy family met with two robbers. One of them attempted to spare the family and Jesus predicted that He would save this robber in return later on the cross. Another "circle" was complete.

11. Even Jesus' sweat produced a miracle which triggered balsam production in that location.

12. Young Jesus met young Judas and the latter hurt Him in His side. This location on His body was the same side that was eventually pierced by a Roman soldier in order to confirm Jesus' death on the cross. Another "Greek drama circle" was complete.

13. The other children dressed Jesus as a King and forced anyone who passed by to come and adore him.

14. Young Jesus had killed some children and adults for their offensive behaviour against him.

15. According to one text, a teacher was trying to teach Jesus Hebrew alphabet, in another text it was the Greek alphabet. However, in both accounts, Jesus was extremely disrespectful to the teacher.

16. A philosopher was amazed about Jesus' knowledge of astronomy and other sciences.

17. Jesus was recognized by his neighbours as being a heavenly being.

In the Bible:

1. Magi came first to Jerusalem where they inquired of Herod about the city in which Messiah would be born. After this, they travelled to Bethlehem.

2. Joseph received a warning from an angel and fled with Mary and Jesus to Egypt before the massacre of the infants by Herod began.

3. Herod very well knew that Messiah should be born in Bethlehem and could not prosecute young John. Since his father Zachariah

was a high priest, the family would be living in the place of his service, which was Jerusalem, not Bethlehem.

4. Simeon is called a "just man", but not one who been a high priest of Israel.

5. Jesus was a common infant, without supernatural abilities.

6. There are no verses about the superiority of Mary above other people; she was a chosen one to bear the promised Messiah, nothing more.

7. The Bible is not written as a dramatic play like in an ancient Greek theatre. We find no "circles of completion" here.

8. Simeon saw only the baby Jesus and his parents. No pillar of light or angels was present.

9. The commencement of the adoration of "holy icons" was determined in non-canonical texts during that time period, and continues to the present day among some (*orthodox*) Christian denominations.

10. The robber who hung beside Jesus on the cross was saved not because he was good to Jesus and His family some years before, but for his faith in the Son of God, whom he recognized as the person of Jesus.

11. No miracles done by young Jesus recorded in the Bible.

12. Judas never met Jesus before he became His follower (when he was an adult).

13. No similar story is found in the Bible.

14. Jesus, whether young or mature, never killed anyone.

15. Jesus had never been disrespectful. The Scripture clearly states that He never sinned. In addition, as a Hebrew boy, He would not have been taught the Greek alphabet first.

16. Those men who interpreted the Law, not scientists, were amazed about Jesus' knowledge of the Law of God.

17. Jesus' neighbours did not acknowledge Him as the Messiah, even after He started his ministry. As Jesus said: *"A prophet is not without honour, save in his own country, and in his own house."* (**Matthew 13:57, Mark 6:4**).

Conclusion

The differences between biblical and qur'anic stories commence with the story of Adam and continue throughout both books. It isimpossible to find common ground between the Bible and the Qur'an when the entire meaning of the same event is very different in both books.

As for the non-canonical gospels, we notice a huge emphasis on Mary's role (including Joseph's part) in the salvation of mankind. Many of these stories do not appear to be realistic or possible in comparison with what we know and read in the Bible. In spite of the influence of the non-canonical gospels on the traditions and beliefs of certain Christian denominations, I believe that they cannot be a reliable source of information about Jesus and are not considered "inspired by God" by the best Bible scholars. Therefore they cannot be included amongst the trustworthy and verifiable sources that are known today as "the gospel".

The Bible is the complete book, inspired by God and directed by the Holy Spirit. It contains all the knowledge we need to know about God, His relationship with all creation, and how we are to respond towards God.

Second Timothy, Chapter 3

*15. And that from a child thou hast known the **holy scriptures**, which are able to **make thee wise** unto salvation through faith which is in Christ Jesus.*
16. All scripture is given by inspiration of God, and is profitable for doctrine, for reproof, for correction, for instruction in righteousness:
*17. That the **man of God may be perfect**, thoroughly furnished unto all good works.*

Second Peter, Chapter 1

19. We have also a more sure word of prophecy; whereunto ye do well that ye take heed, as unto a light that shineth in a dark place, until the day dawn, and the day star arise in your hearts:

20. *Knowing this first,* **that no prophecy of the scripture is of any private interpretation.**
21. For the prophecy came not in old time by the will of man: but holy men of God spake as they were moved by the Holy Ghost.

The last book of the Bible, the book of Revelation, speaks about events that will take place in the Last Days, including the second coming of Jesus, and the conclusion of heaven and earth as we know it today. A stern warning is given to anyone who tries to change the Bible, or add to it or its prophecies in any way. It affirms that no subsequent information could possibly come from God, since the Bible is a "closed" book.

Revelation, Chapter 22

18. *For I testify unto every man that* **heareth the words of the prophecy of this book**, *If any man shall add unto these things, God shall add unto him the plagues that are written in this book:*
19. *And if any man shall take away from the words of the book of this prophecy, God shall take away his part out of the book of life, and out of the holy city, and from the things which are written in this book.*
20. He which testifieth these things saith, *Surely I come quickly. Amen. Even so,* **come, Lord Jesus.**

Galatians Chapter 1

But though we, or an angel from heaven, preach any other gospel unto you than that which we have preached unto you, let him be accursed.

Recommended Reading

Unholy War: Terror in the Name of Islam, John L. Esposito. ISBN: 0195154355. Oxford University Press, USA (May 1, 2002). 208 pages.

The Facts on Islam, John Ankerberg and John Weldon. ISBN 0736911073. Harvest House Publishers (January 1, 2003). 64 pages.

Judgment Day, Dave Hunt. ISBN 978-1-928660-42-2. 464 pages.

Many more books and DVD's can be found on Dave Hunt's web site:

http://www.thebereancall.org/

You may find interesting information by visiting these web sites:

http://www.answering-islam.org

http://www.carm.org/islam.htm